Giddens' theory of structuration

Giddens' theory of structuration is now generally accepted as a very important development because it attempts to supersede the dualisms between structure and agency, structure and process, and determinism and voluntarism. However, it is difficult for readers to come to terms with it. It draws upon a vast range of sources in sociology, anthropology, history, philosophy, politics, geography, linguistics and other disciplines. Many of these sources are themselves difficult, some are not available in English, others are available only in flawed translations. It also includes a large number of neologisms, and has been elaborated in a dauntingly large number of publications.

This book will help teachers and students alike to come to terms with structuration theory. It includes chapters on the basic features of structuration theory; Giddens' relation to American, French and German theorists; the significance of Giddens' critique of historical materialism; the use that structuration theory makes of concepts of time and space; and the model of applied social science which it supports. Finally Giddens himself looks at structuration theory in the past, present and future.

The contributors: Alan Sica, Roy Boyne, Richard Kilminster, David Jary, John Urry, Christopher Bryant and Anthony Giddens.

International Library of Sociology
Founded by Karl Mannheim

Editor: John Urry
University of Lancaster

Giddens' theory of structuration:
A critical appreciation

Edited by

Christopher G.A. Bryant
Professor of Sociology, University of Salford

and

David Jary
Professor of Sociology, Staffordshire Polytechnic

London and New York

First published 1991
by Routledge
11 New Fetter Lane, London EC4P 4EE

Simultaneously published in the USA and Canada
by Routledge
a division of Routledge, Chapman and Hall, Inc.
29 West 35th Street, New York, NY 10001

Typeset by Leaper & Gard Ltd, Bristol, England
Printed and bound in Great Britain by
Mackays of Chatham PLC. Chatham. Kent

British Library Cataloguing in Publication Data

Giddens' theory of structuration: a critical appreciation.
1. Society. Theories of Giddens, Anthony
I. Bryant, Christopher G.A. (Christopher Gordon
Alastair) *1944-* II. Jary, David
301.092

Library of Congress Cataloging in Publication Data

Giddens' theory of structuration: a critical appreciation/edited by
Christopher G.A. Bryant and David Jary.
    p.   cm.
  "Principle works of Anthony Giddens": P.
  Includes bibliographical references.
    1. Sociology—Methodology.   2. Social structure.   3. Giddens,
Anthony.   4. Giddens, Anthony—Bibliography.   I. Bryant,
Christopher G. A.   II. Jary, David.
HM24.G4495   1991
301'.01—dc20   90-34965
                                                                CIP

ISBN 0-415-00796-8
     0-415-00797-6 (pbk)

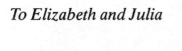
To Elizabeth and Julia

Contents

Figures

Contributors

Roy Boyne is Principal Lecturer in Sociology at Newcastle Polytechnic. He has recently published *Foucault and Derrida* and is also an associate editor of the journal *Theory, Culture and Society*. Address: Faculty of Social Sciences, Newcastle Polytechnic, Newcastle-upon-Tyne, NE1 8ST, UK.

Christopher G.A. Bryant is Professor of Sociology in the University of Salford. His recent publications include *Positivism in Social Theory and Research* and *What Has Sociology Achieved?* (edited with Henk Becker). Address: Department of Sociology, University of Salford, Salford, M5 4WT, UK.

Anthony Giddens is Professor of Sociology in the University of Cambridge and a Fellow of King's College. His publications are listed in Bibliography I (pp. 222–9). Address: Faculty of Social and Political Sciences, Free School Lane, Cambridge, CB2 3RQ, UK.

David Jary is Professor of Sociology at Staffordshire Polytechnic. His recent publications include *Sport, Leisure and Social Relations* (edited with John Horne and Alan Tomlinson). Address: Department of Sociology, Staffordshire Polytechnic, Leek Road, Stoke-on-Trent, ST4 2DF, UK.

Richard Kilminster is Lecturer in Sociology in the University of Leeds. He writes on many aspects of sociological theory. Address: Department of Social Policy and Sociology, University of Leeds, Leeds, LS2 9JT, UK.

Alan Sica is Professor of Sociology in the University of California at Riverside. His latest book is *Irrationality and Social Order* and he is editor of the journal *Sociological Theory*. Address: Department of Sociology, University of California, Riverside, California, 92521–0419, USA.

John Urry is Professor of Sociology in the University of Lancaster. His recent publications include *Social Relations and Spatial Structures* (edited with Derek Gregory) and *The End of Organized Capitalism* (with Scott Lash). Address: Department of Sociology, University of Lancaster, Lancaster, LA1 4YL, UK.

Acknowledgements

We gratefully acknowledge the help that Anthony Giddens has given us in the preparation of this volume. Throughout he has kept a proper distance whilst always offering friendly support. In particular we thank him for discussing his work with us at length in Cambridge on 26 April 1989, and for agreeing to our request that he write a final chapter which looks forward as well as back.

We have a debt to all our other contributors, too, for the evident care with which they have responded to the briefs we gave them. Figure 1.1 is taken from *Studies in Social and Political Theory* by kind permission of Unwin Hyman, with whom the copyright remains. Figures 1.2, 5.4 and 5.5 are reproduced from *The Constitution of Society* by kind permission of Basic Blackwell publishers. In addition we thank Michael Mann and Cambridge University Press for permission to reproduce Figure 5.10, Tony Spybey for his input into Figure 5.2, Julia Jary for her work in preparing both the Index and Bibliography II, Sheila Walker for retyping two contributors' chapters, Mike Curston at the British Library for bibliographical assistance, Chris Rojek of Routledge for commissioning us and our colleagues at Salford University and Staffordshire Polytechnic for their interest. Most important to us of all, Liz Bryant and Julia Jary have encouraged us to keep working at this book whatever the difficulties and however many weekends it consumed. Accordingly, it is to them that it is dedicated.

Chris Bryant, Salford
David Jary, Stoke-on-Trent

Chapter one

Introduction: coming to terms with Anthony Giddens

Christopher G.A. Bryant and David Jary

The need for a critical appreciation

The world of sociology does not know quite what to make of Anthony Giddens and his theory of structuration. There are a number of reasons for this. For a start he has written so much – twenty-three books alone between 1971 and 1989 (eleven sole-authored, four sole-edited, four joint-edited and four collections of his own articles and essays) – that it is difficult to take it all in. Many readers are also discouraged from trying to keep up with his output by the evident repetition (although most items do contain something novel if one cares to look closely). There is also a reluctance in some British quarters to concede that we have a star in our midst, so habituated have we become to the notion that the big names, especially in theory, are always foreign – first European (Spencer apart), then American, now, more often, European again. There has also been uncertainty as to both the originality and the utility of structuration theory, countered by a belief that there must be something to be said for the product of someone with such a command of languages (especially French, German and Italian), and such a knowledge of other disciplines (psychology, philosophy, linguistics, geography, history, politics and economics in particular), who can lecture so fluently without notes, and who can also find time to join with others to start a major new publishing house (Polity Press) and establish the first new faculty in the University of Cambridge for over half a century (Social and Political Sciences). Doubts about this or that may remain, but the scale of the enterprise and the virtuosity of the man compel respect.

In Chapter Eight Giddens affirms that structuration theory is the label he attaches to his 'concern to develop an ontological framework for the study of human social activities' (p. 201). Ontology here refers to 'a conceptual investigation of the nature of human action, social institutions, and the interrelations between action and institutions' (ibid). The originality and utility of structuration theory are matters to which we and our contributors will return. For the moment let us just say that we believe it to be a considerable achievement in social theory that deserves our critical appreciation. But what does Giddens himself claim for it? Here he displays a curious ambivalence that may well not have helped its reception. On the one hand, he presents it as an approach to social science that avoids the dualisms of subject and object, agency and structure and structure and process, which have so bedevilled other social theories. On the other hand, he makes no exclusive claims for it and he clearly has no wish to impose it on anyone; he believes it provides a basis for good sociology, but does not believe it provides the only basis for good sociology. It is an approach that has been hammered out with great single-mindedness at least since *New Rules of Sociological Method* (1976a), and arguably longer. Yet those who submit to the rigours of the major 'summation' of structuration theory in *The Constitution of Society* (1984a) find that it is possible to be a structurationist without knowing it in so far as empirical studies there cited in illustration of its principles and value were done by others without reference to it; those who turn to the recent co-edited overview of leading theoretical traditions and trends, *Social Theory Today* (1987b), find an endorsement of post-empiricism in the 'Introduction' but no claims for structuration theory as such; and those who work with his vast new textbook, *Sociology* (1989a), find no profession of structuration theory, nor even a single reference to 'structuration' (even if the theory does suffuse the whole book). This combination of conviction and reticence is unusual and disorienting. The explanation for the paradox may well be personal. Giddens would seem to be a grand theorist in spite of himself – a grand theorist who finds pretentions of grandeur overbearing, who is deeply serious about his work but who finds repellent anything suggestive of arrogance or pomposity.

Kilminster (see Chapter Four) argues persuasively that Giddens' theorizing is synthetic but not eclectic. It is, however, almost always singular, and therefore hard to grasp in all its implications. Giddens' critique of historical materialism is a case in point. Such critiques, as Wright has observed, tend to be either attacks from outside the Marxist tradition intent on exposing falsity, perniciousness or theoretical anachronism or reconstructions from inside, intent on overcoming weaknesses in order further to advance the Marxist project (Wright, 1983:11). Giddens' is neither; instead it is an appreciative critique from a non-Marxist who seeks to appropriate what is valuable in the Marxist tradition for an alternative theoretical framework of his own. It is the work of someone who endorses post-Marxism without ever having been a Marxist (see the interview in Mullan, 1987:113, 94). Sociologists are often unsure what to make of Giddens because he is too big to be ignored, and too singular to be labelled with confidence.

We have no illusions about delivering in one collection of essays the manageable Giddens, but we do think it possible to help colleagues and students decide for themselves what to make of him. In the rest of this Introduction we will say something about his intellectual formation; we will then outline some of the basics of structuration theory and indicate where it is possible to read further on some of its most important features; next, we will highlight points of particular significance in each of our contributors' essays; finally we will say more about what we make of structuration theory ourselves. We will offer those judgements now, and not in a concluding essay, in order to leave the last word to Anthony Giddens. We are pleased that he has accepted our suggestion that he should write an essay which is as much prospective as retrospective.

Life and early work

Giddens is disinclined to make much of his background and he denies that there have been major influences upon him, but the basics would seem to be these. He was born in 1938 in Edmonton, North London, went to the local grammar school and then to Hull University. He had not done well at school and intended to read at Hull a non-school subject, philosophy, having been refused entry to English. On arrival he found little philosophy on offer that particular year and switched to two other non-school subjects – sociology and psychology. At these he excelled, graduating with first class honours in 1959. He says he greatly enjoyed Peter Worsley's teaching in sociology and George Westby's in psychology. Worsley's version of sociology was more anthropological than most, and Westby's teaching in psychology covered Freud and social psychology but not the more dominant experimental psychology which Giddens found disagreeable. He had had ideas about entering the Civil Service, but, having graduated with distinction, he went instead to LSE and did an MA thesis entitled *Sport and Society in Contemporary England* (1961), supervised first by Asher Tropp and then by David Lockwood. In 1961 he started as a lecturer in sociology at Leicester University. He

3

acknowledges that whilst many other sociologists at that time thought the sociology of sport to be a trivial concern, the leading figures at Leicester, Ilya Neustadt and Norbert Elias, did not. At Leicester he taught neither the second-year course in classical sociological theory (apart from three lectures on Simmel) – this was Neustadt's preserve; nor the third-year course on more recent developments in theory – this was given by Percy Cohen whose *Modern Social Theory* (1968) is based on it. Instead, he was primarily responsible for the third-year course in social psychology in which he chose to link 'social personality' to a number of other topics including socialization, language, attitude formation, identity, institutions and national character.

We do not wish to make too much of this early experience but some features are worth noting. First, Giddens' version of sociology has always been open to developments in anthropology and social psychology. Having been introduced to these at Hull, he found at Leicester a sociology department with in-house teaching not only in anthropology but also in psychology (the psychology department there not being trusted to provide a suitable course). Indeed, it was through in-house psychology courses that Leicester sociology undergraduates first encountered Mead, Becker and Goffman. With hindsight, the contribution of Elias to this conception of sociology is plain enough but it was not visible to students at the time and one of us, Chris Bryant, managed, not untypically, to leave Leicester in 1966, after three years as an undergraduate, and a fourth as a postgraduate and tutorial assistant, without appreciating Elias's part in it, and without knowing anything about Elias's (con)figurational sociology. Giddens has told us that Neustadt was the greater intellectual influence – he was later to co-edit a *Festschrift* for him (Giddens and Mackenzie, 1982a); but he also says it was Elias who impressed him as a model of what a sociologist should be – the single-minded scholar willing to pursue a large-scale personal project, heedless of distractions, over very many years.[1] There are two respects in which the influence of Neustadt can readily be identified. Giddens has said that when he wrote *Capitalism and Modern Social Theory* (1971a), he wanted to contest the then prevailing Parsonian view of social theory in which Marx was treated as a precursor only (Mullan, 1987:95). Such a view may have been common elsewhere but it had never shaped the theory course that Neustadt constructed at Leicester. Neustadt was also a dedicated teacher – 'Teaching Sociology' was even the title of his inaugural lecture (1965); and so is Giddens – the author of both a short introduction to, and a massive textbook in, sociology (Giddens, 1982d, 1989a, 1990a). (The textbook even has separate UK and US editions with different illustrative material to maximize its appeal to students.)

Giddens has mentioned to us that he regards all his work as one continuous project, which we are calling 'the making of structuration theory'. In addition to their merits as commentary, Giddens' writings prior to *New Rules of Sociological Method* (1976a) have thus also to be seen as part of a larger venture, the critical appropriation of earlier traditions in order to secure a base upon which to build theoretical constructions of his own. There are certainly some, especially in Britain and the Netherlands, who argue that Giddens owes more to Elias than he acknowledges. (Kilminster, incidentally, discusses the Elias/Giddens issue on pp. 97–103.) We have no reason to question Giddens' claim that he never knew enough about Elias's (largely unpublished) work for it to have been a major influence, although in 1961–62 he did attend Elias's first-year lecture course at Leicester, which was organized around the theme of development, and he did read Volume I of *The Civilizing Process* in unpublished translation and later in German (Elias, 1939). (In 1962–64 Elias was, in any case, in Ghana.) But there is a more profound sense – provision of a role model – in which the influence of Elias may have been decisive.

Giddens taught at Simon Fraser University, near Vancouver, in 1966–67. There he saw how difficult it was for a European Marxist head of department, Tom Bottomore, to cope with students whose radicalism far exceeded his own. In 1967–68 Giddens moved on to the University of California at Los Angeles. Southern California, he says, was a revelation; old European structural sociologies of class and authority shed little light on the revolution of everyday life associated with the hippies and with new social movements including the student and anti-Vietnam movements. He recounts how a trip to a beach populated with large numbers of people in strange garb brought home to him that European sociology, and the agenda of the European left, had their limitations. It was then that he first conceived the project that has become the making of structuration theory, the first part of which was the critical appropriation of elements of the European tradition, the second specification of the parameters of modern life and the third work on anthropological issues.

In 1969 Giddens left Leicester for a university lectureship at Cambridge and a fellowship at King's College. He belatedly acquired a doctorate at Cambridge in 1974 and eleven years later became the second holder of the chair of sociology in succession to John Barnes. He has remained there ever since, but has also made numerous visits to universities and other institutions in North

America, Europe and Australia. According to *Footnotes*, the news-letter of the American Sociological Association, Giddens will be teaching half and half at the University of California at Santa Barbara and Cambridge from 1989–90 (Appelbaum, 1988). Our understanding is that he has not yet committed himself to any such arrangement in the long term.

The pre-*New Rules* writings include a number of articles on suicide (Giddens, 1964b; 1965d, e, f; 1966). These are interesting for their commitment to a sociology of suicide which discards Durkheim's rigid division between the sociology of suicide rates and the psychology of individual suicides. The essay on Simmel (Giddens, 1965a) is also worth noting because Simmel's concept of 'sociation' is evidence of a desire, which Giddens shares, to avoid the dualism of the individual and society. It is in *The Class Structure of the Advanced Societies* (1973), however, that the concept of 'structuration' makes its first appearance. It does so in a discussion of class structuration in which no attempt is made to distinguish structuration in general from class structuration in particular. Giddens differentiates between the mediate structur-ation of class relationships, which refer to 'the factors that inter-vene between the existence of certain given market capacities and the formation of classes as identifiable social groupings', of which the most notable is mobility chances, and proximate structuration, whose sources are: 'the division of labour within the productive enterprise; the authority relations within the enterprise; and the influence of ... "distributive groupings"', i.e. 'Relationships involving common patterns of the consumption of economic goods' (Giddens, 1973:107, 108, 109). We have never found the mediate/proximate distinction very helpful and it is notable that Giddens never uses it again, but references to class *structuration* do signal a concern to theorize the unending variation in class formation; it is never some fixed schedule of classes he seeks but rather actual formations under particular conditions. As Giddens indicates in Chapter Eight, consideration of class formation raised 'in an acute form the question of the relation between agency and structure', especially with respect to the way in which 'knowledge is somehow incorporated in social relations in a constitutive fashion' (p. 203).

The making of structuration theory: the duality of structure

'Structuration' in a more expanded sense, and with it the theory of structuration, first appear in 1976–77 in *New Rules of Sociological Method* (1976a) and in 'Functionalism: *après la lutte*' and its

Appendix 'Notes on the theory of structuration' (Giddens, 1976c; 1977i; page references to 1976c are those of the more accessible reprint in 1977a). 'To study structuration', Giddens states, 'is to attempt to determine the conditions which govern the continuity and dissolution of structures or types of structure' (Giddens, 1977a:120). Structuration also 'refers abstractly to the dynamic process whereby structures come into being' (ibid:121). As such structuration theory differs from both structuralism and the philosophy of action. The limitation of structural*ism* – whether in its functionalist, Marxist or modern structuralist variants is that it regards the 'reproduction' of social relations and practices 'as a mechanical outcome, rather than as an active constituting process, accomplished by, and consisting in, the doings of active subjects' (ibid). By contrast, 'The characteristic error of the philosophy of action [along with most forms of interpretative sociology] is to treat the problem of "production" only, thus not developing any concept of structural analysis at all' (ibid). Structuration theory attempts to supersede these deficiencies by showing how 'social structures are both constituted *by* human agency, and yet at the same time are the very *medium* of this constitution' (ibid). This is what is meant by 'duality of structure', the central concept in Giddens' structuration theory, and the means by which he seeks to avoid a *dualism* of agency and structure. Giddens stresses that 'to enquire into the structuration of social practices is to seek to explain how it comes about that structures are constituted through action, and reciprocally how action is constituted structurally' (Giddens, 1976a:161). It is also, crucially, to conceive structures not 'as simply placing constraints upon human agency, but as enabling' (ibid).

It is important to note how from the *New Rules* onwards Giddens' use of the term 'structure' differs from most previous usage in sociology. He refers not to 'the descriptive analysis of the relations of interaction which "compose" organizations or collectivities' (its conventional use in functionalism), but rather to 'systems of generative rules and resources' (with some affinities to those in linguistics) that members draw upon, but also thereby change, in their continuous production and reproduction of society (Giddens, 1976a:127). Whereas in structural-functionalism the two terms 'structure' and 'system' are normally regarded as 'more or less equivalent', in structuration theory they are sharply distinguished; 'social system' alone refers to the surface patterns of interactions, leaving 'structure' to what is called, after Ricoeur, the 'virtual order' of 'generative rules' and 'resources'. Unlike Althusser's structuralism, however, structuration theory never makes human subjects the mere 'bearers' of structures.

This leads to a further difference between structuration theory and structural-functionalism. Within both theories 'homeostatic feedback loops', defined by Giddens as causal factors which have a largely unintended feedback on system reproduction, play an important part in the reproduction of social systems (Giddens, 1977a:115). However *intended* 'self-regulation' and 'reflexive self-regulation' (causal loops in which the feedback is *affected* by actors' knowledge) are only crucial in structuration theory. In consequence there is no place in structuration theory for the kind of 'reified', 'quasi-biological' and teleological references to functions, dysfunctions and system needs, which Giddens takes to be the characteristic error of structural-functionalism.

The key contrasts between functionalism and structuration theory at this stage in Giddens' development of the latter are set out in Figure 1.1. The separation of 'system' and 'structure', and the notion of a 'duality of structure', provide an analytical framework in which constraints still operate but in a non-functionalist and non-structuralist way. Giddens supplies an illustration of this in his stratification model of action (see Figure 1.2), in which three levels or layers of consciousness and action are framed as 'reflexive monitoring of action' and 'discursive consciousness' (what actors are able to say about the conditions of their own action); 'rationalizations of action' and 'practical consciousness' (what actors know tacitly about the conditions of their own action but cannot articulate); and 'motivation for action' and 'unconscious motives/cognition' (repressed semiotic impulses, affecting motivation, but usually barred from consciousness). The model makes clear that all three levels of action and consciousness are potentially implicated in the production and reproduction of social systems, and that, notwithstanding the existence of unacknowledged conditions and unintended consequences, any model that seeks to explain social systems simply in terms of unintended reproduction is unbalanced.

The blending of enablement and constraint that structuration theory sets out to achieve is also evident in Giddens' representation of the duality of structure in social interaction in Figure 1.3. (Figure 1.3 is adapted from Giddens, 1984a:29; there are also versions in Giddens, 1976a:122; 1977i:132.) 'All processes of the structuration (production and reproduction) of systems of social interaction involve three elements: the communication of meaning, the exercise of power, and the evaluation and judgement of conduct' (Giddens, 1977i:132–3). The terms on the first row of Figure 1.3 'refer to analytically distinguishable aspects of structure.

FUNCTIONALISM	STRUCTURATION THEORY
Basic concepts	**Basic concepts**
(a) *System* – interdependence of action, conceived of *only* as homeostatic causal loops	(a) *System* – interdependence of action, conceived of as: (i) homeostatic causal loops; (ii) self-regulation through feedback; (iii) reflexive self-regulation
(b) *Structure* – stable pattern of action	(b) *Structure* – generative rules and resources
(c) *Functions and dysfunctions* – contribution of system 'parts' to whole in promoting system integration or disintegration	(c) *Structuration* – generation of systems of interaction through *duality of structure*
(d) *Manifest and latent functions* – intended (anticipated) contributions and unintended (unanticipated) contributions to system integration	(d) *Production and reproduction of society* – accomplishment of interaction under bounded conditions of rationalization of action, i.e. actors produce social action (as a 'skilled performance') but do so in situations in which there are also 'unacknowledged conditions'

Figure 1.1 Key concepts of structuration theory and functionalism compared
Source: adapted from Giddens, 1977a:122

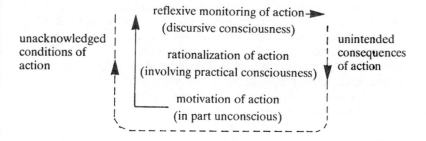

Figure 1.2 Stratification model of consciousness and action
Source: Combines figures from Giddens, 1984a:5, 7 which first appeared in Giddens, 1979a:56

9

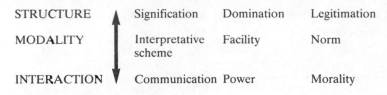

STRUCTURE	Signification	Domination	Legitimation
MODALITY	Interpretative scheme	Facility	Norm
INTERACTION	Communication	Power	Morality

Figure 1.3 Analytical elements of the process of structuration
Source: Adapted from Giddens, 1984a:29

Structure as signification involves semantic rules; as domination, unequally distributed resources; as legitimation, moral or evaluative rules.' In all cases 'rules and resources' are 'properties of communities or collectivities rather than of actors' (ibid: 133). By 'modalities' Giddens refers to the 'mediation of interaction and structure in the processes of social production and reproduction' (Giddens, 1976a:122). Thus the terms 'interpretative scheme', 'facility' and 'norm' attach to the 'knowledge and capabilities (including resources) that actors are able to call upon in the production of interaction' (Giddens, 1977i:133). Interpretative schemes, for example, include the 'modes of typification' that – consciously as well as tacitly – actors draw upon in interactions. Under the heading of 'signification' and 'semantic rules', Giddens includes 'all types of rules that are drawn upon as interpretative schemes to make sense of what actors say and do, and of the cultural objects they produce' (ibid). Under the heading of 'legitimation' and 'moral rules', by contrast, he includes all 'types of rules that are drawn upon as norms in the evaluation of conduct' (ibid). The remaining modality, 'domination' and power, refers to the facilities and (material and non-material) resources 'that may be brought to a situation of interaction; they range from command of verbal skills to the application of means of violence' (ibid:134). The 'resources' involved are again treated as the properties of structures; 'actors "possess" resources in a parallel sense to that in which they "know" rules' (ibid). Finally, and the brevity belies the significance, 'power' is defined as 'transformative capacity'.

In his rejection of both positivism and subjectivism, Giddens has declared where he stands on certain epistemological issues, but it is to ontology that his work on structuration theory is principally devoted. What is at issue is how the concepts of action, meaning and subjectivity are to be specified, and how they relate to notions of structure and constraint. Sociology – like social science as a whole – is conceived by Giddens as neither a natural science, nor a non-science, but rather as a science with a character of its own that reflects its subject matter. It is a central theme of *New Rules* that social theory 'must incorporate a treatment of action as rationalized conduct ordered reflexively by human agents, and must grasp the significance of language as the practical medium whereby this is made possible' (Giddens, 1976a:8). It is in this context that hermeneutic concerns come to the fore. Giddens stresses that social science has to accommodate a double hermeneutic – two 'frames of meaning': (1) 'the meaningful social world as constituted by lay actors', as well as (2) the second order understandings of social scientists (Giddens 1984a:374). He also insists accommodation of the double hermeneutic need not issue in relativism in so far as mediations between frames of meaning are possible. (Giddens' position here has continuities with Gadamer's, but is opposed to *some* versions of hermeneutics, radical forms of conventionalism and Winch's particular interpretation of Wittgenstein's second philosophy.)

Central Problems can, like *New Rules*, 'be read as a non-functionalist manifesto' (Giddens, 1979a:7), but as Giddens says in Chapter Eight, there are also differences. Whereas *New Rules* moves from examination of interpretative sociology to construction of a position that recognizes that it is not enough to attend only to the interpretation of meaning in social analysis, *Central Problems* moves from scrutiny of structuralism and post-structuralism to a position that acknowledges that inattention to 'time' and 'place' is equally a deficiency.

The extent of Giddens' indebtedness to social phenomenology and ethnomethodology is apparent from his talk of 'skilled performers', 'actors', 'knowledgeability', 'practical knowledge', 'modes of typification', etc. Equally plainly, the conception of structure with which he proposes to replace conventional structural–functional notions has direct affinities with structural conceptions in linguistics, and structuralisms related to linguistics, in which structure is something like an underlying message or code explaining the surface appearances of myths, linguistic expressions, etc. Just as the rules of language, in contributing to the construction of a well-formed phrase or sentence, reproduce that language, so structures of rules and resources, in consequence of the duality that renders them both the medium and the outcome of social interactions, reproduce institutions and social relations. The achievements of linguistics and related forms of structuralism are, according to Giddens: a 'decentring of the subject' (the expunging of all metaphysical notions in which consciousness of the subject is taken as either given or transparent to itself); 'an attempt to transcend the subject/object dualism' (ibid: 47); and an emphasis on important aspects of the 'relational character' of social totalities as well as language (utilizing such notions as Saussure's concepts of *langue* and *parole*, paradigmatic and syntagmatic relations and synchrony and diachrony.

Giddens would not dispute that his own structurationist approach to sociology is anything other than part of the more general 'linguistic turn' that has marked philosophy and the social sciences in recent decades. But his own focus on language differs from the structuralism of theorists such as Lévi-Strauss. For structuralists of the latter sort: (a) social relations can be analysed not merely as *like* a language but *as* a language; and (b) social relations can be entirely reduced to language or to underlying relations conceptualized in terms of analogues with linguistic structures. For Giddens, by contrast, the true importance of the new emphasis on the role of language in social life is: (a) the attention it brings to the intersection of language and society, not the reduction of society to language; and (b) the opportunity it provides for the broad use of linguistic models, without any suggestion that linguistic theorists such as Saussure or Chomsky have got their models of 'language' or 'structure' exactly right.

Giddens' main criticism of structural linguistics and derivative forms of structuralism is the same as that of Clarke: 'the creative power of the subject has to be taken away as soon as it is acknowledged and given to a mechanism inscribed in the biological constitution of the mind' (Clarke, 1980:171, quoted in Giddens, 1987i:79). Lévi-Strauss, Giddens points out, willingly accepted Ricoeur's characterization of his work as 'Kantianism with an absent subject' (Giddens, 1976c in 1977a:117). For all their interest in 'competence and performance' the same might be said of Chomsky and those like him. Giddens complains that structuralist conceptions tend ultimately to 'dispense with the active subject altogether'; more particularly, they fail to see that the mastery of both language and social action involves a 'creative' grasping of rules that are applied, interpreted and also sometimes transformed, in particular contexts. Wittgenstein and Garfinkel provide more apt starting points for both a fuller understanding of the nature of language, and a better sense of the relation of language to social life, than either the structuralists or, for that matter, the post-structuralists (cf. Giddens, 1987i). To know a language is not only to know syntactical rules, but also 'to acquire a range of methodological devices, involved both with the production of utterances themselves and with the constitution and reconstitution of social life in the daily contexts of social activity'

(Giddens, 1987i:79–80). That neither structural linguistics nor structuralism offers a satisfactory model for the analysis of social relations is only to be expected given that they fail even to provide an adequate model of language. Post-structuralism, according to Giddens, is also open to objection. In Derrida and others, 'mentalism' and 'formalism' may give way to notions that admit the importance of time and location in analyses of both language and society, but the outcome is a view which sees *only* movement.

One of the most distinctive emphases in Giddens' structuration theory, which first appears in *Central Problems* and is carried forward in both volumes of *A Contemporary Critique of Historical Materialism* (1981a, 1985a), is his insistence on bringing 'time-space relations' into the very core of social theory (Giddens, 1979a, Ch. 6). Three points stand out. First, recognition that time-space relations are 'inherent in the constitution of all social inter-action' avoids the 'repression' of time and agency associated with the sharp distinction between synchrony and diachrony favoured by structuralists and functionalists (ibid:3).

> According to the theory of structuration, an understanding of social systems as situated in time-space can be effected by regarding structure as non-temporal and non-spatial, as a *virtual order of differences* produced and reproduced in social inter-action as its medium and outcome.
>
> (Giddens, 1979a:3)

Second, bringing time-space relations into the core of social theory builds upon the Wittgensteinian and ethnomethodological premiss that structures are produced and reproduced in specific contexts. Structures are instantiated in social interactions and systems which are not only located in, and shaped by, time and space as an environment *external* to social relations, but which also, in turn, so shape the social content of time and space as to make them *internal* to social relations.[2] Thus, as identified by Lévi-Strauss there exists both reversible and irreversible time, the *durée* of day-to-day experience and the *longue durée* of institutions as against the irreversible time of the life course.

Third, examination of the work of 'time-geographers' such as Hägerstrand and Janelle, and also of Goffman, gives further impetus to the formation of a new sociological perspective in the study of large-scale 'places', 'settings', and 'time-space paths' or 'strips' of social action defined by their particular arrangement of time and space. Structuration can now be restated in terms of: 'The structuring of social relations across time and space in virtue of the duality of structure' (Giddens, 1984a:376).

Giddens argues that structuration theory so conceived enjoys distinct advantages – not least in the analysis of increasingly global patterns of social and economic change – such as: (a) escape from the restrictive notion of 'society' as a unitary self-reproducing structure; (b) sensitivity to the importance of intersocietal relations, including such neglected topics as warfare; and (c), following from the above, commitment to an analysis of social change and world society, which is at once non-functionalist, non-structuralist and non-evolutionary. This last also provides the parameters for a radical reformulation of historical materialism.

Volumes 1 and 2 of Giddens' *A Contemporary Critique of Historical Materialism* are discussed at length in Chapter Five, but in brief he concludes that:

1. there exists no necessary overall mechanism of social change, no universal 'motor of history' such as 'class conflict';
2. no universal periodizations of social development are possible, these being ruled out by intersocietal systems as well as by human agency;
3. societies do not have needs other than those of individuals, so notions such as 'adaptation' cannot properly be applied to societies;
4. while 'class conflict' *is* central in capitalist society, there is no teleology that guarantees the emergence of the working class as the universal class, and no ontology that justifies denial of the multiple bases of modern societies represented by capitalism, industrialism, surveillance and the industrialization of warfare;
5. as a subject concerned pre-eminently with modernity, sociology addresses a reality in which, unlike earlier societies, reflexive monitoring is inherent.

In his discussion of these themes, Giddens is at pains to make clear both the similarities and the dissimilarities between his theory and that of Marx. Similarities are evident, for example, in Marx's statement in the *Grundrisse* that:

The conditions and objectifications of the process [of production] are themselves equally moments of it, and its only subjects are the individuals, but individuals in mutual relations, which they equally reproduce and produce anew ... in which they renew themselves even as they renew the world of wealth they create.

(Quoted in Giddens 1977i:129)

Giddens' ambivalence towards Marx, however, is revealed in his warnings that 'there are no easy dividing lines to be drawn between Marxism and "bourgeois social theory"', and that 'no one today ... can remain true to the spirit of Marx by remaining true to the letter of Marx' (Giddens, 1979a:1).

As described by Giddens, *The Constitution of Society* 'provides a summation of [his] previous writings, setting them out in a developed and coherent manner' (Giddens, 1984a, Preface). One of its more striking claims is that 'the vague term "approach" ... actually conveys very well ... the methodological import of structuration theory ... [C]onceptual schemes that order and inform processes of inquiry into social life are in large part what "theory" is and what it is for' (ibid). Given this conception of theory, it is not surprising that Giddens should summarize the ten basic points of structuration theory at the beginning of the chapter that discusses empirical research and social critique (Giddens, 1984a:Ch.6). It is not practical to list them all here, and in any case most of them only elaborate arguments familiar from earlier works. But a few do deserve a mention. In particular, point 4 says that: 'Routine, psychologically linked to the minimizing of unconscious sources of activity, is the predominant form of day-to-day social activity ... In the enactment of routines agents sustain a sense of *ontological security*' (Giddens, 1984a:282, italics added). Point 6 stresses the situated character of interaction in terms of its 'positioning' (discussed further by Bryant in Chapter Seven, p. 199). Point 8 reminds us that 'the degree of closure of societal totalities – and of social systems in general – is widely variable' (ibid:283). There are degrees of systemness, and societies less often have clear-cut boundaries than the era of nation-states has led us to suppose (an issue taken up by Jary in Chapter Five). The theme of point 10 has also not been stated quite so forcefully before: 'There is no mechanism of social organization or social reproduction identified by social analysts which lay actors cannot also get to know about and actively incorporate into what they do' (ibid:284).

All these points suggest, we learn, three guidelines for research. First, all social research has an 'anthropological' aspect to it by virtue of the double hermeneutic. In consequence: literary style matters; social scientists are communicators who 'introduc[e] frames of meaning associated with certain contexts of social life to those in others', drawing upon 'the same sources of description (mutual knowledge) as novelists or others who write fictional accounts of social life' as they do so (ibid:285); and 'thick description' of connected levels and dimensions of meaning is sometimes called for. Second, all social scientists, including those who concentrate on institutional analysis, need to remain 'sensitive to the complex skills that actors have in co-ordinating the contexts of their day-to-day behaviour' (ibid.). Third, given the need to remain 'sensitive to the time-space constitution of social life', social analysts can no longer let time be the preserve of historians and space that of geographers; instead a disciplinary coming together is called for.

Finally, the constitutive character of the ideas that it produces makes sociology an inherently critical discipline. In Giddens' view, sociology always tends to undermine 'ideology' or 'the capability of dominant groups or classes to make their own sectional interests appear to others as universal ones' (Giddens, 1979a:6). But when asked how his theory compares with other versions of critical theory, including the Frankfurt School's, his reply is clear. Structuration theory cannot be expected to furnish the moral guarantees that critical theorists sometimes purport to offer.

The chapters in this volume

Giddens' structuration theory involves a critical appropriation of many other theories, and we are not the first to be struck by his willingness to engage with different national traditions (cf. Bernstein, 1986a). With this in mind, we asked our first three contributors to make Giddens' relation to developments in America, France and Germany, respectively, a central theme of their essays.

Alan Sica (Chapter Two) pays particular attention to the early stages in the development of structuration theory. Though ultimately unconvinced that Giddens' conception of the duality of structure can deliver all it claims, he finds much to praise in Giddens, not least in his dissection of the functionalisms of Parsons and Merton and his refusal to marginalize the theoretical claims of Garfinkel and Goffman as relevant only to micro-sociology. More generally, he is impressed by Giddens' interpretative skills and his ability to synthesize, or perhaps better, to fuse the horizons of European and North American approaches. Sica also describes how the initial reception of Giddens' work in America was muted, partly because its empirical pay-off was not immediately evident. Today, by contrast, interest in, and respect for, Giddens and his work is widespread. Even so, Sica wonders whether it is structuration theory or Giddens' very great skills as an interpreter of different sociological traditions that wins the more attention. For himself, he wonders, too, whether the conception of the duality of structure that lies at the heart of Giddens' theorizing can resolve the dualisms of agency and structure, freedom and unfreedom, which beset both sociology and life itself, or indeed whether they are resolvable at all.

Roy Boyne's discussion (Chapter Three) of Giddens' response to French structuralism involves him first in a consideration of Foucault. Boyne's argument is that Giddens' use of Foucault is entirely coloured by his own concerns, which are to assert the knowledgeability and agency of individual actors, to combat the retreat from 'reference' into subjectivity, and to perpetuate the project of 'rationalist grand theory'. Boyne's second move is to question Giddens' anathematization of functionalism, especially when it is extended to cover all forms of structuralism. He suggests that Giddens' 'abstract concept of agency' understates structural influences while at the same time mythologizing capitalism; instead the degree of knowledgeability of actors, and the extent and kinds of agency, ought all to be settled empirically case by case.

In retrospect, Boyne contends, we are often able to show how the 'subjects' required by social systems were produced though no-one intended them. He hammers home his point by arguing that Derrida's work has so undermined the 'twin notions' of agency and reference as to render them incapable of providing the secure basis for a 'rationalist' general theory of the kind he believes Giddens seeks. Finally, Boyne also examines Giddens' conceptualization of the unconscious, finding it merely 'a metaphoric rendition of the basic assumptions underlying the theory of structuration' (p. 53). For Boyne consideration of the 'post-structuralism' of Foucault and Derrida can only lead to the conclusion that 'any philosophy of the subject must in the end be indeterminate between the subject as structured and the subject as agent' (p. 68). He remains unconvinced that Giddens' theorizing achieves this openness.

While all our contributors register some doubts about structuration theory, Boyne is by far the most critical. For our own part we will merely record that we do not believe Giddens has sought to ground a rationalist general theory. (In similar vein, McLennan (1988) points out that Giddens rejects *both* radical pluralism and objectivism.) The status of structuration theory, given Giddens' professed distaste for (the unprofitability of) epistemological argument, is, however, a difficult issue to which we return later (pp. 24–9).

In the course of his account of structuration theory as a world-view, Kilminster deals (Chapter Four), as we asked, with Giddens' relation to Habermas, Gadamer and Elias – the last having a German intellectual formation even if he has also lived in Britain and the Netherlands. Kilminster's summary characterization of structuration theory in the first two paragraphs of his section on

'Systematics or sociogenesis' (pp. 102–3) is as penetrating as any we have seen. He portrays structuration theory as a metatheory of action relevant to all the social sciences (and notes Giddens' interest in Parsons' earlier such venture). He also argues that it embodies a world-view whose constituents have been chosen for their contribution to its 'prescriptive force as a moral–political platform of the social criticism of modernity' seen through the eyes of the self-directing individual (p. 102). Giddens' version of sociology, he continues, is dedicated to examining 'which conditions of action will maximize the capacity of knowledgeable actors to make a difference in this society when they are differentially socially endowed with access to resources' (pp. 102–3).

Kilminster argues that Giddens discusses Habermas in a curiously disengaged way, partly because the double hermeneutic provides him with a simple notion of critical sociology that makes the complex demands of critical theory unattractive. Gadamer's hermeneutics, centred as it is on the mediation of the frames of meaning of social scientists and those they study, is clearly more congenial to him. Like ourselves, however, Kilminster is struck by the contradiction between a philosophical anthropology in which human beings are always the same and a discontinuist view of history, which invites specification of different character types for different epochs. The latter is something that Elias, unlike Giddens, attends to and Kilminster makes plain his preference for Elias's sociogenetic approach over Giddens' structurationism.

Chapters Two to Four focus on the formation of structuration theory. The three chapters that follow address wider issues of use and application. First, David Jary (Chapter Five) deals with the structurationist underpinning of Giddens' account of historical change and world society, and his critiques of historical materialism and evolutionary theory. While recognizing the flair and considerable interest of Giddens' account of history, Jary questions whether Giddens' conclusion that social change is merely episodic and contingent follows logically from his adoption of structurationism. In suggesting otherwise, Jary argues that the core ideas of structuration theory – time-space distanciation as well as the duality of structure – do not in themselves issue in any specific historical conclusions. Rather, historical accounts can only be the product of detailed empirical inquiries and the construction of specific theories. In Jary's view, Giddens' reluctance to engage in either of these, together with his readiness to place his accounts merely within a general interpretation of the implications of 'time-space distanciation' and the duality of structure, renders his historical accounts suspect. For related reasons, Giddens' dismissal of

alternative theories, including historical materialism and evolutionary theories, is also challengeable – especially so once it is also
recognized that such dismissals often result from caricatures of the
alternatives. A close inspection of these alternative approaches
reveals that they often embrace broadly structurationist conceptions of a duality of structure and time-space, while arriving at
conclusions that are far less restricted than Giddens'. In sum, Jary
does not dispute the general value of Giddens' formulations of the
duality of structure and time-space distanciation, but he does insist
that more variants of historical analysis are consistent with them
than Giddens himself supposes.

John Urry (Chapter Six) offers an appraisal of the import,
applications and omissions of Giddens' general approach to time-
space analysis. He reviews Giddens' selective adoption of the work
of time-geographers, including his specification of the constraints
that time and space impose on human action (see pp. 162–3), and
his elaboration of the key concepts of 'locales', regions and zones,
'time-space edges', and 'power-containers'. His verdict is that
although Giddens can be credited with making a major contribution to the new emphasis on time-space analysis in sociology – a
contribution that has even fed back into human geography – the
new emphasis 'would probably have happened anyway' without his
intervention (p. 160). In addition, Urry points to a number of
deficiencies in Giddens' conceptualizations of time-space. These
include the one-sidedness of Giddens' focus on modernization
through 'distanciation', the lack of any detailed reference to variations in local context or 'place', the neglect of 'post-modern'
tendencies such as nostalgia and pastiche and inattention to those
ways in which modern capitalism is *dis*organized. Urry also repeats
his previous judgement that Giddens, for all his emphasis on
human agency, still fails to supply adequate accounts of the social
processes whereby actors actually constitute structures and fails to
give social movements and collectivities other than states the
extended treatment they deserve (Urry, 1977, 1982).

The 'applications' of which Christopher Bryant speaks in
Chapter Seven have to do with relations between sociology, social
criticism and society. One of the attractions of structuration
theory, according to Bryant, is that it affords a dialogical model of
applied sociology that avoids the deficiencies not only of earlier
engineering and enlightenment models but also of the more
promising interactive model developed in America by Weiss and
others. 'In particular, Giddens' theory of structuration is allied to a
[post-empiricist] model of social science that is consistent with
interactive application in a way in which the [more positivist]

model of science favoured by those who first identified interactive application is not' (p. 177). The key to this is the double hermeneutic; it yields a sociology that cannot but be critical in so far as it helps individuals to see how practices could be other than what they are. Giddens is, however, more inclined to celebrate the transformative potential of human beings than to specify how that potential might be realized; this could change if he were regularly to pay more attention to what in *The Constitution of Society* he calls the 'positioning' of individuals (Giddens, 1984a:83–92). Bryant also notes Giddens' respectful references to the counterfactual normative theorizing of Rawls and Habermas but adds that Giddens would do well to engage in some such theorizing himself if the philosophical anthropology that informs his work is not to remain incomplete and in some respects arbitrary.

By way of conclusion, we asked Anthony Giddens to comment on four areas: the origins and development of structuration theory; its future direction; the use made of structuration theory by others; and the relation of structuration theory to the current state of, and future prospects for, sociology.

In relation to the first, Giddens stresses that structuration theory is intended to be neither a grand synthesis nor a research programme but rather an ontology of social life. He offers interesting comments on the part *Class Structure, New Rules, Central Problems* and *The Constitution of Society* have each played in its formulation. He reaffirms that 'Wittgenstein's specification of "difference", as mediated in the *Praxis* of language games', seems to him 'superior to that filtered through signifiers or "discourse" as understood in post-structuralism' (p. 205), and that social sciences are irremediably historical and incapable of generating any patterns of universal causation.

On the future development of his work, Giddens is revealing. He discloses that in writing *The Constitution of Society* (1984a), he came to see much more clearly how sociology has a greater constitutive involvement with modernity than other social sciences and humanities because it addresses the way human beings 'reflexively monitor their actions and thereby processes of reproduction' (p. 207). In his current writing he is 'concerned to relate the theme of the inherent reflexivity of modernity to a concrete institutional analysis of modern social life' (p. 207). *The Consequences of Modernity* (1990b) uses notions of trust and risk, security and danger, in an account of the extreme dynamism of modernity. In particular, it looks at the disembedding of social relations from local contexts of action in each of the four 'institutional clusterings' of modernity identified in *The Nation-State and Violence* –

'heightened surveillance, capitalistic enterprise, industrial production and the consolidation of centralized control of the means
of violence' (Giddens, 1985a:5). In this context the self, too,
becomes a reflexive project, and post-modernism is seen as but
one outcome of the requirement that everything about modern
societies may be challenged, that there are no guarantees. Volume
3, together with a newly projected fourth volume of *A Contemporary Critique of Historical Materialism*, Giddens informs us, will
extend his analysis of these issues. Volume 3 will deal with the
future of capitalism and socialism; and volume 4 will explore
further the nature of critical theory, developing a distinction
between 'emancipatory politics' (including 'emancipation from
oppression') and 'life politics' (the politics of 'self-actualisation').
Intriguingly, Giddens declares that: 'What is needed is the creation
of models of ... utopian realism' (p. 211). Should he now articulate such models himself, he would, in the eyes of many critics in
this volume and elsewhere, remedy one of the conspicuous omissions in his whole oeuvre. Finally, he also announces an intention
to write a theoretical book on religion centring on the tension
between the principle that 'nothing is sacred' and the persistence
or rediscovery of attitudes of religiosity.

On the use others have made of structuration theory, Giddens
says he prefers 'those usages in which concepts, either from the
logical framework of structuration theory or other aspects of my
writings, are used in a sparing and critical fashion' (p. 213). In
chapter 6 of *The Constitution of Society* (1984a), Giddens
discusses work conducted without reference to structuration theory
but which is true to its principles. Here he endorses three studies,
by Burman (1988), Connell (1987) and Dandeker (1989), which
have consciously taken up and used elements of structuration
theory.

Finally, Giddens makes a very strong case for the indispensa-
bility of sociology – particularly sociology that is ethnographically
sensitive and theoretically reflective – in an age of high modernity.
On the one hand, such a sociology is in part constitutive of social
relations; on the other, new social movements such as the women's
movement and the greens are, together with processes of globalization and profound change in both the west and in Eastern
Europe, redefining the sociological agenda. 'Theoretical reflection
in sociology ... takes place at the frontiers between what "is" and
what "might be" in social life' (p. 219–20). It is precisely because
what is and what might be are again so problematic that the challenge to sociology is so great and the actual and potential value of
a reflexive and constitutive sociology so enormous.

Christopher G.A. Bryant and David Jary

The achievement of structuration theory

Giddens is by no means the first or the only writer to try to overcome the dualism of structure and agency. On the contrary, Elias,
1939, 1970; Touraine, 1965, 1973; Berger and Luckmann, 1966;
Bourdieu, 1977; and Bhaskar, 1975, 1979, among others, have
attempted it (cf. Layder, 1981; Thrift, 1983; Bryant, 1987b). It is
not practical to include a comparative examination of them all
here. Instead, we shall confine our remarks to a brief statement of
Giddens' achievements as we see them, before pointing up what
we believe to be the most serious omission in his work. (Perhaps
we ought also to mention that Giddens is not even the first to use
the term 'structuration'. On the contrary, as he occasionally
acknowledges himself, the term is French in origin. He has told us
that he thinks he first encountered it in Piaget. We have not tried
to trace its provenance, but we do think Giddens could have made
clear that Gurvitch's important usage, which he read in the 1960s,
has at least some elementary affinities with his own (Gurvitch,
1958; cf. Bryant, 1989:324–5). Giddens' only 'acknowledgement'
of Gurvitch consists of a rejection of his concept of 'destructura-
tion' (Giddens, 1979a:70).)[3]

In the opening lines of *Central Problems* Giddens tells how
some ten years earlier he 'conceived the project of examining the
residue of nineteenth-century European social theory for contemporary problems of the social sciences' (1979a:1). Ideas of Marx,
Durkheim, Weber and other nineteenth- and early twentieth-
century luminaries must, however, 'be radically overhauled today:
any appropriation ... has to be a thoroughly critical one' (ibid:1).
Giddens has reviewed mid-twentieth-century writers, especially
Parsons, in a similar spirit. The first claim we would make for
Giddens is that he has been more thorough in his critical appropriation of past writers than any of his rivals mentioned above. Sica in
Chapter Two commends his critical exegeses and muses that these
might prove his most enduring contribution to sociology. That is
not our view, but we do note how widely they have been cited, and
with one exception, to which we will return, we do believe them to
be shrewdly judged. It is notable that no-one has suggested any
significant figure or literature that Giddens might have combed but
has not. In so far as he largely ignores the early Americans, he also
confirms the Parsonian view that the founders of social theory are
indeed European – even if he includes Marx where Parsons does
not.

One element of Giddens' critical appropriation of past writers
about which do we have serious misgivings, though not always the

22

same ones as Boyne in Chapter Three, is his anathematization of functionalism (and, by extension, evolutionism). We hold no brief for functionalism as an 'ism', a comprehensive theoretical system that can yield explanations for anything and everything in social life, but nor do we believe that all functional arguments are worthless – save for the very general service functionalists have rendered social science by drawing attention to the unacknowledged conditions of human action and the unanticipated consequences. What Giddens objects to are teleology (the attribution of social goals and societal strategies in the absence of any plausible means whereby real historical actors could possibly have knowingly adopted those goals and strategies); explanations in terms of need satisfaction (for example, 'industrial capitalism "needs" large numbers of people either to work in unrewarding manual labour or to be part of an industrial reserve army of the unemployed' – therefore the existence of such people is explainable as a response to these needs (Giddens, 1984a:294)); and the attribution of rationality to social systems instead of to people.

We have no wish to contest the rejection of (macro-level) teleology. (Nor would we question his acceptance of micro-level teleology – the goal directed action of individuals.) On the other hand, reference to need satisfaction is sometimes defensible. Much of what Giddens objects to is failure to heed Durkheim's injunction to consider separately the cause of something and the function it fulfils. In the example given, the function does not explain the existence, but the existence does serve the function. Giddens, however, has another objection. What it amounts to is that functionalism typically shades into a structuralism that explains the existence of, in this instance, a supply of wage labourers without taking sufficiently into account the (implications of the) purposive action of the men and women concerned. Now this may be true, but it does not have to be like that. Functional argument not only ought not to displace causal argument, it also ought not to eclipse interpretative understanding and the analysis of purposive action. (Functional argument is one *lay* practice social scientists can ill afford to abandon!) Thus we agree with Wright when, in response to Giddens' strictures on the use of functional arguments by Marxists, he declares that: 'While the functionality of a given institution is never a *complete* explanation of that institution, I see no reason why arguments about functionality cannot constitute an aspect of a proper explanation' (Wright, 1983:15). Finally, we are not sure that functionalists do attribute rationality to frictionless social systems, complete with re-equilibrating mechanisms, and then compare them with real societies. Of course, the connection between model and real society is problematic – but then so is the connection between structure and system in Giddens.

In a way the second great virtue of Giddens' attempt to supersede the dualism of agency and structure, its extended and systematic character, is related to the first, the comprehensive critical appropriation of past theories. The common factor is the thoroughness with which Giddens pursues his goal. In speaking of the extended and systematic character of structuration theory, we are offering hostages to fortune. Our claim is essentially that the framework of sensitizing concepts that Giddens' ontology of social life offers will prove its value not just in the provision of standards with which to assess sociological analyses and researches generally, but also in the way it is used by others to give their work the bearings it requires. The forty-two concepts in the glossary to *The Constitution of Society* (1984a) do provide a more elaborated framework than anything to be found in Elias, Touraine, Berger and Luckmann, Bourdieu or Bhaskar. Giddens has himself given three examples in Chapter Eight of how some of them have been profitably used by others. We have not tried to maximize our own collection of examples, but we can certainly add the following to Giddens' three: Spybey (1984) and Rose (1988) on the analysis of organizations, Macintosh and Scapens (1987) on management accounting and Gruneau (1983) on the history of sport and leisure (cf. Jary and Horne, 1987).

The most basic question one can ask of Giddens' structuration theory is what sort of theory is it? One of the reasons why it has been hard to answer has to do with Giddens' disinclination to date to enter into not only epistemological debate but also moral and political argumentation. In setting out what the problem is, and why we think Giddens' current position is untenable in the longer term, we will draw upon an interesting exchange between McLennan (1984, 1988) and Ira Cohen (1986).

Halsey has recently written that 'most rival theorists are at least able to agree that empirical research in sociology can proceed without waiting for epistemological accord' (Halsey, 1989:354). The alternative, after all, remains the indefinite suspension of social research. What we question is whether social ontology can for long be as detached from epistemology as Giddens would imply. How do we know that humankind and the social world are as Giddens says they are? What makes his framework more than just one among many from which we may choose as we please? And why should other parties to dialogue treat what sociologists say, even when it is true to the principles of structuration theory, as any more or less worth heeding than what journalists, or politi-

Coming to terms with Anthony Giddens

cians, or prophets, or poets or ordinary citizens say? Now one answer would be that social science knowledge claims have a different status from other claims to know and that this deserves respect. In his refusal to disown social *science*, Giddens confirms that he believes this himself, but he is very reluctant to specify what these claims rest on. He thus denies himself one of the commoner gambits of the ontologist, which is to argue that the world must be like it is said to be for it to be possible for us to have the knowledge of it we do have, a gambit that depends on prior justification of some claim to know (based on experimentation, prediction, technological application, vindication in social practice or whatever). Another answer would have to do with the merits of the arguments in favour of the philosophical anthropology that informs structuration theory and supplies it with its (as yet underdeveloped) critical potential; but here, too, Giddens has tended to eschew systematic argument.

In an interview published in *Theory, Culture and Society* in 1982, Giddens was asked how he would ground the sort of critical social science he sought (Bleicher and Featherstone, 1982:72). He answered that he did not know but added that one has to steer between two unrealizable strategies: the first is pursuit of a secure epistemology or a secure normative theory from which to issue forth and study the world; the other is the rejection of epistemology and coherent normative theory in favour of some very strong sociological theory of how the world is (such as Barnes' strong thesis in the sociology of science (Barnes, 1974)). Instead he recommended a middle way: 'I want to follow the strategy of ... firing critical salvos into reality' (ibid:72); and 'to set up the idea of two houses, neither of which is a safe house, the factual house and the moral critical house, that you move between' (ibid:74). More challengingly, he said he wanted to work 'within a sociological commitment which would seem to [him] to suggest that some things are clearly noxious and other things clearly desirable and that it isn't necessary to ground them in order to proclaim this to be so' (ibid:72).

Now, even allowing for the infelicities of interview responses, there would seem problems with the position Giddens here adumbrates. These were taken up by McLennan who charges Giddens on two counts. The unfair charge is that he 'oscillates between the idea that there can be no epistemologically secure or coherent basis for [social theory], and that it is futile to reject epistemology' (McLennan, 1984:124). It is unfair because Giddens does consistently support both arguments; there is no oscillation involving alternate endorsement of the one and rejection of, or uninterest in,

25

Christopher G.A. Bryant and David Jary

the other. The fair charge is that any middle position is at least insufficiently justified. (In the course of his exchange with Ira Cohen, McLennan shifts the emphasis from the former to the latter.) In particular, McLennan complains that Giddens' critical orientation does not extend to specification of '*which* structures, *what* agencies, in what *sequences* go to make up the object of enquiry of social theory' (ibid:125, author's italics). Giddens offers, for the most part, neither positive nor normative theories, but rather fashions concepts that satisfy the *desiderata* of social theory (such as simultaneous avoidance of objectivism and subjectivism).

The one possible exception, according to McLennan, is the positing of 'virtual orders' – the structures (of rules and resources) that exist only in their instantiations in the structuration of social systems and the memory traces that constitute the knowledgeability of social actors. The trouble with these, he continues, is that they remain both substantively cloudy 'because Giddens does not specify the concrete social elements which are to count as predominantly structural', and theoretically cloudy 'because it is not at all obvious what "virtual" existence means ...' (ibid:127). Others, including Layder (1981), Thompson (1984b) and Urry (1982) also ask how it is possible to investigate a structure of rules and resources 'when that structure never produces an unmediated set of effects' that would confirm its existence (Urry, 1982:102). We think Giddens is sometimes clearer than McLennan and others allow. The general idea of 'virtual orders', which are inferrable only from their actual effects, is graspable even if it is hard to put it to operational use. Moreover, as Jary indicates in Chapter Five, Giddens does seek to define 'structural principles' for particular (types of) societies. What Giddens does not do is specify them with sufficient clarity to test them. Thus, in our view, it is not Giddens' concept of structure *per se* that is suspect but rather some of the examples of its use that he sets before us. As Layder, Thompson, Urry and others suggest, Giddens' underspecification of modes of production, social classes, the state, etc. makes it hard to know how to move from such structures of rules and resources to actual, more-or-less systemic, patterns of interaction. To this we would add that it is equally hard to move the other way.

It is worth noting that, as Cohen expresses it, both Giddens and Bhaskar 'focus on social practices and the characteristics of collectivities as potentials that are realized in diverse ways in the perpetuation and transformation of social life across all historically situated cases', and both 'refer to these analytical potentials in ontological terms' (Cohen, 1986:128; Bhaskar, 1975, 1979). But Giddens nowhere endorses the 'scientific realism' of Bhaskar and others. Instead he contents himself with saying, as he did to us, that he is a naive realist; there is a world out there and the ease with which one can bump against it is for him, as for Durkheim, confirmation of its facticity.

Giddens' ontology of the social, it appears, has its limits. In consequence one does not have to share McLennan's sympathy for objectivist conceptions of social science in general, and historical materialism in particular, to want clarification of what it is structuration theory actually delivers. Unlike Parsons, Giddens has never wanted empirical researchers to incorporate his whole conceptual vocabulary in their work. What matters is not the terminology but the structurationist orientation to the constitution of society that that terminology expresses. As we have already indicated, it is possible, in Giddens view, to be a structurationist without knowing it. The formal elaboration of the theory may inspire some to go on to formulate explanatory theories which are true to its principles, but it also serves its purpose in so far as it provides standards against which the strengths and weaknesses of theories generated independently of it may, at least in some respects, be measured (even if these standards are, for McLennan, mere *desiderata*). As Cohen says, however, 'the analytical components of structuration theory provide no explanatory propositions pertaining to substantive theory or history itself' (which makes his claims for their 'explanatory adequacy' somewhat obscure) (Cohen, 1986:127). It is only in substantive theory construction that answers are offered to McLennan's questions: Which structures, what agencies and what sequences? In his *A Contemporary Critique of Historical Materialism* (1981a) and elsewhere Giddens himself engages in substantive theorizing. The structurationist input is indispensable, but it in no way displaces the usual argumentation about contexts, connections and evidence.

Cohen is right that Giddens has consistently located his work within what is now called the post-empiricist tradition (Giddens 1976a:139–48; 1977j in 1977a:75–80). Since Cohen wrote, Giddens and Turner have supplied the following excellent summary of post-empiricism:

> the idea that there can be theory-neutral observations is repudiated, while systems of deductively-linked laws are no longer canonized as the highest ideal of scientific explanation. Most importantly, science is presumed to be an interpretative endeavour, such that problems of meaning, communication and translation are immediately relevant to scientific theories.
>
> (Giddens and Turner, 1987b:2)

Cohen argues, we think correctly, that:

> one of the most important results of post-empiricism has been to overturn the Cartesian duality of objectivism and relativism. While no neutral algorithm exists for the choice between theories (cf. Kuhn, 1970, pp. 199–200), this does not imply that science is an irrational enterprise. Rather scientists are obligated to submit good reasons for the acceptance of their programme in preference to competing schools of thought. The criteria to which these reasons refer are established as the result of the historical development of the community of inquiry within which justificatory arguments are made. This implies a rejection of the thesis of the incommensurability of meaning between theories (see ... Bernstein, 1983, pp. 79–93). On this basis the rational appeal to scientific criteria involves a limited degree of rational persuasion (Bernstein, 1983).
>
> (Cohen, 1986:129)

In this context, Giddens' relative indifference to epistemology, and his refusal to abandon the idea of social *science*, are both easily understood. They are part of a division of labour in which he gets on with the development of structuration theory, whilst others agonize, both instructively and inconclusively, about the principles and practices of justification. We have some sympathy with this view – just because Giddens has done most things it does not follow that he should be required to do everything – but in one respect at least it is imperative that he does do more.

Cohen attributes a 'metaphysical core' to structuration theory. We have preferred to speak of Giddens' philosophical anthropology, Kilminster of his world-view. Weber might simply have referred to his values. Whatever the language, the question arises of how to justify the choices made. As Cohen says:

> Epistemological criteria are not the only principles which theorists can invoke on behalf of their programme. Mary Hesse (1980, Ch. 8) points out that the underdetermination of theories, and the theory-laden nature of empirical accounts, creates the opening for the justification of theories on value-related grounds.
>
> (Cohen, 1986:131)

Natural scientists, at this point, often enter the pragmatic criteria of successful prediction and control. Social scientists cannot expect to do likewise and should refer instead, Hesse suggests, to ethical values and political goals. What is wrong with Giddens, according to this view, is not his evident espousal of particular values but rather his unconcern to justify them. In the absence of normative counterfactual theorizing, or some other means of justifying claims about being, structuration theory will keep the take-it-or-leave-it character that disturbs McLennan and also Bryant in Chapter Seven). It will do so because Giddens cannot rely on others to supply the justifications for him. The post-empiricist community of inquirers may make a virtue of the ethical and political factors that inform social science but it does not yet have any settled means of assessing different, and contesting, values.

In the end there appears to us an unresolved – almost Weberian – tension in structuration theory. On the one hand, Giddens seems to offer it as an open-ended, and non-compulsory, framework – what Boyne (Chapter Three) says it should always be but often is not (Conception A). On the other, he develops it into a forceful expression of a particular historical view – an expression, moreover, that is relentless in its strictures against, and exclusion of, alternatives (Conception B). There would also seem to be a third reading in which an overriding ontological emphasis on the historicality of human action and human societies 'resolves' the tension between A and B; reflexiveness, knowledgeability, unpredictability and contingency not only limit the role of laws and generalizations, but are also here a cause for celebration (Conception C). Kilminster alludes to C when attributing to Giddens a world-view in which the self-direction of the individual is a central feature. None of these three conceptions is without difficulty.

Earlier we remarked that Giddens' curiously ambivalent advocacy of his own theory may not have helped its reception. The same might be said of his shifts between Conceptions A and B. Instead of meeting criticisms of B head on, he too often reverts to A and the declaration that his is only one approach. Conception C, too, clearly requires a fuller normative justification than it has so far received. Refusal to think through the different epistemological implications and ontological bases of A, B and C has enabled Giddens to move between them without inhibitions; but in doing so, he has often left his readers unsure what it is they are dealing with and how it can be justified.[4] Giddens has reaffirmed to us his general support for synthesis *and* pluralism, but his syntheses are syntheses on his terms (and as such often involve a highly selective reading and raiding of the work of others), and his respect for pluralism is a singular one in so far as it does not extend to justification of his own theory let alone anybody else's. In consequence, it constitutes more a recognition of the inevitability of pluralism than a principled advocacy.

Without suggesting that there could ever be a final resolution of all the issues raised by the conception of a 'duality of structure', we

Christopher G.A. Bryant and David Jary

do believe that more could be done to establish a satisfactory grounding for theorizing in structurationist terms. The outcome of the kind of post-empiricism favoured by Giddens and ourselves should be renewed prominence for synthesis and pluralism as two sides of a *continuing* dialectic in social theory (cf. Feyerabend, 1981; Bernstein, 1983; Jary, 1981, 1989).[5] Such a viewpoint would encourage a more principled formulation of the epistemological assumptions that underpin the ontological claims of structuration theory, without this involving bids for theoretical closure of the kind Giddens rightly wishes to avoid.

In conclusion, we must signal clearly that, for all our criticisms, we have no wish to contest the generally positive response that Giddens' structuration theory has elicited. On the contrary, we endorse Urry's (1986) verdict that it is 'the most systematic, interesting and sustained attempt so far found to develop an approach to social theory that transcends the dichotomies of determinism and voluntarism, society and the individual and object and subject' (Urry, 1986:435). This is why we invite our readers to come to terms with Anthony Giddens' structuration theory. It is also why we hope criticisms of it will, where necessary, lead Giddens and others to state its epistemological assumptions and ontological claims with greater clarity and precision.

Notes

1 On Neustadt and Elias at Leicester, see Marshall (1982) and Brown (1987).
2 In the Heideggerian terms sometimes employed by Giddens, social structures and social systems are to be seen more as 'binding' time and space than as located in them (cf. Urry in Chapter Six; Gross, 1982; Joas, 1987).
3 There are other areas of structuration theory where Giddens would seem to understate continuities between his own and others' work, e.g. on time and social theory (cf. Martins, 1974) and on historical sociology (cf. Tilly, 1981). More generally Giddens sometimes understates the continuities between classical social theory and structuration theory (cf. Giddens, 1987d).
4 Structuration theory has been criticized both for collapsing structure into agency and eschewing systematic theory (e.g. Layder, 1981) and for overemphasizing general theory at the expense of either action or contextuality (e.g. Thrift, 1985a). Attacked from both sides, Giddens sometimes claims, as he did to us, that he has got the balance about right. This is, of course, a *non sequitur*. Our view is that unresolved tensions between Giddens' several conceptions of structuration theory – along with a certain looseness in the formulation and testing of empirical

30

propositions framed in its terms – indicate that Giddens does sometimes move from an emphasis on agency to an emphasis on structure in ways that are underargued whether in his general theory or his substantive accounts. This issue is explored further by Jary in Chapter Five.

5   One significant reason for saying this is that the 'duality of structure' – like Bhaskar's 'relational' and 'transformational' model of society – affords a model of science (including social science), in which both pluralism of theories and mediation between theories have their place.

Appendix: The location of summaries of the main elements of structuration theory provided by Giddens

1. *New Rules* (1976a): pp. 126–9, 160–2, for indication of the initial terms of Giddens' appropriation and 'correction' of interpretative and social phenomenological perspectives, together with his conception of the 'double hermeneutic' and his formulation of 'new rules'.
2. *Central Problems* (1979a): pp. 45–8 for a useful 'résumé' of structuralism and its relation to structuration theory. (On structuralism, Giddens (1987i) is also especially useful.)
3. *Contemporary Critique* (1981a): pp. 1–29 for an overview of both the elements of structuration theory and its implications for the treatment of 'time-space' and historical change. (On 'time–space', Giddens (1987j) is also useful.)
4. *Constitution of Society* (1984a): pp. 1–40 for 'an exposition of the main concepts of structuration theory', and pp. 281–8 on the implications for research. This volume also contains a very useful 'glossary' of key terms and main 'neologisms' in structuration theory (pp. 373–7).
5. *Nation-State and Violence* (1985a): pp. 3–5 for an overview of Giddens' argument on the nation-state and violence and on the 'four main institutional axes' of modern societies. (On these general themes Giddens (1984b) also provides a valuable overview.)

Chapter two

The California–Massachusetts strain in structuration theory

Alan Sica

When Giddens made his first appearance on the American theory scene, it was in the form common to previous writers who chose to stay firmly within traditional boundaries, with books on Weber, Durkheim, social class, classical theory and the like. His class-analysis book was not highly regarded by those empirically oriented Americans who knew a great deal about the subject, because he did not add anything to their data bases, did not use their methods and he rubbed their noses in the fact that the most interesting theorizing about social class was being carried out abroad. In fact, his book is so chronically lacking in attention to American research into class – and for a time after Blau and Duncan (1967), Americans thought they owned class analysis – that it was amazing it even saw print in the US.

Graduate students, like myself at the time, looking for a high-level primer on class theory welcomed Giddens' effort as the most useful then on the market, but older researchers, up to their elbows in census data, were not impressed. The only book of his early period (between 1969 and about 1975) that stood out in its excellence was his primer on classical theory, and its many printings surely made it his own best seller. Yet here, too, the audience was the huge crowd of graduate students and young instructors who flocked to sociology in its heyday (1970–74), and not older teachers whose theory textbook choices ran to works like Martindale's or Timasheff's. Thus, Giddens, established himself early on as a student and interpreter of classical theory – even his class-analysis book is steeped in this material – whom readers in the US with already defined interests in these matters recognized as a bright and reliable guide, but whom others, of the more regular American type, could easily disregard. His name for instance, very seldom appeared in any bibliographies of articles that were published in the three main journals (*American Sociological Review, American Journal of Sociology, Social Forces*). And this remained true for many years, even after Giddens retired somewhat from his role as hermeneuticist and had begun propounding his own theory about contemporary social life.

Therefore it came as quite a shock in 1976 when *New Rules of Sociological Method* (1976a) appeared, that short, brittle manifesto of hermeneutically informed analytic principles, and by far the earliest major theory to make use of this 'new' body of ideas. For in this book Giddens not only began putting together the rudiments of structuration theory (the term itself first seen in *The Class Structure of the Advanced Societies*, 1973), but also brought in crafty co-operation of Goffman, Garfinkel, Cicourel, Schegloff and others from the California orbit of micro-theory. This was a bold stroke for Giddens, and coupled with his critique of Parsons and functionalism, gave him a 'purchase' (as he but not his American friends might have phrased it then) on important theoretical material from the States that only a few years before would have seemed out of place in his writing. Even in his 1977 book of essays, *Studies in Social and Political Theory*, he begins by explaining that: 'The studies which compose this volume are essentially organized about a critical encounter with European social theory in its "classical" period' (1977a:9). It is not that Giddens had up to that point never been introduced to the micro-dimension of theorizing. One must remember that Norbert Elias, surely the most creative analyst of interaction, using historical materials, that this century has seen, taught at Leicester along with Giddens in the latter's first years of professional work. But the discovery, for Giddens, of what southern California had to offer – perhaps due to his teaching summer school there for some years – must have done something that his thorough engagement with traditional European and British theory had not.

Robert Howard (author of *Brave New Workplace* (1987) and a talented left-wing journalist) studied with me at Amherst College for a year and then travelled to Cambridge on a Marshall scholarship to work with Giddens the following year (1976–77). He wrote about Giddens' surprising new book, apparently drafted very quickly, that he had seen in manuscript, and the use made in it of 'hermeneutics' – a word he first heard in my seminar on social theory at Amherst. It was with this book that Giddens joined his older concerns with the new threads from the US (plus Gadamer and Ricoeur), and came up with a hermeneutically informed programme for the field. The fact that few people in the States paid much attention to his nine 'new rules' (Giddens, 1976a:160–2) could not completely obscure the fact that Giddens had moved away from exegesis for its own sake and towards something more

33

nearly 'original' in the sense that we now take the word. He never again carried out first-class interpretation of general theory (with the possible exception of his later attention to Habermas), apparently satisfied that he had given whatever he had to contribute along those lines. But the new Giddens suddenly – for so it seemed in the US – began writing in a systematic way that, for all its left-wing subtextual implications, shared with Parsons' conservatism a method of examining everything in the social world through a single lens, and then forcing others' positions through a sieve that gave them a similarly reformed consistency.

As I have pointed out elsewhere (Sica, 1983; Shapiro and Sica 1984:14–18, 1896), Giddens' style – again, as in the case of Parsons – in some important ways shapes his approach to theorizing, and one aspect of this came out clearly in works that followed *New Rules*. Rather than examining a fairly small group of works carefully, as he had done in his theory primer, he began to take in every conceivable source, especially those that were springing up in Europe and had more to do with philosophy and literary criticism than social theory proper. Quantitatively he quickly outdid Habermas, for although the latter has never hesitated to appropriate the work of all and sundry for his own purposes, he has shown a marked distaste, even hostility, for certain strains of contemporary theorizing. Giddens has opened his arms more widely and only recently began to lambast post-structuralist, post-modernist arguments in a way not dissimilar to Habermas.

But to return to the American case. It is not quite accurate to think of Giddens as a British theorist, especially if one considers writers like Gellner, Winch, Rex, Morris Ginsberg or even the immigrant Dahrendorf. And if there is a characteristic of his original theorizing that sets him apart from his English colleagues, it is his interest in ethnomethodology and functionalism. As John Heritage pointed out in his chapter on ethnomethodology in a book that Giddens co-edited and published: 'Anthony Giddens' writings ... have been a consistent exception to the generally negative tone of response to ethnomethodology' (Giddens, 1987b:225 n.4). Already in 1974 Giddens had included a chapter by Garfinkel – the only American of ten authors – in his *Positivism and Sociology* (1974a), and his own press, Polity, reissued Garfinkel's only book nearly 20 years after its first publication in the US. There is a special affinity between Garfinkel's brand of phenomenological investigations (and that of some of his followers), and Giddens' generally macro-orientation, one that is perhaps reminiscent of that between Durkheim – concerning whom Giddens has published four books – and social psychologists of his own day.

But long before this warm fellow-feeling surfaced, Giddens was dealing seriously with American social theory, specifically Parsons' and some of his followers, which Giddens labelled simply as 'functionalism'.

As I have pointed out elsewhere, regarding:

> his connection, however formal, with Parsons´ (which he would probably discount), one can use Giddens against himself, as he often uses Marx. He observes that Marx partook of his ideological opponents despite efforts to the contrary, simply because one becomes part of the enemy even as one consumes him.

(Sica, 1983:1261)

From Giddens' earliest published analysis of theoretical materials (e.g. ' "Power" in the Writing of Talcott Parsons', 1968), he has put much of himself into dissecting either Parsons or Durkheim. By comparison, his consideration of Marx or Weber has been slight and incidental. It takes no feat of imagination to see that if one is more temperamentally or otherwise drawn to Durkheim than to other classical figures in the history of social thought, then some attention to Parsons becomes almost inevitable, inasmuch as the latter's best efforts at exegesis and theoretical elaboration fell well within the functionalist perspective that Durkheim single-handedly legitimated. And thus it has been the case with Giddens, particularly during his first years as theorist and student of others' ideas, that his attention to Parsons has had within it a noticeable ambivalence that is probably tied up with an equally uncertain reverence for Durkheim.

There are other, more mundane reasons for Giddens' preoccupation with Parsons when he was 'young' – just how young few folks know, since he has carefully omitted from all standard sources the vital statistics other theorists nowadays do not hesitate to disclose. Surely one was the need, during the liberating 1960s, to identify with that stream of writers who opposed the 'orthodox consensus' initially stigmatized by Atkinson (1972) and Gouldner (1970). Just as with Gouldner, who spent much of his book tearing at Parsons on political grounds, Giddens could see that the fixture at Cambridge, Massachusetts was the only authentically prominent theoretical target within American sociology – if one discounted Marcuse and others on the left who, it turned out, were a passing fancy for those in the mainstream of social science. To make a name for himself he had to go after Parsons, and this he did, even if – again, as with Durkheim – his tone was serious critique rather than dismissal (Mills) or evisceration (Gouldner). He took Parsons at his word, that is, as a writer who in the grand manner had been trying for forty years to construct a social theory that would hold the esteem of philosophers, other social scientists, even historians. If Parsons' perpetually mentioned conservatism – a version of theoretical conservatism that was not, incidentally, always linked in his life or work to political conservatism of the ordinary American kind – bothered Giddens, it did not cause him to throw aside Parsons' case entirely. In fact, it forced the young critic to pay closer attention than he otherwise might have to those features of Parsons' work that he hoped to radicalize and use in his own theorizing.

This first foray into functionalism of the American brand is not terribly combative, as one would expect from a young critic. But it alreadys bears the marks of Giddens' lifelong style of exposition. It is measured, utterly clear, free of sarcasm or open hostility – which, given other writings Parsons had inspired, is itself an achievement of sorts – and reliably informative up to a point. He sets himself the task of asking Parsons' writings for their specification of 'power', dutifully notes the highpoints of doctrine (even when they seem absurd on their face), and then, much towards the close of the article, begins the task of criticism. He even allows himself an occasional exclamation point, as in: 'But what slips away from sight almost completely in the Parsonian analysis is the very fact that power, even as Parsons defines it, is always exercised *over* someone!' (Giddens, 1977a:341). He shows good sportsmanship in the extreme by defending Parsons against those who see his work as nonsense or worse. But in the end he turns to a metaphor from the Maoism of the age, reminding his reader that it is 'in this sense that power can grow out of the barrel of a gun' (ibid:345), and that power does indeed have about it some 'zero-sum' qualities that Parsons so refused to acknowledge. It is only in closing that Giddens begins to reach for a bit of profundity, as when he observes: 'Parsons's own analysis shows an ingenuous tendency to see nothing beyond the processes which are overt.... Power now becomes simply an extension of consensus.... But this is surely inadequate' (ibid:346). And in an undated postscript to this article, probably written eight years later, he defines power as 'transformative capacity', and then takes a page from Habermas: 'From this aspect, freedom from domination in systems of interaction appears as a problem of the achievement of rationally defensible forms of authority' (ibid:349). It is instructive that this sentiment, if slightly reworded, would fit equally well within Parsons' idea of power, even though he never became as philosophically or linguistically sophisticated as Habermas when confronting the problem of power in democratic environments – the inevitable need to explain away its bleak consequences for most of the subjected populace. The point, though, relative to Giddens, is that he was willing to discuss the matter with his theoretical colleagues in an entirely gentlemanly way, and steadfastly refused to become as vituperative as had so many other readers of Parsons' miserable prose. It is this quality that stood Giddens so well in the US – it seemed so entirely British in the best sense – as he made his way through Parsons twenty years ago.

Giddens had a good year in 1972, publishing his pamphlet on Weber (Giddens, 1972b), his first selection of Durkheim's works, and two important essays – in addition to just having brought out his theory textbook to warm response. It was in doing research for the latter, his first book, that he came upon contradictions between what he learned to be so and the received wisdom that plays havoc with simple historical fact. He was becoming hermeneutically sensitive to exactly the sort of problems associated with textual analysis that Schleiermacher and others of the interpretative tradition had been writing about for centuries. He did not, however, explicitly imbibe hermeneutical theory – his references to works of that tradition are infrequent and not connected to their 'principles' of interpretation – which gives his work the power of hermeneutically skilful renderings, but at the same time a more-or-less naive cast. It is as if he had taught himself what 'good' analysis of texts means, and was willing to throw the weight of his youthful renderings against much more established writers, especially those whose careers were played out in the US. Giddens had learned what all good readers do when they turn from secondary to primary works, that no matter how 'accepted' a capsulization of a given theorist might be, it is invariably wrong, either by distortion, omission or ideological slant. It was in this frame of mind that he wrote the 'Four Myths' paper (Giddens, 1972e) and spoke out directly against misinterpretations of classics, especially Durkheim, and it so happened that his targets were principally Americans of high repute. Since American sociologists were not at that point priding themselves on their knowledge of theory's history or its fine points, it may have surprised Giddens more than his colleagues in the States that standard characterizations of classic thought were often caricatures.

It was from this point that Giddens begins to take off the kid gloves in dealing with Parsons, whose *Structure of Social Action* he calls 'probably ... the most influential study of the development of social theory produced in the last thirty years' (Giddens, 1972e in 1977a:209). Naturally, Giddens needs to set up the king before

Alan Sica

knocking him off the throne, but there does seem to be in his treatment of Parsons a fairly serious residue of respect for the elder's early achievement. Giddens holds that Parsons misunderstands Hobbes, that his 'exposition of Durkheim's sociological concerns is highly misleading' (ibid:210), and that he was more concerned to establish his own artificial lineage than to explain exactly what his predecessors had thought. This argument became common in American journals a few years after Giddens' piece appeared in England, and it is probably the case that his early de-Parsonizing helped in this campaign to reclaim the classics from functionalist fancies masquerading as history. Of course, no interpretation or close reading is innocent, as literary critics now point out obsessively. And Giddens was beginning to formulate his own particular appreciation for Durkheim so that 'structuration', a term coined 'for want of a better word' in his class-analysis book (Giddens, 1973:105), might take the form he could defend. Yet for the time being, in this early essay, he does what most nascent theorists do when starting out; that is, he takes apart the preceding generation's story of what happened and why it mattered for the express purpose of 'advancing' social thought. Had masses of readers read and believed Giddens' attack on Parsons, the latter's resurrection in the 1980s would have been much harder to accomplish. But his critique was published in the premier issue of a radical British journal that few Americans then read, so its power on sheerly intellectual terms was diffused before influencing readings of Parsons in the ensuing decade as it should have.

For Giddens, the set of arguments Parsons makes about Durkheim that turn around the problem of order, the role of moral rationality in modernizing societies, the central motif of Durkheim's entire labours and so on, add up to gross distortion and miscomprehension. And since Parsons's exegesis of Durkheim is probably the best he did – very much like Alexander's book on Parsons in his four-volume set – Giddens implicitly wonders how carefully Parsons thought through the texts he was trying to convey sympathetically. Though he stops short of saying so, it seems clear that Giddens' entire article (and parts of others he wrote at the same time) is an attack on Parsons' interpretative ability, upon his very intelligence. And other American theorists do not fare much better when Giddens looks at what they have said about Durkheim and compares their findings with his own, more carefully contextualized version. The analyses of Durkheim tendered by Robert Nisbet, Irving Zeitlin, and Lewis Coser, among others, do not stand up well under Giddens' cross-examination. Durkheim's alleged link to political conservatism is shown to be illusory, and

38

Nisbet's throwing together of disparate writers 'whose ideas were really quite widely divergent' (Giddens, 1977a:214), in an effort to establish a conservative lineage for Durkheim, Giddens shows to be unsupported by the facts. Moreover, it is not Parsons' Hobbesian problem that worried Durkheim, nor the link to the right that is central to his work, but rather 'the "Kantian problem" of the moral imperative' (ibid:216) that kept him busy for 30 years. Giddens interestingly links Durkheim's thought to Freud's, in that the discomfort between self and society was more profound and antinomic in Durkheim's work than those writers on the right wing, like Nisbet, cared to believe. In short, many American analysts of his ideas were applying concepts and historical connections to other writers that were simply too crude or irrelevant to the contextuality of Durkheim's opera to do him justice. It was this kind of error that Giddens happily pointed out, some years before the excellent Durkheim scholarship of the 1970s surfaced, forever banishing simplistic misunderstanding of 'Durkheim's functionalism presented *in abstracto*' (ibid:217).

Giddens then pulls to pieces related mythologizing, especially concerning the gulf between 'early' social thought – anything prior to the Second World War – and the 'brilliant' accomplishments of Parsons and his generation during the period of American world hegemony. Here Giddens shows his perhaps unknowing indebtedness to classical hermeneutic theory, e.g.

> In order to understand the framework of Durkheim's sociology, it is undoubtedly important to examine the socio-political context in which he wrote – and it is certainly the case that there is a close relation between his political and sociological views
>
> (ibid:218)

Nowadays, with presses collapsing under the strain of printing book after book of exegesis, this viewpoint has become ordinary, both in England, where it never went far out of style, and in the US. Because Parsons and his peers were so intent upon making sociology out to be a fundable science with practical applications, concerns like Giddens' in 1972 seemed extremely antique. In those days, non-specialists had taken over 'theory', and anyone with graduate training felt qualified to write spectacularly ignorant articles on the founding fathers. Surely one of the reasons Giddens took so long catching on in the States, despite his yearly publication of a book or two, and why even now he can comfortably be ignored by many researchers in areas that might well profit from his ideas, is because of his old-world insistence that context, intellectual lineage, philosophical grounding and moral–ethical programme mattered enormously to earlier writers, and that contemporary readers push aside these elements of their work at grave risk. And Giddens has not over the years made friends in the States by writing bluntly, even if always in very gentlemanly terms, regarding what he and his British colleagues see as appalling ineptness in the Colonies, e.g. 'Durkheim is often regarded, especially by American sociologists, as the founder of empirical sociology.... This view is manifestly false' (ibid:219).

What is most interesting about this period of Giddens' writing, however, is not that he was straightening out the record *vis à vis* a load of distortions and confusions imported into it by sloppy or deceitful Americans. After all, other scholars working in the US – H. Stuart Hughes, Hans Speier, Kurt Wolff, Hans Gerth – were perfectly capable of that task. The peculiarity of Giddens' most serious hermeneutic labours (since shortly after this, by the mid-1970s, he had stopped working through classic texts with the sort of careful scrutiny evident in his youthful articles and books) is that the French and German side of textual critique is completely missing. Had he taken on scholars working in those countries on the same material, or had he used critical techniques then well worked out on the Continent, it seems his game would have better matched the calibre of his weapon. As it was, he was shooting lame beasts, since most Americans who bothered at all to write of these matters did it with their left hand while the right went about the more serious business of advancing social 'science'. One wonders, for instance, why his only rival in the realm of serious social theorizing, Habermas, does not appear in his work, except incidentally, until 1977, when he published an article critically recounting the Gadamer-Habermas debate (Giddens,1977d). In it one reads many lines of cautious praise, then gentle rebuke, culminating in dark foreboding for Habermas's future as theorist: 'How successful this approach is likely to prove, however, ... remains to be seen' (Giddens, 1977d in 1977a:156); '... it is difficult to resist the conclusion that several of the problems I have indicated remain deeply embedded in Habermas's most recent writing' (ibid:164). Yet in most of his work, Giddens confronts classical thought directly or with steady reference to Parsons and other Americans, as if interpretative wars going on nearby in languages Giddens knows well did not merit inclusion in his own reconstructions. In a strange way, then, Giddens went about building his own reputation by discrediting the weakest community of interpretation, not those writers then hard at work in Europe who together, even if in vastly different ways, were putting together a body of interpretative theory and practice that during the 1980s would transform all hermeneutic labours that sought widespread credibility.

Why he chose to work this way is not clear from his own writing. In fact, Giddens is not in the least a confessional or self-revealing writer. Only his first book wears a dedication – to a set of initials; his acknowledgments are crisp and brief in all his many volumes; he does not discuss why he decides to pursue this rather than that set of texts, and he assumes an authorial voice that by contemporary French standards is positively Walter Scott. (Compare his conventional prose with, say, the post-positivist style of Ben Agger in *Socio(onto)logy* (1989) or Lawrence Hazelrigg in *A Wilderness of Mirrors* (1989a) and *Claims of Knowledge* (1989b.) Giddens is not 'known' as a theorizing person in the way that Merton was, or Mills, Gouldner or Sorokin had become, in that their styles were immediately recognizable, and revealed more of themselves than they probably even wished. There is throughout Giddens' work, and nowhere more so than in his running critique and/or co-optation of American theory, a distanced neutrality, a disciplined patter elegant enough to seem very smart, and tight enough to close off objections before they can gain a foothold. Whereas it is easy to pinpoint Parsons' blunders, even when he was writing at his most evasive (e.g. about power), finding the holes in Giddens' widely cast net is something like discovering the flaws in Habermas. Yet, of course, the latter is notoriously opaque and overwritten, while Giddens' analyses always come across as sane, well-considered, carefully constructed, even charming. If Parsons' arguments see often times hilariously remote from easily perceived social reality, and Habermas's posture so abstracted from the everyday – even when he writes 'about' the everyday! – that its connection to existence seems imagined and unreliable, Giddens' work calms the troubled heart with its rhythmic, patient, fatherly clarity. His enthusiasms are clearly stated, but never insistent, and his willingness to bring everyone of any use into his story is the mark of a friendly host. These characteristics, which, just perhaps, he may have picked up as much from American friends as from English scholarly mores, run throughout his theorizing and exegesis, and are as evident in the early essays just discussed as in later work. If this mindset, combining tolerant absorption with gentle criticism, has become attenuated somewhat in his most recent responses to post-structuralism and also Habermas, for many years it became the hallmark of Giddens' work, and built an audience for it that responded as much to its non-intellectual qualities of style as to its theoretical substance.

In addition to the shelf of books that Giddens has added to the libraries of theorists, several of his articles – always later republished in one of his books of essays, to be sure – have point-edly revealed his quality of mind. When he is good, he is among the best. Such an article, it seems to me, is 'Functionalism: *après la lutte*' (*Social Research*, 1976c), which is distinct from many of his previous essays in that it first appeared in the US, and argues very powerfully against a set of American theorists. The essay served as an advertisement for *New Rules* (1976a), to which he refers constantly, and which was published almost simultaneously. This is a deservedly well-regarded piece of intellectual dissection, and along with his introduction to his 1972 Durkheim reader, and perhaps also his 1976 *American Journal of Sociology* article on classical theory and the origins of the discipline, numbers among his most important shorter labours (Giddens, 1972a; 1976b). It would be pleasant to think that whenever Giddens faces his American colleagues head-on, and invariably to disagree with them, that he works the most seriously. But that aside, his picking apart of Merton, Stinchcombe and others in the bastion of functionalist hegemony, deserves careful rereading, because in it he says a great deal about his next decade of writing and also makes claims there that, though repeated dozens of times subsequently, seem equally subject to critique as were Merton's hopeful observations about his own way of doing social theory that Giddens hoped to dispose of once and for all.

It would be tedious and impractical to evaluate the success of Giddens' frontal assault on structural-functionalism, since it would call for rehearsing Merton's, Stinchcombe's and Nagel's positions – in fact, those of every contributor to the volume Giddens spends most of his time working from, the Demerath and Peterson book (1967), frozen in that mindset of long ago – and then doing the same for Giddens. In typical style, he attacks points of logic and definition that he finds wanting. This is Giddens' most British, one might say Winchian, proclivity, and one that has not influenced American sociology very much. To show, for instance, that Merton's use of 'structure' is loose, or that, more importantly, his most famous distinction between manifest and latent functions 'does not withstand close scrutiny' (Giddens, 1977a:107), cuts very little ice in a research environment where Merton's ideas had, up till the early 1970s at least, inspired more empirical research than virtually anyone's, and certainly much more than Parsons'. In the US, as Giddens must have known from teaching here, ideas of unusual clarity and empirical usefulness, the sort that become standard textbook lore for introductory students, are extremely difficult to dislodge. Even though Giddens' rhetoric against Merton here and elsewhere in the article is aggressive, he does not manage to dethrone the sitting king of the 'middle range' mainly because his attack remains on the logical level. In an academic world where Wittgenstein is worshipped, it may well be enough to make points off the other fellow's illogical remarks, or his inconsistencies of definition. But in the US – and this accounts substantially for Giddens' inability to reign supreme in theory – what is required in order to humble contending theoretical claims is not only logical attack, but especially empirical reference. It is here that Giddens was and continued to be very weak, at least until *The Constitution of Society* (1984; US publication, 1985), where for the first time he tries to show, by using other people's research, that his theory could deliver the empirically grounded goods (see Sica, 1986).

It is indeed true, as Giddens observed in 'Four Myths' that 'Parsons usually only seems to reply to his critics elliptically' (Giddens, 1977a:381, n.50). But one wonders why Giddens was not more aware of this sort of dilemma in his own theorizing, especially since he was clearly not content – as opposed, say, to Winch or Gellner – to remain a British theorist, but wanted badly to crack the American ideas market. This is still another resemblance between Giddens and his nemesis in Massachusetts, in that both were willing and able to spin abstractions morning till night, but neither paid nearly the kind of attention that would have made a difference to potential critics who invariably wanted to know how the proffered theory might clarify or invigorate their research into contemporary life. There is a strange kind of intellectual blindness at work here, or simply an inability to contend seriously with large-scale objections to one's ideas. Parsons suffered from this much worse and for much longer than Giddens. And with his most recent works, he seems to be breaking out of this enclosed sphere of self-validation. This contrasts sharply with Merton. It was to his lasting credit and the principal source of admiration among his colleagues that he was willing to state his ideas always in terms of research agendas, even at the grave risk of simplifying his conceptualizing beyond what would have been most pleasing to him intellectually.

If, for instance, one considers Merton's dissertation or his playful *tour de force, On the Shoulders of Giants* (1965), it can hardly seem credible that Giddens in a few lines is able to prove that Merton did not see things very clearly, and that therefore 'the limitations of functionalism ... are irremediable' (Giddens, 1977a:96); or that: 'Merton's discussion is ambiguous' and: 'All this shows that what initially appears as a neat, inclusive distinction, between manifest and latent functions, papers over various basic problems concerning the nature of intentional action and its implications for social theory' (Giddens, 1977a:108). It may be the case that Merton's 1949 notions needed some redirection as of nearly 30 years later, but Giddens' agile deflation comes off as too simple and, to use an Americanism, too slick. However, just as in his lectures at professional meetings, where 'whole paragraphs' roll out of Giddens with practised ease and precision, apparently without notes or prompting, this article seems to make many points against functionalist orthodoxy with a level of orderly deconstruction that escaped other important critics of the 'school'.[1]

Naturally, Giddens wants in the end to advance his ideas as capable of doing what functionalism failed to do, but along the way he brings up an important theoretical point that is worth pursuing. Up to now I have argued that the article was not as convincing in the US as Giddens may have wished due to features of his working style that may appear extrinsic to its intellectual content. But now it is on the theoretical level *per se* – if one can isolate things in quite this way – that I find a central difficulty to Giddens' theoretical proposals.

In the first paragraph of his article, Giddens sounds an alarm that probably rang louder in his own environs than it did in the US, and he continues to ring it throughout the article and into an appendix – 'Notes on the theory of structuration' (1977i) (which seems an out-take from *New Rules*). Giddens exclaims:

> For whatever the limitations of functionalism ... it always placed in the forefront problems of institutional organization, and was firmly opposed to subjectivism in social theory. I believe this emphasis still to be necessary, indeed all the more urgent in view of the upsurge of subjectivism and relativism that has accompanied the waning influence of functionalist notions in the social sciences.
>
> (Giddens, 1977i in 1977a:99)

This opening identifies the bugaboo that will throw its ugly visage into the article at many turns, and seems to unify in one way Giddens' subtextual strategy of critique, while at the same time revealing, I think unwittingly, one of Giddens' most fragile, insistent 'domain assumptions' (Gouldner, 1970:31ff.). Throughout the post-war history of American sociology, much more so than in Britain, a central, highly charged tenet of its extra-intellectual *and* intellectual programme has been to banish 'subjectivism' from its province. Without going into the necessary detail for an historically responsible explanation of why this has been the case, let us simply recall the rough treatment accorded Freud and the 'Machiavellians' (Mosca, Pareto, Michels, also Sorel) during the 1950s. Even Parsons' attempt after the war to bring Freud into the realm of legitimate social theory did little to assuage American sociology's suspicion of explanations for social action that hinged on the unconscious or the irrational. (Richard LaPierre's *Freudian Ethic* (1960) is a barbed but eloquent statement of the counterFreudianism of the time, and firmly based on sociological premisses.) It is not too difficult to see that mass irrationality – or so it was evaluated after the war by liberal social scientists – which the fascists all over Europe put to such effective, horrifying use, posed a set of exceedingly dark issues that American empirical sociology, nor its theoretical wing, were in a position to analyse. No one from within the discipline, for instance, produced a work that rivalled Reich's *Mass Psychology of Fascism* (1933b) or *Character Analysis* (1933a) and even the collective expatriate venture, *The Authoritarian Personality* (Adorno *et al.*, 1950) was not warmly received by sociologists in the States, despite being written here. Reich's early work as a therapist in Vienna with patients from the sexually repressed working class – precisely those for whom fascism apparently held such appeal – gave him insight into the personality/ social structure nexus, particularly with regard to sociopathology, that Americans refused to take seriously, even as they carried out sociological research on racism, political violence and other topics that fit naturally with Reich's (Reich, 1972).

Giddens has never taken very seriously this 'unsociological' dimension of social or political life. He was not, for instance, a contributor to the important volume edited by Wilson (1970) called *Rationality*, probably because he was then too little known to warrant inclusion. And yet, it 'makes sense' in terms of his subsequent writing that he would not wish to share pages with colleagues who pursued these vexing matters (which have become ever more heated over the ensuing twenty years), exactly because of the position laid out in this article. Giddens quoted Merton's early manifesto to the effect that: ' "Social function" refers to *observable objective consequences*, and not to *subjective dispositions* (aims, motives, purposes)' (Giddens, 1976c in 1977a:99, original italics). This reasonable argument, designed, of course, to give sociology a bailiwick separate from that of psychology, is not in tone or substance at one with Giddens' opening remarks. When Giddens lashes out at the 'upsurge of subjectivism and relativism', about the need to remain 'firmly opposed to subjectivism in social theory', he is surpassing the significance of Merton's functionalist position, and edging perilously close to ideological fires that have their origin in non-intellectual tinder.

He is quite clear, after offering capsule summaries of the three functionalist theorists, how he intends to better their programme:

What I propose to do in the sections which follow is provide a *decodification* of functional analysis, an examination of certain fundamental weaknesses in functionalism in the concern, not to reject its emphases in favour of subjectivism, but to encompass them within a different theoretical scheme.

(Giddens, 1977a:105)

And later, in another summarizing statement he reminds his readers that: 'it is of the first importance to avoid the relapse into subjectivism that would attend an abandonment of the concept of structure' (ibid:117). Then he poses the question that has concerned him above all others during his mature period of theorizing: 'How can we reconcile a notion of structure with the necessary centrality of the active subject?' His answer, of course, is structuration theory.

It is this very ambition that has fired Giddens' engines for many years and won for him an audience of respectful, if not worshipful, listeners. None the less, I have for some time been skeptical of his 'solution', as expressed, for instance, in this evaluation of his *A Contemporary Critique of Historical Materialism* (1981a):

But his ultimate claim – to have overcome the limits of subjectivism and objectivism – seems wishful to me. I do not understand why acknowledging the recursive nature of language, structure, even domination, or pointing out that social actors are not dopes, can relieve us of our Scylla and Charybdis. Truly overcoming the theoretical and practical limits of the subject moving among objects is the unique opportunity of those about to die. Squaring circles is for magicians.

(Sica, 1983: 1261–2)

What makes 'Functionalism' such an important article in an attempt to understand Giddens' relationship to American ideas (and, I would argue, his oeuvre at large) is its openly stated theoretical predilections, some of which have guided him for years and give his schemas their ability to convince the sceptical. But, of course, they also give ammunition to his opponents.

The problem with veiled references is that, over time, readers can no longer be certain whom the author had in mind when composing his argument. So when one now reads in the Giddens of 1976 that subjectivism (undefined) and relativism were suddenly on the 'upsurge', it is not easy to know which texts or intellectual currents were bothering him. He is keen to 'reject' subjectivism in all its nasty forms, but does not name names. In a sense it is immaterial if he had in mind Marcuse and the euphoric left, Laing and the hysterical school of psychiatry or even positivists of some kinds who subscribed to no particular 'values' – as they were once called – and wanted merely to get to 'the facts', thus becoming relativists. The important matter is that he wanted badly to be perceived, especially I think by his American readers, as a friend to the *truly* sociological view of reality. If others had gone the easy way of psychologism and a unilevel comprehension of social life verging on solipsism, one in which 'structure' seemed to evaporate or become transformed into mere interpersonal agreement, Giddens would have none of that, and rallied his forces around an almost Mertonian veneration for structural explanation that would have won easy approval from Durkheim. There were in the 1960s, when Giddens came of academic age, many good reasons for rejecting the intrapsychic as the ultimate reality. It became too easy for authorities to attribute politically motivated deviance to 'personal problems' (e.g. if the Viet Cong had just been 'nicer, more reasonable folk', we would not have had to bomb them so much). And yet Giddens is well versed enough in the literature around Durkheim's time (Tarde, LeBon, Masaryk, *et al.*) concerning the magically complex roles of the solo human within aggregate humanity that he could never genuinely dispense with the social-psychological purchase on the subject matter of social theory.

It seems, in fact, that he wanted to overcome the same kind of Kantian antinomies that worried Durkheim, and simply to have his cake (structural determinancy in social life) after having eaten it (the recursively reproduced 'patterns' of social life). It is in this quest for a theoretical platform that could liberate him from the blindspots of both Marxism and Parsonsism that he stumbled onto the hypersubjectivism of American theorizing, especially that of Blumer and his followers, but also Garfinkel's. It is interesting that throughout Giddens' work, the former almost never receive laudatory reference, while the latter does rather well. From this side of the Atlantic, it seems capricious to privilege one over the other in that both are known here as the bedrock of micro-analysis, and when added to Goffman's dramaturgy, flesh out whatever the US has recently had to offer that remains theoretically persuasive in explaining the social-psychological. Something in Giddens' worldview rejects the subjective as a worthy locus of inquiry, and therefore also casts aside theories that, it seems to him, 'have shirked analysis of structure' in favour of 'agents' intentions and reasons' (Giddens, 1976c in 1977a:121, 123). It is no doubt true, as he conjectures, that American theorists in this heavily pragmatic tradition, are less overtly interested in structure than some of their conventional colleagues, for the reason that overattention to pattern leaves individual wishes and efforts in the shadows. Or, put differently, and more in keeping with Giddens' lineage, it is much harder to think about constructing a more liberating society if one follows the work of William James than that of, say, Rosa Luxemburg. It is surely tidier and politically more comforting to stay with structure than to descend into the complex darkness about which James wrote.

And yet if this is true, why does he then smuggle back into structuration theory the micro-analysis of Garfinkel, sometimes with frank reference to this body of work, but much more often quietly, as if no-one will notice that he has retrogressed from the high ground of structural disassembly to the marsh of: 'generative rules and resources that are both applied in and constituted out of action ... the totality of largely implicit, taken-for-granted rules that structure everyday discourse and mutual understandings of action as "meaningful"' (Giddens, 1977a:118). This is a straight borrowing from ethnomethodology, even if done *sotto voce*. Here Giddens reinvolves himself with 'the subjective' because he knows that a general theory of action will surely fail that does not come to terms with it. But he fondly thinks, it seems, that by inventing a new vocabulary, by bringing in the ubiquitous 'duality of structure' or 'reflexive rationalization of conduct', he can make good his escape from both calcified Marxism without a subject (Althusser) or sloppy-hearted Parsonsism, which is all norms, values and wishes.

Just as the pre-socratics struggled to define the ultimate nature of causality in the physical and social worlds, exhausting all the logical possibilities and leading to the unbridled idealism of Plato, Giddens has tried to find that 'virtual' point where the subject thrives and structure patterns this thriving, yet each remain somehow genuine and inviolable. And to do this, he has had to rely heavily on American impulses, particularly Garfinkel, but also as a spur to his own countercreativity, symbolic interactionism. Though he may not approve of theorists who deal mainly in 'the properties of individuals' instead of those belonging to 'collectivities or social systems' (ibid:126), it is to this very sphere that he returns again and again, with ever more qualifications and redefinitional ingenuity. When he dismisses functionalism's failure to account for 'the transformational capacity of self-reflection within human affairs' (ibid:128), he is using European philosophical phraseology to transmit his concern for social life in the flesh – the 'skilled creation of situated actors', always being 'produced and reproduced' (ibid) – that has been foremost in the American socio-logical imagination since the earliest works of Cooley at the turn of the century.

When some writers, then, refer to Giddens as a child of the left (e.g. Joas, 1987:14–15), and go on to locate him firmly within a European family tree of intellectuals, I sense that his authorial strategy of deflection and feinting has tricked them, as he probably hoped it would. As I read his work, ever since those earliest important essays that stretched for originality, he was simply a fine hermeneuticist until he came to terms with post-war American theorizing. It may be true, as I argued elsewhere, that he took key points of structuration theory from Ricoeur (Sica, 1986:344) – Joas (1987:13) adds Piaget – but throughout his later theorizing, whenever the question of self/society appears, one can hear the unnamed echo of ideas long popular in southern California, and even important remnants of others dreamed up in Cambridge, Massachusetts. Giddens has never wanted to be tagged as a follower of anybody because he clearly hoped to start a theoretical tradition of his own, and also perhaps due to his authentic reserv-ations about what other writers had to say. So whereas the typical theory writer links him or herself to some recognized, totemic figure or school, Giddens never has. But if, for example, one studies the table he provides in 'Functionalism' (Giddens, 1977a:122), contrasting his theory with that of the functionalists, there is precious little on his side of the ledger that is funda-mentally original to him. He has surely refined and corrected their ideas, but 'structuration theory' is incomprehensible without the prior American notions, not unlike thinking about Baran and Sweezy's *Monopoly Capital* without *Das Kapital.* And it is for this reason that I have argued for considering Giddens as an American theorist at least as much as one from abroad. He has not let on when he took this and that from the colonists, but he has stayed true to their major theoretical intentions, which is more important anyway.

When working through a dozen volumes of a writer's output, and then having to extract from them everything germane to a theme – in this case Giddens' response and indebtedness to Amer-ican ideas – the chance of hermeneutic error is very good indeed. In fact, failure is almost a certainty. The most that can be hoped is to open a way into the woods, as Heidegger said, which might have become overgrown or left unnoticed. I have chosen to work care-fully through Giddens' earlier works for two reasons. First, I suspect that younger writers, especially those who are energetic, creative and ambitious, take more time and use more care in preparing their first public statements than is later the case, so that studying earlier works often yields an understanding of an author's position that in more mature productions has been carefully papered over. For instance, everyone, including Giddens, now believes that Parsons' first book was his best – see Camic's (1989) Herculean analysis in a recent *American Journal of Sociology* – and this is not unusual among those who ponder social life. Second, and more to the point in terms of Giddens, it was in his earlier works that he tried most seriously to reconcile what he knew of the European classical line (especially involving Durkheim) and the American work of the post-war period that he came to know face to face. In his last half-dozen books he has spent more time working through European philosophy and literary criticism, geography, history proper and other materials suited to his contra-Habermasian project. Of course, he was not alone in this shift of attention, for even in the US, it is yesterday's and the day-before-yesterday's European theorizing that has become more conducive to advanced thinking – Jeffrey Alexander and Richard Rorty notwithstanding.

More recently, Giddens has turned again rather lightly to American ideas, as in his interesting dissection of Goffman (Giddens, 1987c), where once again he turns the tables on conventional wisdom and claims that Goffman was systematic, not just a brilliant essayist. There have also been short treatments of the Schutz/Parsons letters (Giddens, 1979e), a demystifying look at Marcuse (Giddens, 1982j), plus Braverman (Giddens, 1982m), in addition to endless repetition and amplification of Garfinkel's ideas, reanalysed and renamed, in his *Constitution of Society* (1984a) and elsewhere, often at great length. Yet for all this sustained recent productivity, there is a sharpness and precision to the earlier work that is less evident in works of the 1980s, and also less willingness to give other theorists their due. Perhaps part of this is simple ageing. But I suspect that Giddens has become somewhat impatient with the quality of ideas that have recently surfaced in communities of social theorists, and his irritated dismissal of others' notions (e.g. of the entire post-modernist discourse), his increasing impatience with Habermas, shows that he might be willing to return once again to some American ideas for inspiration. And if the sparkling concision for his early work can be recaptured, and then mixed with his matured vision of what a general theory of social life must entail, such a return to the colonies might well benefit us all.

Note

1   The most elaborate monograph yet to have appeared on Merton is Sztompka's (1986), a volume in the series of works about theory and theorists edited by Giddens for Macmillan (UK) and St Martin's (US). The author thanks Giddens for 'the idea of my taking up this challenging endeavour, as well as for many insightful and important editorial suggestions' (p. x). Perhaps Giddens would evaluate Merton more generously in the wake of this book than he did a decade before. (See Sica, 1987.)

Chapter three

Power–knowledge and social theory: the systematic misrepresentation of contemporary French social theory in the work of Anthony Giddens

Roy Boyne

Introduction

The following discussion has four parts. In the first part, we will consider the implications of two of Michel Foucault's most important texts – *L'Histoire de la folie à l'âge classique* (of which *Madness and Civilisation* is a partial translation) and *Discipline and Punish* (1975) – for the project of formulating a general social theory. Although the focus will be on the work of Anthony Giddens, and in particular on the theory of structuration, the points made here would be of equal relevance to the work of such writers as Jürgen Habermas in Germany and Jeffrey Alexander in the United States. The general form of the argument will be that Foucault's work is deeply subversive of 'grand' social theory of a rationalist kind because the rationalist quest for apodictic truth and general adequacy cannot avoid conferring transcendent validity upon discursive forms that history teaches us are almost certainly transient. This section ends with a brief commentary on Giddens' critique of Weber, to the effect that his undervaluation of Weber is at least partly explained by the severe limitations placed upon agents' knowledge implicit in both the latter's substantive sociology and his methodology of social science.

Giddens' critique of functionalism forms the topic of the second part of this chapter. It is important to engage with this critique, not only because it is internally contradictory, but also because if it remains unchallenged, it can have the effect of sealing the theory of structuration against decisive counterarguments that can be dismissed as erroneously functionalist.

In the third part of the chapter, the focus turns from the functions of social theory to the idea of the agent. It is basic to any theory of the knowledgeable social agent that the notion of reference (in the case, for example, of the referent of the agent's knowledge and intentions) be understood as ontologically unassailable. Yet the work of Jacques Derrida has cast clouds of suspicion over such confidence. We will see, through an examination of Derrida's essay, 'Plato's pharmacy' (Derrida, 1981), that the twinned notions of agency and reference are insufficiently secure to found a general social theory.

The last part of the paper continues the interest in the social agent by addressing the question of the unconscious. Anthony Giddens understandably rejects any notion of the unconscious that would have the effect of reproducing the primacy of social structure in the very constitution of the social agent. Such, it might be thought, would certainly be the case with Freudian notions of the superego and the Oedipus complex. It will, however, be shown that the concept of the unconscious favoured by Giddens is little more than a metaphoric rendition of the basic assumptions underlying the theory of structuration. This leads us back to the first three parts of the chapter, which seek to demonstrate that the theory of structuration is unacceptable.

Foucault and the functions of theory

How much has the character of social theory changed over the last three decades? We have recently been told (Giddens and Turner, 1987b:2) that it has changed a great deal, and that the hold of logical empiricism is now thoroughly broken, replaced by an altogether different philosophy of science that denies the possibility of theoretically neutral observation and asserts that all science is interpretive. This picture misleads. It provides the illusion of dramatic change by concealing, behind an epistemological screen, the relation between social theory and its other – the social world that it purports to theorize about.

In his work on the history of madness, Michel Foucault gave a compelling account of the relation between power and social scientific knowledge (Foucault, 1961). Back in the seventeenth century, in response to a developing mass of political, economic and administrative pressures, Louis XIV decreed that the streets of Paris should be cleared of beggars, criminals and social deviants. Something like 6,000 people were rounded up and confined in the General Hospital. Over a period of about a century and a half, an uncontrolled process of precipitation took place in this and many other similar institutions. At the end of this process, certain categories of people – the poor, the criminal and the insane – had been altered and then, shrouded by a new aura, more firmly established than ever before within the emerging social order of capitalism.

Three social scientific discourses – economics, criminology, psychology – emerged to confirm the validity of this splitting apart of what formerly had been more or less an indiscriminate mass defined only as undesirable, troublesome and unproductive.

What does this illustrate? If we concentrate just on the insane, we can see that a latent function of the science of mental health has been to turn to political and cultural advantage the unintended consequences of politico-administrative manoeuvres begun long ago. Even more than this, the very ground of both political legitimation and political subversion is established through historical processes over which no single individuals exercise control. At the most superficial level, we can see, for example, that the state may derive political legitimation from supporting particular regimes within the mental institutions founded on its territory. We can see that credibility may be gained from support for research into the 'desperate' condition of the mentally ill. We recognize and acknowledge the intelligence of an administration that demonstrates its understanding of the human condition by allowing insanity as a defence in criminal cases. Moving deeper, we can also see that reform and protest movements seek to legitimate their objectives in the terms of the very discourse that establishes, through what might be called historical processes without a sovereign subject, the very phenomena that are the object of their attention. Going deeper still, powerful new criteria of legitimacy are created by virtue of new institutions that declare not merely the abnormality of those within them, but also, in the context of an ever more rational and efficient social order, the normality and sanity of those without.

Now, this particular concatenation of effects and functions was not planned. It cannot be ascribed to one social agency, not the state, nor the bourgeoisie, nor the working class. Nor, as a specific historical outcome, can it be ascribed to the knowledgeable practices of sets of social agents over time unless one accords priority to the changes in social structure that determine what knowledgeability is at any one point in time. This does not mean that historical movement and change cannot be investigated and interpreted. It may be beyond the reach of social agents who are, as we all are, part of it, but we can pause and look back, and even learn from the processes that we see at work. The general point remains, however, that the rich and complex workings of our societies are the legacy of historical processes without a sovereign subject (and the case of mental illness is just one of many examples that might have been used to make that point). We are dealing here with the condition of history.

Faced with this condition, it is hard if not impossible to speak of the 'knowledgeable social actor' – which is, of course, the very heart of Giddens' theory of structuration – as the solution to socio-logical theory's search for adequacy. But there is a further level we need to explore. If it is being suggested, and it is, that social agents are in some way captivated, seduced or partly blinded by forces that are in some way contained within the discourses in which they are embroiled, we should ask how this works. Let us continue with the example of mental health here.

While the modern discourse of mental illness may be seen as, at least in part, an outcome of a complex set of political, economic and cultural processes, one suspects that the ironies of the situation are lost on most of the practitioners of the various disciplines concerned. Perhaps the deepest irony arises for the humanist psychiatrist who would willingly blame the less-than-perfect mental condition of his or her patients on the unreasonable demands that modern society makes on us all. Such a psychiatrist, while critical of modern society, nevertheless deploys concepts like psychosis and neurosis, treats the patient in terms of this or that therapeutic regime and fervently hopes for the patient's progress and eventual cure. What is ironic here is that the psychiatrist's form of knowledge is one of those legacies of the complex machin-ations of social power in pretty much the same kind of way that the patient's condition is also a legacy of different, although not unrelated, forms of social power. It is probably the case that practi-tioners within the fields of mental health are mostly unaware of their complicity with the disingenuous relation between knowledge and power. For them it is largely irrelevant that the discourses within which they work have been sedimented by a historical process entirely saturated by a blind and aleatory power. It is diffi-cult to say that this is a state of affairs that can be remedied. What alternative frameworks are available for such practitioners? Are there any that escape the circuit of power–knowledge–power? Answers to such questions will be neither definitive nor comfort-able, but it is important to begin from the recognition of how little control we have, rather than how much implicit and explicit know-ledge we deploy. We should also recognize that the depth of the problems that emanate from a historically informed, rather than a generically abstract view of agency ought to fuel innovative attempts to penetrate beneath or beyond the level of what lay actors explicitly or implicitly know.

What is of prime concern here is not the historical accuracy of Foucault's account, but rather the cogency of the lessons that it provides. One of these lessons is that the same ironies are present in regard to the whole range of social problems besetting modern societies. Which state apparatus would not take credit were it to promote even a partial solution to the problem of homelessness or of drug abuse, and which of the social scientists contributing to such 'advances' would not bask in the glory of unrecognized and probably unavoidable historico-political collaborationism?

How hard it is to respond to such indictments of social science! How hard to provide an honest answer to the question of the point and purpose of social science under conditions where all social scientific concepts are compromised by their past history and by their present function of perpetuating the circuit of power–know-ledge–power. Much the easiest course is to show how much social theory has changed over the last thirty years. It is comfortable not to inquire too deeply into the historical functions of contemporary social theory, and much more constructive to repeat the traditional formula, which has not changed at all, that once the philosophical underpinnings are right then we can properly understand the present and proceed intelligently to address the future. We are all guilty of allowing social theory to assist in the legitimation of historical blindness and political amnesia.

There is a price to be paid for this. Paul Veyne wrote:

> The medieval zoologists were occupied, or ought to have been occupied, with what is zoologically interesting: all animals. They could have been more or less conscious of the ideal of their science, and at any moment a zoologist could have risen among them to appeal to that idea; it may also be that the zoologist's ideal has evolved. But that evolution will by right have been purely scientific and have constituted something that science had within itself.
>
> (Veyne, 1984:53)

To what ideal can social theorists appeal? If social theory does play a part in reproducing society as a circuit of power–knowledge–power, can it appeal, under the sign of the intellectual's commit-ment to truth, to any ideal other than the perpetual exposure of that circuit? Any other appeal would not be to an ideal but to the illusion of an ideal.

We can try to test this out. Giddens has announced that post-structuralism is dead. It could not survive because it was always unable to deal with human agency, which is the precondition of structure. From the standpoint of structuration as the key to the science of society, the ideal to which the social theorist will refer when required will be the service of social theory on behalf of the future. This future will not be a particular future, but an abstract future to be determined through the exercise of the deliberative power of human agents. 'For in the notion of agency resides the capacity to restructure the social universe' (Giddens and Turner, 1987b:6). This is an illusory ideal for social theorists. It is illusory because it ignores the circuit of power–knowledge–power through lack of reflexive awareness of its own contribution (largely one of omission rather than commission) in shaping the concrete people that human agents are.

This can be illustrated by considering Foucault's work on prisons. There was a time when the power of the sovereign, of the single figure of the ruler, lay at the symbolic heart of the law. This power was expressed in such institutions as the royal prerogative and in such practices as the violent affirmation of this personal power in rites of public torture and execution. With the progression of European history through the seventeenth and eighteenth centuries, the disfunctionality of such a regime, in the context of an emerging social formation characterized by the need for precise attunement of the masses to the needs of capitalist production, can now be seen to be obvious. A social system in which royal specificity confronts the undifferentiated mass of the population may have been appropriate in feudal times, but it is anachronistic within a society on the threshold of a complex division of labour. It is, however, no easy matter to design and institute a new array of social practices. The masses were not composed of abstract human agents; the people were concrete living individuals with particular behavioural predispositions. In retrospect, we can see that new social subjects were required for the successful transition from feudalism to capitalism. We can also see that the social reforms that were debated were hardly aimed at producing a new form of social subject with particular characteristics such that they would have internalized new norms of dress, rationality, earnestness, competitiveness, punctuality and so on. Foucault examines the historical process whereby such new social subjects were produced. He focuses upon prisons, the education system and sexuality within the bourgeois family. He shows that a basic task of social analysis is to elucidate the concrete nature of social subjects at any one time.

Does not this rough description of Foucault's work on historical subjectivity cast some doubt over the idea that the abstract concept of human agency should form the conceptual basis for social theory? There are four points to be made. First, societies are not composed of abstract agents; they are composed of human individuals with, in broad terms, a historically determined set of characteristics. Second, and following from the previous point, the formulation of social theory as founded upon the abstract notion of human agency may function to block off realistic appraisals of possible social futures, since it will tend to undervalue structural constraint at both the social and personality level. Third, the assertion that human agents knowledgeably, but not intentionally, produce and maintain social structures can lead to an assertion of the power and ability of human agents to shape these structures and thereby exercise control over their future; this hidden utopianism can function to preserve existing structures of society, since actual involvement with failed projects of structural change will serve to confirm the personal inadequacies of the would-be agents of change, with the result that social change is confirmed as the responsibility of the other, or even as beyond rational control, and societies are thus fated to remain as they are or to change as they will without hope for the repair of all their tragic imperfections. Fourth, the assertion that abstract human agency should form the basic starting point of contemporary social theory is in perfect accord with the demands of late capitalism for total adaptability and directed multifunctionality on the part of its social subjects.

Now, none of these points has much force if it is the case that the theory of agency advanced as the projected foundation for the human sciences is formulated as an heuristic that is meant to focus attention on the historical nature of actual social subjects. If, however, it is considered that a crucial part of the basic theory of agency is that *all* social subjects are in some way knowledgeable, then the problems mentioned arise in full force. The point is that the degree of knowledgeability, whether implicit or explicit, is not something on which one can philosophically legislate; it is a matter for empirical enquiry. As soon as this is admitted, of course, then the opening assumption that social agents in some sense know the social structures that they have created is also open to question.

Let me summarize so far. An examination of the work of Michel Foucault produces *inter alia* two basic insights that are crucial for a contemporary assessment of the state of social theory today. The first of these is that the human sciences play a legitimating role within modern society; they form part of the circuit of power–knowledge–power. They feed on the phenomena that are produced as a by-product of the workings of social power; they produce knowledge of such phenomena that, by virtue of being documented and thereby glossed with the patina of what has rigorously and methodically been shown to be the way things are, tend to become treated as natural rather than historical; this new knowledge of the objective social world takes its place within the field of social power, the workings of which generate new phenomena that the scientific attitude will once more seek to understand. The circuit of power–knowledge–power is a spiral, but how many of the agents on its path think themselves to be proceeding in a linear fashion: brick-house realities like personal survival, political ambition and technological progress are not so easy to deconstruct. The second insight is that social subjects are made; their practical skills as members of society come to be what they are as a result of historical processes over which human agents exercise very little degree of control. Such a view does not imply that human agents are not knowledgeable. It does, however, mean both that there are degrees of knowledgeability, and that there are no philosophical barriers to the postulation of realms beyond the limits of that knowledgeability.

Anthony Giddens has read Foucault. He has commented upon his work. Let us now see what he has had to say. We find, first of all, a considerable degree of admiration: 'The contributions of Foucault to the analysis of surveillance are perhaps the most important writings relevant to the theory of administrative power since Max Weber's classic texts on bureaucracy' (Giddens, 1981a:170). Furthermore, this is no isolated judgement. It is repeated almost word for word in the following year (Giddens, 1982g:221). This approval of Foucault's work is conditional. It is not taken as a contribution to the project of a general social theory, but to a subclass of social theory – the theory of administrative power. It is taken, then, to be a theory of the third rank, operating not at the primary level of foundational clarification of a philosophical kind, nor at the secondary level of general social theory, but below and subordinate to both of these superior levels. Within such a hierarchical schema, it is perfectly appropriate to pick from it certain themes, ideas and demonstrations, while criticizing and discarding the rest. This is just what Giddens does. Allowing the third-level utility of Foucault's notion of surveillance and his demonstration of the relevance of panopticism, he rejects any claim that Foucault might have for a revision of theoretical thinking in general. The reason for the rejection is that Foucault's work exemplifies the confusion that structuralism helped to introduce into French thought, between history without a 'transcendental subject' and history without 'knowledgeable human subjects' (Giddens, 1981a:171). For Giddens, the plain fact is that history is explained on the basis of the situated activity of practically-knowledgeable agents. While he agrees with the contemporary dismissal of Hegel's 'Absolute' subject, he cannot accept the dismissal of knowledgeable agency that Foucault's work seems to imply.

The question to be asked, however, is whether Foucault's

'histories' do demand the rejection of such concepts of agency. Giddens does not seriously ask this question. But when Foucault tells of the execution of Montigny in 1737, recording that the local fish-wives walked in procession holding aloft an effigy of the condemned man, the head of which they then cut off, is he clearly denying the knowledgeable agency of these women? When Foucault (1980:38) said that there was a moment in the economy of power when it became understood that it was more efficient and profitable to place under surveillance than to punish, he very clearly was not denying the knowledgeable agency of those holders of power who came to see which way the wind of historical change was blowing.

What is at issue here is Giddens' refusal to renounce the social-theoretic search for the one single perspective that will provide the God's eye truth of society. His debate with Alex Callinicos (Giddens, 1985e and Callinicos, 1985) provides a telling example of two absolutists in confrontation with each other: the Marxist and the theorist of agency each presenting themselves as if the ideal which each pursued were different, when in fact in both cases it is the same – the single true paradigm of social being.

The last decade has seen a welter of attacks on this ideal of truth, the work of Foucault, Lyotard, Deleuze and Derrida has demonstrated that the corrupt nature of that ideal has to be very seriously considered within social theory. The connection between truth and power has even been demonstrated to the satisfaction of Giddens himself. But what is his response? He has a triple strategy. The first part of it we have already seen, which is the treatment of countervailing accounts of the social world as only bearing signifi-cance at those lower levels of theoretical relevance where they do not pose problems to recuperative manoeuvres of selective assimil-ation. The second strategy is a diversionary critique of Weber and Nietzsche. The third strategy is the critique of functionalism. Let us deal first with Weber and Nietzsche.

In a famous formulation, Weber wrote that: '"Classes", "status groups", and "parties" are phenomena of the distribution of power within a community' (Weber, 1922:927). Weber also wrote, apparently on quite a different topic, that, 'An ideal type is formed by the one-sided *accentuation* of one or more points of view and by the synthesis of a great many diffuse, discrete, more or less present and occasionally absent *concrete, individual* phenomena, which are arranged according to those one-sidedly emphasised viewpoints into a unified analytical construct' (Weber, 1904:90). If we place Weber's two assertions side by side, we can see that the second qualifies the first. The first assertion about power assumes a contextualized validity only if it succeeds 'in revealing concrete cultural phenomena in their interdependence, their causal conditions and their *significance*' (Weber, 1904:92). For Weber, then, the aim of concept formation in the social sciences is the elucidation of cultural significance. It is not the production of absolute truth. This is made extremely clear in Weber's judgement upon Marxism:

> The eminent, indeed unique, heuristic significance of these ideal types when they are used for the assessment of reality is known to everyone who has ever employed Marxian concepts and hypotheses. Similarly, their perniciousness, as soon as they are thought of as empirically valid or as real (i.e. truly metaphysical) 'effective forces', 'tendencies', etc. is likewise known to those who have used them.'

(Weber, 1904:103)

The point here is not precisely that Giddens' discussions of these matters from 1971 onwards have deployed a powerful exegetical competence to the exclusion of serious reflexive application; nor is it exactly that his social theory has leaned heavily towards the ideal of formulating some finally definitive theoretical account of the social world, which is something that Weber warned against; it is that the critique of Weber as compromised by his political context and his psychological predispositions (Giddens, 1972b:58), and the critique of Nietzsche, Weber, Foucault and others as exponents of a 'reductionism of power' (Giddens, 1982g:227) functions, in quasi-bureaucratic mode, to close and file away those cases that, had they been seriously considered, would have given mainstream social theory more than adequate justification for completely reformulating its entire project.

The function of Giddens' critique of functionalism

It has been suggested that social theory has been through a process of recasting. This, we are told, not only applies to the attenuation of the influence of logical empiricism, referred to above, it also relates to 'the decline of the hegemony that objectivism and functionalism once enjoyed' (Giddens, 1984a:361). The decline of functionalism is something that Giddens strenuously applauds, for the influence of functionalism has been 'largely pernicious' (Giddens, 1984a:xxxi). In fact, more than perhaps any other social theorist, he has sought to contribute to this process of decay by repeating and elaborating upon what is presented as the definitive critique of functionalism in social theory. There is something disturbing about this crusade against functionalism. To show what this is, it is necessary briefly to rehearse the main critical arguments that provide crucial premises for Giddens' 'non-functionalist manifesto' (Giddens, 1979a:7).

There are first of all something like eight interconnected points that Giddens makes against functionalism:

1. 'Functionalists discount agents' reasons' (Giddens, 1981a:18).

2. Functionalism reduces 'human agency to the internalisation of values' (Giddens, 1976a:21). [Since I only propose to try and examine the general significance of Giddens' critique of functionalism, I will merely note the possible contradiction with point 1.]

3. Social systems are comprised of practices, not roles; the functionalist stress on the latter serves to underpin its normative emphasis (Giddens, 1979a:117).

4. Functionalism fails to treat social life as actively constituted through members' doings (Giddens, 1976a:21).

5. Functionalists make much of the notion of unintended consequences, but since functionalism disregards agents' intentions, it has no criterion by which to discern what they are (Giddens, 1984a:xxxi).

6. Functionalism treats power as secondary (Giddens, 1976a:21). [It is perhaps a cheap shot to remark that the functionalists are criticized for a relegation of power, while, as we have seen, the neo-Nietzscheans are criticized for treating it as primary.]

7. Functionalism fails to deal adequately with the conflicting interests of agents, and even on its own ground this is especially important since such conflicts give rise to tensions in the negotiation of norms (Giddens, 1976a:21).

8. The notion of functional incompatability does not begin to treat the question of the real contradictions which arise out of the conflicts of interest between agents (Giddens, 1976a:127–8).

It is not difficult to see that this list of critical points presents a series of formulations on one basic theme. That theme is the inability of the functionalist paradigm to provide a central space for the notion of human agency. Within the Durkheimian tradition – a lineage that, according to Giddens, leads to the work of the structuralists and post-structuralists – there has appeared to some scholars to be an active eschewal of any concern with human agency (or at least, so the story goes; careful readers of *Suicide* will know that Durkheim did look at agents' intentionality so as to elucidate the individuation of the various forms of suicide – one can argue whether or not this was a matter of inconsistency on Durkheim's part (see Turner, 1983:444)). Giddens contends that the search for a *sui generis* reality above and beyond the level of individual agency is somewhat duplicitous, since it surreptitiously rests on an unexplicated reliance on agency. He shows this by arguing that the categories deployed by the functional analysis of atemporal cross sections of society necessarily rely on assumed temporal processes, and since the temporal order is constituted by agents with causal powers, it will follow that the rejection of any concern with agency, based upon a genetic indisposition, from within functionalism will be cause for the total abandonment of the paradigm. Giddens' basic case is that functionalists cannot exhaustively analyse the phenomena that they assume, both explicitly and implicitly, to comprise the social world.

It would be a fair response to say that if such a test were applied to any social theory, it would be cause for its decisive rejection. Just in case such a response were articulated in a powerful way, Giddens has a further set of arguments against functionalism. These are that functionalism tends 'to encourage unthinking acceptance of societies as clearly delimited entities, and social systems as internally highly integrated unities (Giddens, 1984a:xxvi–xxvii); that the homeostatic processes upon which functionalist explanations rely are both crude and capable of being recast in the language of agency; that functionalism encourages the relinquishment of historicity; and that statements about system needs only have validity, and marginal validity at that, within counterfactual propositions.

Now, I do not propose to try and refute all of these arguments, even though none of them are anywhere near as cut and dried as Giddens seems to think, nor to develop, at least in a systematic way, Stephen Turner's argument that Giddens' critique of Durkheimian functionalism is couched in a language that Durkheim decisively rejected as cloaking reality (Turner, 1983), but rather to follow Weber's lead and reflect upon their significance within the culture of social theory. What this mass of relentless argumentation produces is an effect of stigmatization, such that the exposure of any residual functionalism in an opponent's thought is sufficient to discredit it. Yet this procedure is disingenuous, because the stigmatized characteristics of the object are revealed through a process structured by those same characteristics.

This needs some explanation. At its crudest, we can say that functionalism is repudiated because it lacks coherence, which is

itself a functionalist notion. Or we can put it this way, that functionalism is repudiated because it does not integrate *everything*.
We can put it in a third way: functionalism is repudiated because it
is not functionally compatible with the system needs of a particular
version of social theory.

Thus far I hope to have indicated that the deep grounds for the
rejection of functionalism have to do with the workings of power.
One might rephrase Weber and say that intellectual capital is a
phenomenon of the distribution of power within society. In the
field of the intellect, the workings of power masquerade under the
notion of truth. It is as inconvenient to spell this out as it was to
spell out the connection between the social sciences and the circuit
of power–knowledge–power. Just as the human sciences are both
products of and accomplices with social power, so are the human
scientist's arguments focused as power on a product of power.

Perhaps it is impossible to work with this in mind all the time.
Should the social theorist in his or her own defence say that while
truth and power may be deeply related, if we were to allow that
relation to spoil the game of argumentation, then far more than
social theory would be dissolved since it would penetrate to the
roots of interpersonal persuasion. As such a defence is mounted, it
begins to become clear just what would be at stake. Indeed it
begins to dawn on us just what should be at stake in social theory.
But is this not unfair? After all, Schutz (1962:22) drew a well-
known distinction between actors as embroiled in ongoing action
whose self-understanding would be of the 'in-order-to' variety,
and actors as observers of themselves who could gasp retrospect-
ively the 'because-motive' that led them to do what they did. He
suggested that actors could not hold both understandings at the
same time. Would not the social theorist's position be something
similar? Would it not be the case that the social theorist would be
unable to grasp the power-truth relation while doing social theory?
But what would that mean? What consequences would it have for
the social theorist: at the least it would be a question of *mauvais
foi*, of feigning satisfaction with writings that in retrospect can only
be seen to be radically incomplete. Furthermore, what consequences arise for a theory that places the knowledgeable social
actor at the centre of the stage, given that this actor only knows
half the story at any one time? But, perhaps Schutz's formulations
run astray. Perhaps it is possible to make use of the concept of
truth while foregrounding its complicity with social power. If,
however, this is possible, it has yet to be achieved; which does not
mean that it should not be strived for. The point here, of course, is
that such an initiative within social theory would probably have to

make use of the functionalist paradigm in articulating the connections between forms of discourse and forms of social power. Thus, such an initiative would be ruled out by a social theory such as the theory of structuration. It is again a question of emphasizing how little control social agents may have, how easily they can fall prey to using truth as a weapon without realizing what it is that they do, and how what is done may function to reinforce further the discursive system that holds them fast.

Deconstructing the agent

One of Giddens' basic complaints about structuralism and post-structuralism is that they 'consistently failed to generate an account of reference' (Giddens, 1987a:85), and furthermore this retreat from reference has never, it is claimed, been established by philosophical argument. Leaving aside the important point that withdrawal from concern with reference *need not* be established by philosophical argument, and further, that unnecessary concern with the philosophical legitimation of research programmes may well preclude their full development, the fact is that there has been philosophical argument in abundance in Derrida's work bearing on the inherent elusiveness of the referent.

In order to demonstrate this, we cannot, unfortunately, draw upon Giddens' own account. While the preparatory exegetical work for his own intellectual project was carried out meticulously on the writings of Marx, Weber and Durkheim, his deployment of ideas from structuralism and post-structuralism has tended to be somewhat piratical – he has taken what he wanted without any real concern for where it came from or for the value of it within its proper context. Indeed, he has then so characterized such borrowed ideas that their original context has been presented as inimical to their proper development and use. The 'liberation' of ideas such as *différance*, surveillance, spacing, to name but a few, is further achieved by elaborating, in counterpoint, upon the incoherence of their erstwhile theoretical frameworks. Some years ago, it would have been *de rigueur* in certain circles to point to the epistemological confusions involved in borrowing just one idea from another theoretical discourse; Althusser's notion of problematic is rather less favoured now. Today, the theme of theoretical violence has been overlaid upon that earlier one of epistemological integrity. Shifts in intellectual fashion do not, however, mean that earlier currents of thought do not contain much that is significant.

To show Derrida's philosophical argumentation at work, let us examine, briefly but not without care, one of his most influential essays. In his essay, 'Plato's pharmacy' (Derrida, 1981), he finds a secret ambivalence in Socrates' account of writing. Socrates thought writing to be ignoble, an inferior replacement for original thinking expressed in speech. We can think of a number of arguments to confirm the Socratic view. Is there not something suspicious, for example, in the employment of speech-writers by contemporary politicians? Would an authentic politician, a leader to be trusted, present someone else's words as their own? How can a mere reader, even the most consummate actor, defend that thought that is essentially another's? Such reflections might lead us to infer that writing is a perilous business leading to a devaluation of the quality of social life. Should we be happy with a practice that allows us to counterfeit qualities that we do not have? How understandable it would be, under the influence of such views, to see a blank sheet of paper as a threat. Writing is poison!! On the other hand, writing can be an irreplaceable aid to memory and communication. Thus writing is ambiguous, indeterminate between good and evil, poison and cure. It is hardly coincidental that Socrates refers to writing as *pharmakon*, a Greek word that can mean either poison or remedy. But, even on the remedial side of this opposition, a question must be put. For a drug is an unnatural thing; something that interferes with nature. This at least was Plato's view. And just as the medicinal use of drug therapy may cause more serious problems than the condition treated by the drug, so we can also see that writing may not strengthen memory at all, but that it might cause it to weaken through disuse – to read one's thoughts at a later date is not necessarily to know them as one's own, nor is it necessarily to know their truth.

The Socratic discourse against writing is directed at the art of sophistry. Just as the sophist may pretend to have knowledge, so might writing simulate truth. Thus, for Socrates, writing is inferior to spoken wisdom, to the felt knowledge of the genuine philosopher. For Derrida it is clear: 'What Plato dreams of is a memory with no sign' (Derrida, 1981:109), a memory in direct communion with wisdom and truth: contact with higher reason would ideally be unmediated by the corruptions of signification.

It is not contradictory that the sophists, too, were suspicious of writing. For them it was a question of effectiveness: live speech is more forceful, penetrates more profoundly into the hearts and minds of an audience. In their case, writing was denigrated because '*logos* is a more effective *pharmakon*' (Derrida, 1981:115). Speech, too, can enter the mind and work on it like a drug, to poison or to cure. Why should socratic speech be any different in this respect? How can it evade that fundamental indeterminacy between poison and cure that marks the phenomenon of writing? Derrida shows that the privilege of Socratic discourse is only sustained through an irredeemable claim of access to a wisdom that cannot be presented, since in its presenting it will always be a question of re-presenting; and it is precisely in re-presenting that the undecidable alternation between poison and cure arises.

What is truth except a representation of truth; and because representation is, like writing, an inferior substitution that might also be a false substitution, who is to say that this is the truth? The answer must surely be that whosoever claims the truth, claims to reveal it in all the glory of its full presence, claims to mime it with utter faithfulness, must be a magician, a *pharmakeus*. For it is only a strictly magical ability, a hypnotic talent, a supreme cleverness that can persuade us that what we have seen is the light rather than its reflection, the presence rather than its representation. It is, for Derrida, this magic, hypnotic power that since Plato and before has concealed the essential incompleteness of the world. Deconstruction will expose this ersatz magic in its necessarily textual operations. It will teach this:

> The absolute invisibility of the origin of the visible, of the good-sun-father-capital, the unattainment of presence or beingness in any form, the whole surplus Plato calls *epekeina tes ousias* (beyond beingness or presence), gives rise to a structure of replacements such that all presences will be supplements substituted for the absent origin.

> (Derrida, 1981:167)

What for Derrida is common to Plato, Rousseau, Husserl, Lévi-Strauss, and others, and what we now find in the work of Anthony Giddens, is a derogation of supplementarity. Within the main tradition of western metaphysics, what is important is the original presence, whatever form it takes: socratic wisdom or the human agency celebrated in Giddens' social theory, to provide just two examples. The original presence is held to determine its empirical manifestations, its signs, marks, language, writing, the structures within which it operates and for which it is responsible. The philosophical task has always been to restore that origin, and the philosophical prejudice has been continually to disparage the phenomena subsequent or supplemental to that presence.

It should now be perfectly clear why Giddens cannot take post-structuralism seriously. A serious reading of Derrida would find him forced to respond to the charge that the theory of structuration is perfectly in harmony, and therefore (to put the matter in more disturbing terms) in league with the project of western reason. What is that project? It is simultaneously to offer and postpone access to the fundaments, expressed as truth or God or deliverance from evil or some such other formulation. It is a powerful rhetoric that functions superbly as a cloak over the workings of social power, and it is based on a false promise.

If we turn to what Giddens has to say about Derrida and structuralism, we find that he is not prepared to offer a criterion of distinction between them. The reason for this is, deeply, that the offering of the criterion that does distinguish them would be self-indicting. For that criterion, is precisely the philosophically established dismissal of appeals to the referent, to the origin, to agency as the *real basis* of social life. For ultimately, such appeals have no substance. They are magical incantations.

In the light of this discussion of Derrida, we can also see that Giddens' version of the post-structuralist decentring of the subject functions to avoid confrontation with the core of Derrida's analysis. Giddens says:

> The theme of the decentring of the subject is without doubt one which must be taken seriously by anyone interested in modern philosophy or social theory. But while the basic perspective surely must be accepted, the particular mode in which it is elaborated within structuralism and post-structuralism remains defective ... structuralist and post-structuralist accounts of the decentring of the subject are inevitably closely tied to the versions of language and the unconscious associated with structuralist linguistics and its influence.
>
> (Giddens, 1987i:89)

But this quasi-functionalist vision of post-structuralism misses the point, which is that the decentring of the subject within post-structuralism rejects the philosophy of the subject as a version of the origin and recasts the subject as a supplement, something both added to and replacing the absent origin. The question of language is a side issue in relation to the question of the subject, just as the question of the subject is a side issue in relation to language. And the status of side issues is precisely supplemental, they will function indeterminately as additions and replacements. The post-structuralist argument is not that the decentring of the subject is the first step on the road to a more adequate philosophy of the post-Cartesian subject, it is that any philosophy of the subject must, in the end, be indeterminate between the subject as structured and the subject as agent. That is as near as the essential duplicity of a world that cannot redeem its promises will allow us to get. It means that the programme of transcending voluntarism and determinism is precisely magical, that the theory of structuration cannot deliver what it promises. This is the condition of our form of reason (*maybe* we can go beyond it – that is another story, but certainly not one to be written with the knowledgeable social agent as its hero).

Derrida is well known for his discussions of speech and writing, but it just confuses matters to refer to the primacy of talk in social interaction. We read:

> the priority which Derrida gives to writing over speech has to be questioned. For speech – or rather talk – recovers a priority over other media of signification. Talk, carried on in day-to-day contexts of activity, is the fundamental carrier of signification
>
> (Giddens, 1987i:91)

As Giddens elsewhere admits: 'A critique of Derrida cannot be most profitably approached via a reassertion of the priority of the spoken word over the written' (Giddens, 1979a:35). But even that latter formulation is not exactly the right one; and here we encounter the structure of supplementarity once again. The thing is that Derrida's exploration of writing is just a vehicle for the elucidation of the supplementary nature of social being. Speech and writing are not his subject, the nature of the supplement is. In short, Giddens' promise of access to the principle of agency has all the hallmarks of a social power play – all principles are lacking except this one, and we are even forbidden, on grounds of validity determined by this super-principle of agency, from asking what functions such a promise performs.

Agency and the unconscious

To further understand Giddens' rejection of the spirit of post-structuralism, we have to consider his rejection of the concept of the unconscious. At a simple level, it is easy enough to understand why a theorist of agency would seek to dismiss the idea, since it functions in the work of both Freud and Durkheim to prejudice any claim for the ontological primacy of the knowledgeable social actor. Let us deal with Freud first of all.

Giddens rejects the view that the unconscious structures conscious life. He allows that, since Freud, social theorists have no choice but to reckon with it, but argues that the unconscious is, effectively, produced and maintained by social actors themselves:

> Given that the modes of management of organic wants repre-

sent the first, and in an important sense the most all-embracing, accommodation which the child makes to the world, it seems legitimate to suppose that a 'basic security system' – i.e. a primitive level of management of tensions rooted in organic needs – remains central to later personality development; and given that these processes occur first of all before the child acquires the linguistic skills necessary to consciously monitor his learning, it seems legitimate to hold that they lie 'below' the threshold of those aspects of conduct that, learned later and in conjunction with the reflexive monitoring of that learning, are easily verbalised – thus 'made conscious' – by the older child or adult. Even the earliest learning of the infant is understood in a misleading sense, however, if conceived of as mere 'adaptation' to a pre-given external world; the infant is from the first days of his life a being that actively shapes the settings of his interaction with others.... That human wants are hierarchically ordered, involving a core 'basic security system' largely inaccessible to the consciousness of the actor, is of course not an uncontroversial assertion, and is one which shares a great deal with the general emphasis of psychoanalytic theory; but it does not imply a commitment to the more detailed elements of Freud's theoretical or therapeutic scheme.

The maintenance of a framework of 'ontological security' is, like all other aspects of social life, an ongoing accomplishment of lay actors.

(Giddens, 1976a:117)

What this long quotation illustrates is that Giddens will allow a concept of the unconscious on the basis of early tension management by an unskilled social being. It also shows that the youngest child is seen as already an agent able to accomplish tension management and able from the first to shape interaction with others. The unconscious that Giddens will allow here is the result of the skill of the agent that seems to be present *ab initio*. The need for this unconsciousness is not social. It is organic. It is not social because even the youngest agent is socially skilled. The reason that this blatant Cartesianism (strong language one might think, but isn't a statement like, 'the infant is from the first days of his life a being that actively shapes the settings of his interaction with others', redolent of a Cartesian certainty in the self-sufficiency of the subject?) has remained unexamined is simply that the primacy of agency requires that the agent should not be shaped by forces outside of its potential control.

There is a second angle to the notion of the unconscious that

Giddens is prepared to concede. This pertains to the notion of repression. He writes:

> Everything that I have dealt with so far is 'accessible' to the *awareness* of the actor: not in the sense that he can formulate theoretically how he does what he does, but in the sense that, given that he is not dissimulating, his testimony as to the purpose and reasons for his conduct is the most important, if not necessarily conclusive, source of evidence about it. This does not hold in the case of motivation. As I shall use the term it covers instances both where actors are aware of their wants, and also those where their behaviour is influenced by sources not accessible to their consciousness; and, since Freud, we have to reckon with the likelihood that the revealing of these sources may be actively resisted by the agent.
>
> (Giddens, 1976a:85)

Here again the notion of repression is structured by the activities of the agent who actively resists. Of course, were it the case that the agent was not actively involved in this resistance, if, for example, it was the unconscious itself that determined the censorship and repression, then the primacy of agency would again be broken.

How, then, are we to understand Giddens' statement that social theory needs a concept of the unconscious? The answer is plain enough, and it is that the concept of the unconscious needed by social theory is predicated upon the idea of 'tacit knowledge that is skilfully applied in the enactment of courses of conduct, but which the actor is not able to formulate discursively' (Giddens, 1979a:57). Giddens' discussion of Lacan makes things clear (in so far as any discussion of Lacan could do that): 'the Lacanian formulation of the "it" thinks in the space where the "I" has yet to appear' (Giddens, 1979a:120), allows Giddens both to demand a theory of the subject (a theory of the processes through which the 'I' arises) and to assert that even before the arrival of the 'I', there is still an 'it' that thinks, which is to say that there is still agency. As Giddens puts it: 'if the reflexive monitoring of action only becomes possible in so far as the child becomes a 'positioned subject', there are none the less a range of competencies which precede that development' (Giddens, 1979a:123). As with Foucault and Derrida, Giddens' brief encounter with Lacan and Kristeva has the form of a power play, a raid into enemy territory with the intention of removing from their home territory certain things that can perform a legitimating function upon the return to the home ground. Indeed, Giddens says as much, when he remarks: 'It is still not entirely clear, in fact, given the cryptic and elusive nature of many of Lacan's formulations, how far it is possible fruitfully to detach some of his theorems from the overall scheme of his theory' (Giddens, 1979a:122).

The psychoanalytic concept of the unconscious is not, of course, the only source available to the social theorist for a theory of the unconscious. Particularly in Giddens' case, we must also look to his treatment of the idea of 'conscience collective' in the work of Emile Durkheim. It will be beyond the scope of this chapter to detail the many connections between the concepts of *conscience collective*, collective representations and a sociologically reformulated notion of the unconscious, but some pointers can be provided that may be important for an overall assessment of Giddens' project thus far.

Giddens explained Durkheim's idea of the *conscience collective* as follows:

> There is a fundamental distinction between individuation and individualism. The growth of individuation presupposes a decline in the volume, intensity and rigidity of the conscience collective: individuals are able to develop their own particular propensities and inclinations to the degree to which these are freed from the control of the moral homogeneity of the community, but this in turn entails a transformation in the content of collective moral ideals.... The main thesis of the *Division of Labour* is that while individuation is a necessary concomitant of the dissolution of traditional society, it implies, not the complete eradication of the conscience collective, but its transmutation in the form of the development of new moral ideas: those comprised in the cult of the individual.
>
> (Giddens, 1972a:6)

When writing this, almost twenty years ago, Giddens' exegetical concern was to demonstrate that individualism, in the work of Emile Durkheim, is a social construction that relates to a set of values that are far from egotistical. There were two ways forward. The way that was taken was to repudiate the Durkheimian programme of sociologized Kantianism, merely taking from it the notion of social structure, and to develop a sociology of the will. This has been done in a syncretistic kind of way so as to incorporate and use parts of countervailing theories and perspectives. The result has been the theory of structuration, which no one should doubt has been the most serious attempt to provide one, single, comprehensive, true social theory. In the end, however, the project is a compromise; one might almost say a typically English compromise, the value of which resides mostly in the exposure of the one-sidedness of other perspectives. The way that was not taken was to focus upon the thought that individualism can be seen as a social fact, as a collective representation grounded in some form of social unconscious (or *conscience collective*, to use that earlier terminology). On this path the agent would have been exposed as a collective representation, a mytheme generated, it might have been surmised, by the virtual structures of the social unconscious. This path would have been the risky one to take. But the path of potential discovery was rejected for a grand theoretical exercise that has functioned alongside the stories that social systems need to perpetuate in order to maintain their hold. Perhaps the Durkheimian path of discovery was foolish, and perhaps the foolishness has been perpetuated by the attempts of writers such as Foucault, Derrida, Deleuze and Guattari to break free from what they see as compromised assumptions about the social world. For they, too, have failed to counteract the seemingly inexorable law that finds the workings of power and interest in-validating or recuperating and neutralizing every other-directed thought that they have ever had. The theory of structuration stands testimony to that, since Giddens' work has been underpinned by his skilful appropriation of concepts that in their original context demonstrate the questionable nature of the entire enterprise.

Chapter four

Structuration theory as a world-view

Richard Kilminster

> Syntheses ... do not float in an abstract space, uninfluenced by
> social gravitation; it is the structural configuration of the social
> situation which makes it possible for them to emerge and
> develop.
>
> (Mannheim, 1928:225)

Introduction

Contrary to the misgivings of some commentators, for example,
Hirst (1982), Giddens' theory of structuration, as elaborated in
The Constitution of Society (Giddens, 1984a), is an example not of
eclecticism, but of theoretical synthesis. As an exponent of
synthesis, he shares the sociological stage with other synthesizers,
including Parsons (1937), Lenski (1966) and Collins (1985). As
Stephen K. Sanderson (1987) has usefully pointed out, eclecticism
involves a mechanical juxtaposing of elements of research traditions, whereas theoretical synthesis combines elements in such a
way that the recombination produces a novel fusion, qualitatively
distinct from any of the combined components. The new combination then acquires assumptions, concepts and principles of its
own, forming a new basis for research efforts. Eclectics, on the
other hand, always advocate using multitheoretical approaches in
principle (for example, Merton, 1981).[1] Giddens says explicitly,
and reasonably in my view, that he cannot see the force of the
objection that his work is unacceptably eclectic (Giddens,
1984a:xxii). His involvement with the various schools of sociology
and philosophy is entirely for the purpose of extracting the relevant guiding thread, concept or core insight in order to recombine
it with other elements. He writes:

> The theory of structuration was worked out as an attempt to
> transcend, without discarding altogether, three prominent tradi-

tions of thought in social theory and philosophy: hermeneutics or 'interpretative sociologies', functionalism and structuralism. Each of these traditions in my view, incorporates distinctive and valuable contributions to social analysis – while each has tended to suffer from a number of defined limitations.

(Giddens, 1981a:26)

In this respect he shares the *method*, at least, of Parsons' project in the *Structure of Social Action* (1937), even if he does distance himself from Parsons' systemic determinism, functionalism and naturalism (Giddens, 1976a, Ch. 3; 1984a:xxxvii). There is extensive discussion of Parsons in Giddens' works because in many ways Parsons provided the theoretical point of departure for his reflections, as he did for a number of other sociologists in the 1950s and 1960s such as David Lockwood (1956), Alan Dawe (1970), Percy Cohen (1968) and Harold Garfinkel (1967). Obviously, Giddens is operating in a new context, with a different range of theorists and philosophers from those upon whom Parsons drew to build his general action theory in the 1930s and 1940s. But like Parsons, Giddens proceeds from the raw material of diverse theories to erect a scaffolding of synthesized concepts for the purpose of informing further research; and both resultant schemes are forms of action theory. Neither theorist builds his theory in direct cross-fertilization with evidence as he proceeds; rather, empirical examples are appended illustratively or suggestively.

Parsons wrote that the *Structure of Social Action* was a 'study in social *theory*, not *theories*' (Parsons, 1937:v) and that what unified the discussion was that each author discussed was held to have made in a different way an important contribution to 'this single coherent body of theory', i.e. Parsons' theory of social action. Giddens does not see the same kind of immanent convergence in all the recent writers he discusses, but they are none the less described as 'working on a common range of problems' (Giddens, 1982l:175) and 'they come together in the following conclusions' (Giddens, 1976a:52); or there are 'affinities between' (ibid) various ideas from different traditions. In other words, Giddens, too, borrows valuable contributions from diverse schools to forge what is effectively another 'single coherent body of theory', i.e. structuration theory. He explicitly describes this theory as an example of 'social theory in general' (Giddens, 1984a:xvii). (NB. Giddens denies that his *New Rules* was a work of synthesis because of its selectiveness (Giddens, 1976a:20), but I do not think this is true of the *Constitution of Society*, which integrates into the theory concepts derived from many more sources, including human

75

geography and existential phenomenology, and which he describes as a 'summation' (Giddens, 1984a, Preface) of his previous work on this subject.)

Despite its level of abstraction and method of construction, the theory of structuration is not, however, as divorced for relevance to empirical research as it might have appeared in the earlier versions. Giddens sees his theory as theoretically linking a number of levels of the total social process in time-space which can guide empirical research both in general and at each level: 'Structuration theory will not be of much value if it does not help to illuminate problems of empirical research' (Giddens, 1984a:xxix). The concepts 'should for research purposes be regarded as sensitizing devices ... useful for thinking about research problems and the interpretation of research results' (ibid:326–7). The action concepts in Giddens are more sophisticated than those of Parsons, as are the recommended research techniques for each level. This is because of Giddens' insistence on the reflexive character of the constituting social action of knowledgeable agents and the methodological consequences of the 'double hermeneutic'. But the overall ambition that the theoretical framework should inform empirical research is something he shares with Parsons, who wrote of his own generalized action theory: 'It ... constitutes a crucially important guide to the direction of fruitful research' (Parsons, 1938:89). I appreciate that there are also a number of discontinuities with the work of Parsons, and aims that Giddens does not share with him: for example, Giddens does not pursue universals or other societal constants; and he is critical of Parsons' 'cybernetic hierarchy'. But the comparison does serve to put structuration theory into perspective as a species of action theory with the characteristic assumptions and limitations that implies.

It is a theme of this chapter that there are tenets in structuration theory the presence of which is not explicable entirely by Giddens having been rationally or intellectually convinced of their soundness, as well as other tacit assumptions of which he is hardly aware. Structuration theory is, on the one hand, a metatheory of action, and on the other, a pulling together of a selection of concepts, tenets, assumptions, emphases and normative elements, the unity of which constitutes a world-view. As we will repeatedly see, some of these features derive from the traces within structuration theory, as in sociology in general, of the great ideologies of the nineteenth century – liberalism, socialism and conservatism – and their later developments. Others derive from the institutional location of the project and still others from the moral and political convictions of the author.

Let us begin by looking at the significance of some of Giddens' guidelines for empirical research in *The Constitution of Society* (1984a) in the light of these considerations. Giddens wants to direct research towards hermeneutic concerns, or the mediation of frames of meaning; the skills of knowledgeable actors; and the time-space constitution of social life. These proposals are intended to supplement the more customary sociological focus on institutions. He says that it is the concerns of the researcher that determine the emphasis on any one of these levels and the consequent methodological bracketing of the others. For example, in analysing the strategic conduct of actors, the focus is on the modes in which in their plans and intentions agents draw upon knowledge of the structural properties of institutions. For this purpose these institutions are methodologically regarded as 'given'. But he adds:

> There is, of course, no obligation for anyone doing detailed empirical research, in a given localized setting, to take on board an array of abstract notions that would merely clutter up what could otherwise be described with economy and in ordinary language.
>
> (Giddens, 1984a:326)

The oddity of this comment will be apparent. In the theory of structuration Giddens expends a lot of effort establishing theoretically the links between 'social integration' and 'system integration', i.e. between the face-to-face encounters of co-present actors and the wider social formation of which they form a part. As we have seen, in addition to the hermeneutic research advocated, he also commends research into time-space constitution; but then, in the previous quotation, he seems to throw away this thrust of his work by devaluing its theoretical expression as mere clutter. An unintended consequence of the methodological 'bracketing' recommendation, and this way of representing it, is to provide a legitimation for researchers to remain in their 'localized setting' or small corner of the total societal web. It discourages researchers from any ambitions they may have to make the linkages to the wider and more far-flung social interconnections implied by the theory.

However, if sociologists are substantively, and not just at the level of metatheory, to take this aim on board, then they need to be developing ways of presenting their findings, which show these simultaneous linkages. (They would have to go beyond Giddens, though, if they wanted to represent society as a figuration in Norbert Elias's terminology. This would incorporate the interpenetrating viewpoints of groups across the whole social network not envisageable within structuration theory: more on this later.) Clearly, reaching this goal is not an easy task, but is not beyond the sociological imagination: it is an ambition that unites works as diverse in aims, period and subject matter as Hegel's *Phenomenology* (1807), Marx's *Capital* (3 vols: 1867, 1885, 1894) and Elias's *Civilizing Process* (1939). This piece of Giddens' methodological advice, together with the stress on meaning frameworks, legitimates the fragmented, if scrupulous, empirical research efforts in the institutionalized settings of contemporary sociology.

The methodological recommendations seem to embody a liberalistic timidity about the possibility of representing and theorizing 'social wholes', lest this procedure erases individuals. This uncertainty is reminiscent of the diffidence generated by the publication of Karl Popper's *Poverty of Historicism* in the 1960s and indeed Giddens' recommendations would seem compatible with Popper's strictures against holism (Popper, 1961:79). It is noticeable how many pages Giddens devotes in the *Constitution of Society* to refuting the arguments of the methodological individualists, whose work he takes very seriously: 'they are quite justified in being suspicious of the aspirations of "structural sociology"' (Giddens, 1984a:220). He is not content to let the debate rest where it was left by Steven Lukes in the 1970s, but further worries over exchanges between Perry Anderson and Edward Thompson before concluding that the whole debate presupposes a false antinomy of individual/society. This is true, but it is the worrying that is significant.

The historical involvement of the European sociological tradition with the development of liberalism, both as a political doctrine and as a style of thought, is well known (Mannheim, 1928:216ff.; 1929:276ff.; Seidman, 1983) as are the other connections of sociology with socialism and conservation. In drawing out the liberal strand in the following section, I am not implying that either sociology in general, or Giddens' theory of structuration in particular, is *reducible* to its liberal ingredient. Traces of all three of the great nineteenth-century ideologies can be found woven into the fabric of sociology (Goudsblom, 1977, Ch. 5) and also into Giddens' work. Nor do I intend any pejorative judgement by this observation.

The tradition of European liberalism in various national contexts has placed the freedom and self-actualization of the individual at the centre of the doctrine. Early liberalism was all about protecting the individual from arbitrary power, but later on into the early years of this century the 'new liberalism' developed, amongst other principles, a broader conception of the individual

(Freeden, 1978). In the words of Bramsted and Melhuish, the individual was now viewed as 'potentially unique and spontaneous', a line of thought going back to the Renaissance, and they add:

> Individualism as a 'habit of mind', as the right of the individual to follow his own preferences and tastes within the limits imposed by the law instead of *having them dictated by the conventions of society*, became an additional strand in the liberal attitude.
>
> (Bramsted and Melhuish, 1978:xviii; emphasis added)

The new liberalism was partly a political doctrine, but it was also an ontology of the individual, seen as the unique, bounded and dynamic centre of self-activity, set against arbitrary power in the political realm and against 'society' in general. Liberalism derives much of its force from its foundation in the self-experience and type of conscience-formation of individuals in the increasingly complex networks of interdependencies of urbanized, advanced societies.

It would not be too fanciful to note how easily Giddens' theory of structuration dovetails into this style of thought. One of the central tenets of the theory is that, against functionalism and structuralism, the agent is to be seen not as a 'cultural dope', i.e. not as a mere conforming, approval-seeking reflex of a central value system that the actor has successfully internalized and translated into motivations. Nor is the actor simply constructed by discourses, as the antihumanist structuralists would have it. Giddens counters these distortions with a plea for the dignity of capable human actors who have 'knowledgeability', a reflexive self-monitoring capacity, discursive and tacit knowledge and 'practical consciousness'. Built into the theory are individual agents seen as acting knowledgeably and intentionally, bounded on the one side by objective institutions, and on the other by their unconscious. Giddens (1984a:90–2) lists elaborately the conditions that enable the differential cognitive penetration of wider societal processes to be achieved by aware agents. Like all liberalism, this dimension of the theory seeks to maximize the conditions for rationality so as to minimize, and thus control, the irrational.

Furthermore, for Giddens, the action of human agents involves the possibility of 'doing otherwise', of being able to make a difference in the world – a principle which has for Giddens the status of a 'philosophical theorem' (Giddens, 1982m:30). He realizes, however, that power differentials limit agents' relative capacities to mobilize resources to make a difference. The implication is clear: the unstated value premiss of this view of human action is that individual human dignity, self-expression and freedom *should* be maximized against and within institutional parameters and against unequal power chances. It makes sense of Giddens ending an analysis of worker resistance on the shop floor with the evocative words: 'precisely because they are not machines, wherever they can do so human actors devise ways of avoiding being treated as such' (ibid:45).

Obviously, these commitments work at a tacit level in structuration theory and having located them one needs to explain how and why they got there at the time they did. I cannot go into this question here. Suffice it to say that the liberal strand is the dominant one, providing an exaggerated – even Promethean – conception of the extraordinarily skilled individual agent in social reproduction.

The scope of sociology

Giddens has been influential in establishing within educational institutions in recent years a particular construction of the sociological tradition as consisting primarily of the triumvirate of Marx, Weber and Durkheim (Giddens, 1971a). He gives short shrift to Simmel because his use of evidence is cavalier and his terminology loose (Giddens, 1965a, in Raison, 1969:143); Comte is dismissed as an eccentric nineteenth-century figure whose extravagant works betray a naive faith in science (Giddens, 1975b, in 1982c:68–75);[2] and one can multiply the number of important earlier figures who are barely mentioned, let alone discussed in the same depth: Spencer, Tönnies, Tocqueville, Hobhouse, Pareto, Sorokin, Elias. Standing behind structuration theory is not only a thorough grounding in this tripartite 'selective tradition' (Williams, 1973:9) and its (partial) Parsonian consolidation, but also a staunch commitment to the importance of the sociological enterprise as such. Giddens has grasped that sociology in general has always had the capacity to contribute to an understanding of the feasibility of the plans and goals offered by various political ideologies and groups, despite the fact that many of its most distinguished practitioners have espoused one or other ideology themselves. In this vein he comments as follows on the work of the three nominated greats:

> The writings of both Durkheim and Weber have their origin in an attempt to defend – or rather to reinterpret – the claims of political liberalism within the twin pressures of Romantic hyper-

nationalistic conservatism on the one side, and revolutionary socialism on the other. Marx's writings, on the other hand, constitute an analysis and critique of early capitalism.

(Giddens, 1971a:244)

It is noticeable that Giddens nowhere attempts to muster arguments to ground a specifically 'critical' sociology in the manner of Habermas (1968) or Bauman (1976), because in absorbing the classical tradition he has already assumed that sociology is *inherently* critical. He writes: 'As critical theory sociology does not take the social world as a given, but poses the questions: what types of social change are feasible and desirable, and how should we strive to achieve them?' (Giddens, 1982d:166).[3]

In later formulations of the practical implications of sociological research, he has added the new dimension – implied by structuration theory and the principle of the 'double hermeneutic' – that concepts constructed within sociology itself, through a process of 'slippage' (Giddens, 1976a:162) back into the world of everyday life, can come to be appropriated by lay people whose conduct the concepts were originally coined to analyse (Giddens, 1984a:348–54). Giddens does not give many examples of concepts that have become an integral feature of social life in this way, but perhaps alienation would be one. From a technical concept known and used by only a handful of sociologists and philosophers a few decades ago, it has now become a word that people living in large cities often use to describe a whole range of feelings of estrangement, frustration and loneliness that they experience.

Giddens served his sociological apprenticeship in the high seriousness of the Leicester school of sociology built largely from Continental traditions of theory and research by Ilya Neustadt and Norbert Elias (before his worldwide acclaim) in the 1950s and 1960s (Neustadt, 1965; Marshall, 1982; Brown, 1987). Although not intellectually unified, this department was for a long time the largest outside London. All accounts agree that it generated in its participants considerable enthusiasm for the discipline and cultivated a particularly high degree of self-confidence. Giddens' sociological commitment bears the marks of its origins here, where he taught for six years. It is very noticeable how his absorption of a thorough-going sociological orientation effectively immunized him against getting carried away by any one of the many perspectives, schools, manifestos and fads with which sociology was subsequently deluged.[4] As he says again and again in his many discussions of these schools, he is prepared to learn or borrow from them without becoming a disciple or a partisan of any particular one.

An awareness of this dimension throws light on Giddens' attitude towards the attacks that were made during the 1960s and 1970s against the very possibility of a science of society, which often drew on older traditions of anti-sociology. Of the proliferating schools of recent times, the more radical exponents of three of them in particular – neo-Marxism, ethnomethodology and Wittgensteinism – claimed that sociology was suspect. Briefly the grounds were because sociology was respectively: (a) a bourgeois reaction to socialism and Marxism that justified inequality in capitalist societies; (b) in its professionalized and positivistic mode it illegitimately bootlegged lay actors' meanings into its explanations; and (c) its subject matter properly belonged to philosophy.

How does Giddens react to these attacks? His writings from the early 1970s are saturated with the problems raised by the then current Marxism-versus-sociology controversy, and he is clearly *au fait* with the general outlines of the debate (Giddens, 1971a, Introduction; 1973, *passim*). But he gives it short shrift: 'I do not wish to discuss here the relative merits of these competing views' (Giddens, 1973:17). Following his customary strategy, he says he will, however, take from the debate only the implications 'for the identification of the tasks with which contemporary social theory should be concerned' (ibid). There is nowhere in his writings from this period a systematic discussion of the attacks made against sociology in the writings of, say, Lukács or Adorno, which had been rediscovered and reworked at that time (Kilminster, 1979). Giddens rises above the controversy pointing out both the overreaction by Marxists to sociology in its shallow 'end-of-ideology' mode, and their simultaneous failure to come to terms with the lack of proletarian revolutions in the west and the legitimation of domination in the name of Marx in Eastern Europe. Hence: 'we live in a society that is both "post-Marxist" and "post-bourgeois", although not in a society which is "post-capitalist", let alone "post-industrial"' (Giddens, 1973:19). The point is that Giddens' unstated warrant for transcending these misleading antinomies is a prior commitment to the standpoint of sociology as an overarching and mediating framework, even if it is only implicit.

In relation to ethnomethodology, Giddens rightly points out that the implications of Garfinkel's concepts of reflexivity and indexicality, taken together, led in two directions. One was towards a kind of naturalism, resulting in conversation analysis, and the other was into the infinite regress of the hermeneutic circle. This was the more radical direction of the project of 'Theorizing' associated with Alan Blum and Peter McHugh (Giddens, 1976a:52). This philosophical project abandoned all attempts to generate reliable knowledge of society, and instead celebrated the ongoing process of collective enquiry for its own sake into the collective ontological grounds that make possible any enquiry at all (Blum, 1974; McHugh *et al.*, 1974). From the interpretative sociologies, including ethnomethodology, Giddens borrows four basic ideas for incorporation into structuration theory. These are that: (a) sociology draws on the same resources as lay people; (b) people have pragmatic knowledge; (c) sociological concepts are linked to lay ones; and (d) *Verstehen* should be treated as 'generic to all social explanation' (Giddens, 1976a:52). This tenet is transcribed into the explanatory principle of the 'double hermeneutic'.

But in extracting these principles Giddens does not pick up Garfinkel's profound discussion of the distinction made in German philosophy between *Verstehen* (the state of understanding) and *Begreifen* (the process of coming to an understanding) (Garfinkel, 1967:24ff.) and neither the latter concept nor any equivalent plays any part in Giddens' theory, for reasons that will become clear. The Theorizing tendency, which picked up on the latter concept, is abandoned without discussion, deserving only the comment that Blum and McHugh and their British followers (see Sandywell *et al.*, 1975; Dobson, 1979) are 'intrepid travellers all, now left swirling helplessly in the vortex of the hermeneutic whirlpool' (Giddens, 1976a:166).

It is obvious, however, that this rhetorical comment does not actually engage with the arguments of the Theorizers and, indeed, to my knowledge there has been no serious sociological riposte to the group's programme. Giddens' summary abandonment of them is ironic because they have made much of Heidegger's concept of 'presencing', which has also inspired the development of his own conception of time (Giddens, 1979a:3ff, 54ff; 1984a:45). As Attewell (1974) has pointed out, Garfinkel's theory of members' accounts fuses 'doing' interaction with 'telling' about it. This fusion effectively reduces *Verstehen* to *Begreifen*. So on the strong version of ethnomethodology (e.g. Theorizing) understanding becomes entirely *process*, which conception undermines the sociological project of trying to substitute objective, i.e. scientific, expressions for the ubiquitous indexical ones. This substitution, Garfinkel says, 'remains programmatic in every *particular* case and in every *actual* occasion in which the distinction or substitutability must be demonstrated' (Garfinkel, 1967:6). This is because sociologists' accounts (including their would-be objective expressions) inevitably remain organized features of the research settings that, in organizing, they describe. As Attewell rightly says, Garfinkel's statement, in this radical form, is perhaps the most extreme found

83

in sociology: 'It is as extreme a statement as the declaration of form without content, or subject without object' (Attewell, 1974:202).

Giddens does not take on the challenge of the Theorizing tendency, which took this radical road from Garfinkel. This omission is in marked contrast to his lengthy discussion in the *New Rules of Sociological Method* of the radical Wittgensteinian ideas of Peter Winch (Giddens, 1976a:44–51). 'Theorizing' is, I think, dismissed with an *ad hominem* argument because it does not occur to Giddens that so fundamental a philosophical critique of sociology even needs to be seriously discussed. He is insufficiently worried by the school to take the trouble of refuting it. This abstention is indicative of the strength of his sociological outlook and the stage of development of British sociology at which it was acquired.

Winch, on the other hand, has more professional credibility, even though he was avowedly mounting what was an unsuccessful takeover bid for sociology by philosophy. In his observations on language games, Winch is at least saying something relevant to the empirical understanding of forms of life. It is this anthropological core to Winch's work that interests Giddens (1982d:22ff.). He notes with approval and grateful relief that Winch 'makes a scrambled retreat from a full-blown relativism' (Giddens, 1976a:50) even if it is into dubious biological universals as a bedrock for cross-cultural understanding (ibid:49).

So, there is a solid sociological commitment of a specific kind embodied in Giddens' work. But what else can we discern about its nature? Despite Giddens' advocacy in his recent textbook (Giddens, 1989a, Preface and Ch. 1) that sociology should be a discipline with a fundamentally important historical dimension, a close reading of his other writings reveals inconsistency and equivocation on the subjects of development and sociogenesis. He seems to have overreacted both to the weaknesses of specifically evolutionary thinking in sociology and to philosophers' fears that appealing to the sociogenesis of concepts *ipso facto* undermines validity and rationality. This ambiguity shows itself in two ways.

First, there is no historical, genetic device in Giddens' theory construction that could take account of how the different schools and perspectives across which he abstractly roams *came* to achieve the specificity and institutional salience they possess in the form in which he finds them. Lacking a dynamic principle, he can only logically assess the cognitive value of the perspectives and schools, which he treats as comparable and equipollent. This procedure has a levelling effect on the theories and authors. He is therefore unable, for example, to distinguish true advances in theory from revived dead-ends because in eschewing development he has left himself bereft of any theory of progress or scientific advance that might enable him to accomplish this. Put another way, he does not allow genetic considerations to play any part in concept formation. (I will return to this issue later on.) For now, we can note the fact that quite a long time ago Giddens dismissed the usefulness of the sociology of knowledge in the establishment of valid concepts and has written nothing on the subject. He bade farewell to this tradition using a standard argument:

> But it needs no special perspicacity to see the *petitio principii* involved in the notion that such an exercise can in itself produce a new theoretical framework for sociology; the transmutation of sociology into the sociology of knowledge is a logically impossible endeavour.

(Giddens, 1973:15)

Second, Giddens' conception of the subject matter of sociology is based on an *a priori* commitment to a caesural, or discontinuist, view of history. He writes:

> The modern world is born out of discontinuity with what went before rather than continuity with it. It is the nature of this discontinuity – the specificity of the world ushered in by the advent of industrial capitalism, originally located and founded in the West – which it is the business of sociology to explain as best it can.

(Giddens, 1984a:329)

Elsewhere he writes that he is committed to this view 'whatever continuities may exist with what went before' (Giddens, 1982e:107), which suggests that he is not denying that continuities exist side by side with discontinuities, but that in this balance he is simply wanting to privilege discontinuity.

But to what form of 'caesurism' (Martins, 1974:280) is Giddens committing us here? And does this commitment go beyond mere preference or simple conviction as a reaction, or even revulsion, against archaic evolutionism? Giddens implies that he is intellectually convinced by discontinuism. He says that by a discontinuist view of history he means his belief – derived from Ernest Gellner (1964) – that the transformation of the west over the last three hundred years has no precedent in history and is a break of scale with what went before, greater than any previous break (Giddens, 1982h:107; 1984a:237–8). This clearly delimited configuration of modern industrialized societies provides the terrain for sociology, which emerged precisely as the discipline *par excellence* for explaining this bounded but historically discontinuous and distinctive world. He writes: 'Human history is not, to use Gellner's term, a "world growth story"' (Giddens, 1984a:237; see also 1982h:76ff).

A starting point for raising the problems involved here is a perceptive comment by Herminio Martins:

> Gellner's version of caesurism is particularly attractive to sociologists, not least because in a sense his conception of the modern world implies a rather central place for sociology as against history, and to some extent also asociological conceptions of epistemology and ethics.... As a general characterization of the modern world, of the paramount structure of 'our time', it remains highly plausible.... As a forceful reminder of the strong and in some respects overriding moral obligations incumbent on sociologists and scholars in the contemporary world it remains valid.
>
> (Martins, 1974:282)

Indeed, I think that Giddens' commitment to discontinuism *à la* Gellner is shot through with moral as well as empirical or scientific considerations. It fits very well with his oft-repeated advocacy of the 'critical' vocation of the sociologist to illuminate the structure of this singularly modern world. And it sits comfortably with his related socialist convictions (Giddens, 1982h),[5] which have partly guided his annexation of much of the socialist-Marxist economic ontology into this theory alongside the action components. Predictably, therefore, Giddens uses highly evaluative and emotive language to describe the character of this discontinuous modern world: 'It is much more illuminating to see it as placing a caesura upon the traditional world, which it seems irretrievably to *corrode and destroy*' (Giddens, 1984a:239, emphasis added). And more strikingly on capitalism:

> A philosophical anthropology relevant to socialism must attend closely to what we can retain of the human diversity that is being devoured by the voracious expansion of the 'created space' of capitalism – for in the world that capitalism has originated, time is no longer understood as the medium of Being, and the gearing of daily life into comprehended tradition is replaced by the empty routines of everyday life. On the other hand, the whole of humanity now lives in the shadow of possible destruction. This unique conjunction of the banal and the apocalyptic, this is the world that capitalism has fashioned.
>
> (Giddens, 1981a:252)

It is not surprising that with a moral conviction of this emotional intensity driving his commitment to Gellnerian caesurism, Giddens will be uninterested in developing a more sober picture of the balance of continuity/discontinuity on various levels; or retrieving the developmental baby thrown out with the evolutionary bath-water in order to put on to the agenda structured long-term *develop-ment*. As one can see from the previous quotation, capitalism sometimes assumes in Giddens' hands (as it did for Marx) the character of an unstoppable force spreading like a contagion across the globe.[6] But he has overstated the penetration and effects of global, capitalistic economic relations, which he sees only as *one-way* traffic. With the result that he underplays countermovements, for example fundamentalist religious and political movements in various parts of the world, including, in the advanced societies, movements that seek to reassert national or ethnic identities as a kind of cultural protectionism against the encroaching globaliz-ation that is pulling nations together (Robertson and Lechner, 1985).

Moreover, Giddens' world-view discourages asking what is the longer-run sequential order of processes of differentiation/inte-gration that has shaped the present conditions and foreshadows the next emergent phase (see Elias, 1987); but rather encourages apparently looking only at social and political processes in the national and global present for a diagnosis of the current situation and its possibilities.[7] The sequential order issue is suppressed because of the assumption that the study of long-range develop-mental change can only be evolutionist, i.e. an inquiry that he claims contains the fatal flaw of seeing modernity as an inevitable accentuation of previous trends, as their summation. But this is an overreaction.

To put the corrective briefly and abstractly for present purposes: attention to the sequential order of continuous but uneven strands of development, which provides successively newer sets of preconditions for the emergence of the next phase of soci-etal change, can illuminate the problem of how such combinations result in the production of discontinuity and societal specificity. Continuity and discontinuity are both implicated in social develop-ment and no inevitability or teleology need be implied. A fuller and more finely tuned social diagnosis of the present situation will entail extending the analysis into non-economic bonds (see p. 102) as well as back into the order and sequencing of longer-term contin-uities that Giddens' discontinuism, as a matter of principle, plays down.

Finally, another example of the way Giddens' evaluative

enthusiasm interferes with a sober sociological analysis of human social realities occurs when he is drawn in an interview on the subject of the relationship between human beings and nature. In a Romantic statement inspired by Lévi-Strauss, he declares:

> A ... major feature of modern world civilizations is the loss of a generic relationship between human beings and nature and I think that's really a tremendous loss for the style of life we live because we just live in an essentially artificial milieu in which there is no longer any contact with nature of the traditional kind. I just think to go on holidays, tourism, to go out into the country at weekends, is different from the way in which people have always lived in dealing with nature.

(Giddens, 1982h:68)

It is as though Giddens has not heard of the whole tradition from Marx, Simmel, Lukács and Elias to the Frankfurt School and many others who have in different ways established the historical variability of 'human nature' and questioned the idea that there ever was a time when human beings stood in an authentic relationship to nature. The character of the relationship between human beings and non-human nature, as well as the interplay between human sociality and the biological level that it continues, depends on the stage of social development. In the previous quotation, Giddens unreflectively interposes modern society as an 'artificial' milieu between man and nature, when man is inconceivable outside social relations or severed from biological nature. Society was made possible by a prior evolutionary biological precondition. *'Nature' is as human-made a category as 'society'.* But we would never consider that the natural sciences were sciences of something artificial. Giddens has reproduced a value assumption that, compared with genuine, pristine, real nature, modern society is a merely artificial, synthesized and by implication, a somewhat debased concoction. We are living in a way that cuts us off from authentic communion with nature. Giddens reinforces the old dualism between nature and culture by superimposing it on the traditional/ modern distinction, thereby reproducing it in its most mystifying form.

Philosophy and 'social theory'

In inspecting Giddens' sociological credentials, one is struck by his very conventional view of the relationship between sociology and philosophy, but one also detects a certain ambivalence surrounding this subject. As I will show, he takes for granted philosophers' stipulations of the range of questions to be allocated to the respective academic establishments. This topic is worth attention because it bears upon the status of structuration theory as 'social theory' and affects how we evaluate the 'systematic' as opposed to historical or genetic theoretical strategy which it exemplifies.

Giddens' attitude to this issue can be gathered from these two quotations: 'both empirical social analysis and sociological theorizing involve inherently philosophical endeavours' (Giddens, 1982l:175) and: 'The social sciences are lost if they are not directly related to philosophical problems by those who practise them' (Giddens, 1984a:xvii). As I have demonstrated more fully elsewhere (Kilminster, 1989), the evidence suggests, however, that with the rise of the social sciences and of sociology in particular within European social development, it became more and more difficult for philosophers to justify an autonomous area of competence for their discipline. (Indeed, this problem could be said to have reached crisis proportions in contemporary philosophy (Baynes *et al.*, 1987; Rorty, 1982).)

Sociology gradually took over and transposed on to a new level questions about the nature of knowledge and morality that were previously raised by philosophers or theologians or that were locked up in the great ideologies of the nineteenth century. These matters became embedded in the conceptual structure of sociology and are profoundly preserved within it, carried forward in a reformulated state. Meanwhile, the philosophical establishment retreated more and more into developing their logical and conceptual skills, transforming philosophy mainly into a technical discipline, particularly in the Anglo-Saxon tradition, and erecting barriers of argument and cultivated profundity around themselves to effect the professional closure of their subject.

If this general picture of the historical fate of philosophy has even a grain of accuracy, then we must be more cautious than Giddens in taking for granted the autonomy and cognitive value of philosophy and the range of specialisms within it that we find ready to hand in the current books produced in the field. On one level Giddens seems to grasp the profound evaluative social relevance of the sociological tradition that he sees as a 'critical' commitment, in deference to the current catchword. But there is also in Giddens a failure of nerve in not carrying this awareness through to its conclusion in relation to philosophy.

Giddens brings into play the woolly term 'social theory' which he concedes is 'not a term which has any precision' (Giddens, 1984a:xvii), derived from the Parsonian–Mertonian tradition, in order to build bridges towards philosophy. The 'field' of social theory is said to encompass issues about the nature and conceptualization of human action in relation to institutions and the practical connotations of social analysis, which are deemed to be applicable to all social sciences. 'Sociological theory', on the other hand, is said to be relevant only to advanced industrialized societies and to be a species of social theory. It is a social theory that is said to raise issues that 'spill over into philosophy' (ibid:xvii). The dubiety of the field called social theory can readily be seen if sociology is compared with the science of psychology. In this discipline would anyone ever refer to 'psychic theory'?

The problem I am bringing into focus here is that philosophical concepts, unlike sociological ones, have not been developed in direct cross-fertilization with empirical evidence, and that the importance of this difference is blurred by the acceptance of the legitimacy of the enterprise of social theory. Oddly enough, in one place Giddens acknowledges just this difference. Speaking about divergences between Marx's conception of history and the observations of later critics, he says that he does not think that the divergences can be either validated or invalidated by a conventional empirical test: 'But neither are they refractory to empirical reference in the sense in which philosophical theories are' (Giddens, 1971a:x). But in the *Constitution of Society* he sees the conceptions of human action and agency to be produced by social theory as theorems that 'can be placed in the service of empirical work' (Giddens, 1984a:xvii). The point presumably being that when doing social theory one works up concepts of action and agency found in philosophy in such a way as to render them amenable to empirical research. I say presumably, because this is far from clear.

Furthermore, the subject is made even more vague by his casual and undiscriminating terminology. When describing the texture of the philosophical enterprise that is supposed to connect with social theory, Giddens moves freely between philosophical 'concepts', 'theories', 'issues' and 'debates'. If these terms are studied separately, however, the uncertainty surrounding the status of structuration theory is compounded. Philosophical 'concepts' have, as Giddens has clearly also seen, no direct empirical reference or intention and are hence, in themselves, of no usefulness for research purposes. Indeed, by their very nature, philosophical concepts are held to be part of a transcendental, i.e. *non*-empirical, kind of discourse (Kilminster, 1989). From the standpoint of the sociological view of theory as being involved in an interplay with evidence, surely the phrase 'philosophical theories' is a contradiction in terms. Furthermore, because of philosophy's dubious autonomy historically, it is by no means clear that there are philosophical 'issues' at all, let alone any relevant to the social sciences. Philosophical 'debates' certainly exist, but their cognitive value cannot be guaranteed. They are often arbitrary and of only accidental relevance to sociology.

In the light of the aforesaid, one can then ask: in what does the perceived overlap between philosophers' and sociologists' treatments of issues in the study of social action consist? Both groups are said to have been working 'on a common range of problems' (Giddens, 1982l:175) but surely this is true only in an abstract sense, in so far as all the writers concerned are talking about human action generally and the ways in which sociologists have tried to explain it. Under the rubric of social theory, Giddens is able to move freely between authors as diverse as Weber, Garfinkel, Durkheim, Gadamer, Erikson, Austin, Schutz and Wittgenstein; an exercise that grossly flattens out the distinctive historical and national specificity of their work, as well as eliding the sociology/philosophy distinction. Moreover, because philosophers can only in the nature of what they do develop their concepts and discussions without direct interplay with empirical evidence, we can never be sure whether their assertions or conclusions are not hypostatizations of their own self-experience or that of particular groups in our society or in some other society or period. The apparent convergence observed may also be partly due to the slippage of sociological findings and concepts *into* philosophy, which are then reworked in a different and characteristically philosophical vocabulary. These are then fed back into sociology as apparently independently arrived-at insights.

The status of social theory and its role in Giddens' thinking has to be seen against his depiction of the proper field of sociology. As we have already seen, for Giddens, sociology is the social science dealing only with advanced societies, its concepts being developed in relation to the distinctive character of the discontinuous, modern industrialized world. Hence sociology is 'not a generic discipline dealing with human societies as a whole' (Giddens, 1984a:xvii). But if sociology is not this generic discipline, then which is? Presumably the imprecise social theory, which is said to span all the social sciences. Social theory, therefore, as a 'second-order' range of conceptual reflections on the nature of action occupies a structurally similar place in relation to sociology as conventional wisdom has it that philosophy in general stands to all the sciences. Indeed, as far as I can see social theory is philosophizing by another name.

Structuration theory, as social theory, is born out of a style of thinking that assumes that philosophy is the master discipline unifying the sciences and, as such, it reinforces this role. Giddens cannot entertain the possibility that the master science might be *sociology*, because for him that would smack of Comteanism, scientism and positivism and similar doctrines that, together with the idea of progress, apparently celebrated the superiority of the west. This is why (as we saw in the previous section) he so strenuously rejects all theories of evolution, (Giddens, 1984a, Ch. 5) because they are regarded as part of the same undesirable package of nineteenth-century ideas; but in doing so he also discards a sensitivity to *development*, which is not the same thing.

Giddens' response to the work of Habermas, as the leading exponent of 'critical' theory in the Marxist tradition, is interesting in the light of what I have been arguing in this and the previous sections. Habermas has produced a vast and weighty output over the last twenty-five years and has been highly influential because of the challenging way in which he has reconstructed the Marxian legacy for a generation caught up in the radical politics in the 1960s and 1970s. As is well known, he builds on the work of the earlier writers of the Frankfurt School, and the *Dialectic of Enlightenment* (1947) by Horkheimer and Adorno looms large in his intellectual development. Because of the particular German transcendental philosophical tradition from which Habermas comes and the specifically western Marxist problematics in which his work is embedded, one can only fully understand his work once one has taken account of certain Kantian principles and traced his project back to the Hegelian structure of thinking epitomized by Horkheimer's essay 'Traditional and critical theory' of 1937 and ultimately back to Lukács *History and Class Consciousness* (Kilminster, 1979). Hence, when Habermas employs in his work concepts and insights derived from the philosophy of language, linguistics, developmental psychology and systems theory, these are grafted on to an already consolidated philosophical–sociological standpoint in which Kantian and Hegelian themes are intertwined in interesting and, in my view, contradictory ways.

Much of the centre of gravity of this critical theory tradition is lost in Giddens' otherwise clear and concise discussions of the writings of Habermas. He seems to learn little from Habermas and none of his concepts are directly integrated into structuration theory. Giddens expounds Habermas in a disinterested kind of way, clinically laying out the ideas and evaluating them in the light of his own interest in the nature of knowledgeable human action. And he explains the importance of one strand of the philosophical tradition in which Habermas stands (that which located social sciences as *Geisteswissenschaften*), which is most relevant to the matter in hand. He comes at Habermas as a curious but sceptical observer who wants to take his works seriously because of their eminence, but who in the end cannot see their point.

Giddens' criticisms of Habermas are in fact standard ones, frequently made by critics. He says that the two distinctions labour/interaction and nomological/hermeneutic science in Habermas interpenetrate to such a degree in real life that he questions the usefulness of distinguishing them analytically in the first place. He also questions Habermas's analogy between the relationship of psychoanalysts communicating to patients and social scientists communicating to lay people knowledge about structures of inequality in society. And he wonders if Habermas has not exaggerated the pervasiveness of technocratic consciousness in late capitalism (Giddens, 1977a:135–64; 1982b, Ch. 7).

Giddens is obviously out of sympathy with Habermas's whole project and style, referring to its 'quasi-Hegelian murkiness' (Giddens, 1974a:20). He sometimes makes shrewd substantive objections but often misunderstands or disregards the significance of the transcendental dimension of Habermas's work, i.e. the metatheoretical aspects, to which he gives much less attention. Clearly, if you think sociology is already 'critical', why bother evaluating philosophical arguments designed to demonstrate it? But it is not enough, however, simply to say as Giddens does that the ideal-speech situation, because it is an ideal, cannot be used to analyse concrete linguistic situations; or that its use in evaluating distorted speech presupposes nomological knowledge of that speech situation. Of course it does, in Habermas's terms, because the knowledge-constitutive interests have an analytical, transcendental status.

These comments miss the trickier implications in Habermas (and in Karl-Otto Apel) of the ideal-speech situation as a regulative principle, in Kantian terminology. The ideal-speech situation is partly realized in the distorted speech of the present, but is as yet also unrealized. In the theory of communication its utopian status is held to be more firmly grounded. This model serves as an ideal, a basis for critique and evaluation, as something both to work towards and to employ as a bulwark against bureaucratic socialist elites who might claim that the utopia has been realized in the society that they rule. That is to say, it provides a criterion by which to see through spurious utopias or false claims to 'universality'. For this reason alone in this frame of reference the ideal-speech situation, as a utopia, cannot and should not be taken as being concretely realizable. In other words, it is related to empirical situations both concretely and 'potentially'.

Consequently, Habermas' theory entails that conditions

sustaining some distorted communication must, dialectically speaking, *always* exist for the ideal-speech situation to have its transcendental existence and thus its critical power. There are echoes here of Marx's 'realm of necessity'. For this reason, too, the ideal-speech situation is unrealizable concretely. Paradoxically, once built or created, i.e. realized in practice in the world, the ideal-speech situation would then lose its critical function. It follows, therefore, that in the meantime the critical theorist can only work towards achieving an idealized situation that is inherently unachievable. I have discussed the serious implications of this paradox elsewhere (Kilminster, 1982). The point to be made here, however, is that the particular kind of prior sociological commitment Giddens has desensitizes him to the tensions of critical theory, which require sociological understanding. I, too, would want to reject this programme, but feel that it has to be thoroughly evaluated in its full dignity. This paradox constitutes for the practitioners of critical theory an agonizing spiritual dilemma. They are driven by their conscience to try to achieve an unachievable ideal, against which their efforts are forever condemned to inadequacy. Nowhere is the guilt-driven Protestant super-ego writ larger than in the Kantian dimension of critical theory.

Interaction or interdependence?

As a species of action theory, Giddens' theory of structuration is an attempt to bring together conceptually through a process of reasoning the two levels of action and system. Moving off from a critique of Parsons' theory of socialization via internalization, he sets out to show how the *actual process of interaction* by skilled, knowledgeable actors produces and reproduces the structure and widespread patterning – or degree of 'systemness' – of social relations. This strategy overcomes both Parsons' tendency to reify social systems as well as the powerful objection made by a number of writers, but notably Percy Cohen in his influential *Modern Social Theory*, that 'Parsons is scarcely concerned with action at all, but rather with the conditions that lead up to it' (Cohen, 1968:237).

Giddens then weaves in an action theory variant of the principle of the ubiquity of power in social relations, a human reality established in the sociology of Norbert Elias and also derivable from Foucault and from Max Weber's efforts to show how Marx's analysis of economic power was only one example of a generic phenomenon.[8] Without making it explicit, Giddens is conjuring up a massive weight of sociological tradition when he writes: 'There is no more elemental concept than that of power' (Giddens, 1984a:283). This move enables him to insist that the skilled inter-pretative exchanges of actors are not to be seen as taking place between peers (as Garfinkel implied) but are likely to be skewed or imbalanced by the distribution of power in society at large. And for the sake of completion (and to cover the contemporary demand for reflexivity) Giddens builds in the tenet that both the unintended consequences of action, and agents' knowledge of the mechanisms of system reproduction, can feed back into system reproduction. The essence of structuration theory can thus be grasped from the following two quotations:

> All structural properties of social systems ... are the medium and outcome of the contingently accomplished activities of situated actors. The reflexive monitoring of action in situations of co-presence is the main anchoring feature of social integration, but both the conditions and the outcomes of situated interaction stretch far beyond those situations as such. The mechanisms of 'stretching' are variable but in modern societies tend to involve reflexive monitoring itself. That is to say, understanding the conditions of system reproduction becomes part of those conditions of system reproduction as such.
>
> (Giddens, 1984a:191)

> Power is not, as such, an obstacle to freedom or emancipation but is their very medium.... The existence of power presumes structures of domination whereby power that 'flows smoothly' in processes of social reproduction (and is, as it were, 'unseen') operates. The development of force or its threat is thus not the type case of the use of power.
>
> (ibid:257)

In a similar vein to my remarks in the previous section, a number of critics have suggested that Giddens' stress on people's knowledgeability and reflexive monitoring tilts the balance of structuration theory towards subjectivism. This line is worth pursuing further. Johnson, Dandeker and Ashworth, for example, argue that despite his intention to transcend the subjectivism/objectivism dualism by reframing it as the 'duality of structure', Giddens' ambiguous attitude towards realism means that he remains a subjectivist (Johnson *et al.*, 1984:205–13). And Margaret Archer underlines this by pointing out, from a systems theory perspective, the vaunting power Giddens ascribes to human agency, including that of generating apparently social-structural properties, which are *all* said to be instantiated by action. But she argues that not all such features are equally changeable by agents. These will include some that change quickly, such as taxation rules, others that take longer, such as demographic distributions, to others that are resistant to change such as gender roles and some, like natural resources or language, that are effectively unchangeable. Giddens' overwhelming commitment to the efficacy of reflexively monitored action flattens out these crucial distinctions leaving him unable to deal with *degrees* of constraint. She writes that he thus 'provides an insufficient account of the mechanisms of stable replication' (Archer, 1982:479).

this objection and other criticisms of a similar kind, particularly in the section 'Three senses of constraint' (Giddens, 1984a:174ff). He acknowledges bodily and material constraints, which he distinguishes from constraining negative sanctions and from structural constraint derived from the given context of differentially empowered, situated actors. All these limit the range of options open to knowledgeable agents and some of these constraints, which include structural properties, he says cannot be changed, but these are not named (ibid:176). Essentially he differentiates the issue in a Weberian fashion, claiming that there are different types of constraint that work in different contexts of action; in any case, constraints on one level can also provide the enablement of individual action on another.

Giddens states that it is the *structural properties* of institutions (symbolic orders, political, economic, legal dimensions) that are objective to the individual agent. (The more deeply embedded ones he calls structural principles.) The *structure*, however, as rules and resources, has a paradigmatic existence, and is said to be only instantiated in action and memory traces, providing the 'virtual' order in the patterning of the social practices in the social system. In this sense 'structure' in Giddens' theory is *internal* to actors (Giddens, 1984a:25). But do these definitions meet Archer's criticism about the problematic objectivity of constraints in Giddens' theory?

When talking about these structural properties of institutions in detail, Giddens says that this is only a valid procedure 'if it is recognized as placing an *époché* upon – holding in suspension – reflexively monitored conduct' (ibid:30). What does this mean? Presumably that with the methodological brackets removed, structural properties are *also* – like structure – uniformly *instantiated* in reality in reflexively monitored conduct. Or does he mean that reflexively monitored conduct can go on with institutions existing as an objective backdrop? In which case, what is their ontological status? The first suggestion finds backing in an earlier formulation by Giddens (1979a:80) that seemed to imply that by virtue of the 'duality of structure' these structural properties, too, are instantiated in human action, both constraining and enabling it. The latter interpretation seems to square with Giddens' comment about symbolic orders in semiotics as a constraint in the realm of signification: 'Signs "exist" only as the medium and outcome of communicative processes in interaction' (Giddens, 1984a:31). But these formulations are at odds with the definition of 'structural properties' given in the glossary to *The Constitution of Society*, which only mentions 'institutionalized' and 'structured' features, with no reference to reflexively monitored conduct or to instantiation.

I think that the source of these inconsistencies lies partly in the specific character of the structuralist concept he has used. (I will return to this concept in the next section.) In addition, the problem arises from the nature of structuration theory as action theory. The starting point for Giddens is the bequeathed theoretical problem of how the actions of skilled actors ongoingly produce and reproduce the systemness of wider patterns of social relations. Hence, Giddens has to provide a way of talking about the patterned interconnections between far-flung chains of interdependent groups and individuals that both retains the all-important skilled, knowledgeable actor but does not reify structure as an external source of constraint, thus reproducing the fallacious individual/society dualism. He is trying to deal with *interdependence* in the language of *interaction*.

Let us look more closely at this problem, in the light of Elias's comment that 'the concept of "individual" refers to interdependent people in the singular, and the concept of "society" to interdependent people in the plural' (Elias, 1970:125). The point to be made is that structuration theory does not at any level contain a fully *relational* conception of constraint because of Giddens' failure to incorporate the reality and concept of human interdependence into this theory. Nowhere does he provide a conceptual discussion of the term interdependence. The term appears occasionally in his writings, as when he is expounding the functionalists' conception of the interdependence of parts and whole, or when it is dropped loosely into discussions to mean interaction or interrelation. In other places, he is clearly aware of the socioeconomic meaning of the concept in the theory of the division of labour in Marx and Durkheim (Giddens, 1971a, 1982m:36) but these are the only senses in which Giddens appears to know the concept. Interdependence plays no systematic part in the theory of structuration.

Once he has started down the action theory road, then this approach defines the problems for Giddens and circumscribes their solution. Once the starting point is interacting individuals and types of individuals, rather than the plurality of people in webs of interdependencies, two features come to dominate the analysis.

First, a tendency to see unintended consequences and unacknowledged conditions of action only as conditions or consequences of *individual* actions, not as endemic to the actions of many interdependent individuals in a developing society. The ramifications of these actions reverberate down chains of intertwined people across nations, and across the world and back again. Similarly, the ambiguous 'structural properties' of institutions, which I mentioned earlier, tend also to be regarded as objective only in relation to the individual. Despite his attempt to transcend the individual/society dichotomy by the duality of agency and structure, the ghost of the old dualism haunts the theory because his point of departure is action theory, which carries the dualism at its core.

Second, the interacting individuals in conditions of co-presence (social integration applies here) can only be visualized as connected to other individuals who are not present by using metaphors such as the 'stretching' of social practices ('time-space distanciation'); or by reference to their 'lateral' properties or to the 'channelling of time-space paths of individuals' in system integration (Giddens, 1984a:142). When talking about social integration he sometimes refers to 'absent others' or 'those who are physically absent' (ibid:37). The closest Giddens comes to conceptualizing interdependence is when he makes a distinction in one passage (though not sustained throughout the *Constitution of Society*) between 'social interaction' and 'social relations':

> Social interaction refers to encounters in which individuals engage in situations of co-presence, and hence to social integration as a level of the 'building blocks' where the institutions of social systems are articulated. Social relations are certainly involved in the structuring of interaction but are also the main 'building blocks' around which institutions are articulated in system integration. Interaction depends upon the 'positioning' of individuals in the time-space contexts of activity. Social relations concern the 'positioning' of individuals within a 'social space' of symbolic categories and ties.
>
> (Giddens, 1984a:89).

I have quoted this knotty passage at length in order that the ambiguities and elisions of the theory can stand out in sharper relief.

This quotation articulates the furthest point possible within action theory and yet it still fails to resolve the action/system dualism. Individual interactions in conditions of co-presence seem to be given precedence and form the starting point. These are said to involve reflexively applied procedures by knowledgeable agents whereby integration is achieved. But note the vagueness of the terms 'building blocks', 'social relations', 'symbolic categories' and 'ties' to describe the way integration is achieved on the system level. Unspecified 'social relations' are said to be involved at both levels and the differential 'positioning' of individuals in both is regarded as significant. Despite the word relations, individuals are seen here only in the first person, as positions. There is no conceptual grasp of the perspective from which they themselves are regarded *by others* in the total social web, nor of their combined relatedness. Structuration theory is a one-dimensional view of society that does not permit the sociologist to show this combined interplay of relations and perspectives in all its richness and complex balances of power.

The issue here is this: What is the nature of the social interconnectedness, the unspecified 'ties' that bind people both into smaller networks, and into wider ones that ripple beyond their immediate milieu? To extend the question: What makes it socially possible for people to break off contacts and move on spatially to take up others, then to break these, and so on, in the manner described so vividly by Giddens (and by Simmel before him)? In all cases I would suggest it is their inescapable interdependence with others. Actors do indeed have intentions, plans, goals and knowledgeability and possess differentially valid discursive cognitive 'penetration' of wider social interconnections. But they cannot escape their complex interdependence with others, present or absent, no matter how penetrative their knowledge may be. In John Lennon's haunting line: 'Life is what happens to you while you're busy making other plans.' People's rational, aware actions may have unplanned consequences, which they did not anticipate and cannot control, brought about by the repercussions of the actions of others whom they do not know but with whom they are interdependent. And this process works the other way, not as an 'interaction' or simple reciprocity, but as a functional nexus (see pp. 100–1). Giddens' theorem of individuals 'making a difference' has to be rethought and cleansed of its rationalistic and voluntaristic character.

The complex intertwined nature of the social bonding that binds social and system integration, in Giddens' terminology, is left in woolly vagueness in structuration theory by the nature of its cognitive cast. As we have seen, Giddens can only visualize inter-dependence in its partial economic mode in his discussions of Durkheim and the capitalist wage-labour contract in Marx. But even this dimension is marginal to his structuration theory, as such. He thus fails to grasp interdependence as a much more multi-levelled, complex and *relational* structure, involving human bonding of various kinds, including political, economic and affective bonds. As Elias says of the multiple functions that people perform *for* each other:

> People need each other, are directed towards and bonded to each other as a result of the division of labour, of occupational specialization, of integration into tribes or states, or a common sense of identity, and of their shared antagonism for others or their hatred and enmity towards each other.
>
> (Elias, 1970:175, n.1)

In analysing such multidimensional functional nexuses, one can show how the nature of bonds between individuals and groups changes over time as part of wider societal changes. For example, the parent-child bond goes through a number of stages during the lifetime of the two people, as the balance of power shifts from one to the other as part of the changing play of forces across the family network and society as a whole.

With his concept of the 'dialectic of control' (Giddens, 1984a:283), Giddens has conceptualized the important fact that subordinate groups can, through making use of resources open to them, exercise some control over superordinate ones, even if the balance is highly asymmetrical. This welcome concept, though not in essence original, contributes much to the debate about the nature of social power and, rightly, has a high profile in the theory of structuration. But it has not the same explanatory force as grasping such a skewed balance-of-power relationship as one of functional interdependence in the previous sense, whereby each group or unit is dependent on the other *for its very social existence*. And sometimes groups or larger social units will be driven into bitter conflict with each other by the structure of their related-ness, despite their mutual understanding of their relationship. Giddens can only grasp this kind of interdependency-in-antagonism in the weaker and more voluntaristic form of: 'control ... as the capability that some actors, groups or types of actors have of influencing the circumstances of action of others' (ibid). But this formulation overlooks that these groups or actors are *already* locked into forms of bonding with those they are trying to influence, and they with them, vice versa, forming a functional nexus in a wider web of interdependencies. As Elias says: 'Underlying all intended interactions of human beings is their unintended interdependence' (Elias, 1969:143).

Structuration theory embodies a rationalistic image of people whose affective life – and readiness to connect with others on this dimension of bonding – is bracketed out by the methodological prescription that the reflexively monitoring actor is bounded by institutions on the one side and by the unconscious on the other, which is said – following ego-psychology – to be little implicated in practical conduct (Giddens, 1984a:50). Giddens' indebtedness to this school of psychoanalysis and, within it, to Erik Erikson, helps focus the model of the rational agent at the centre of the theory. Erikson's work, and that of this school in general, is famous for broadening the scope of psychoanalysis to include the ego's conscious interests and the individual's relationships with collective symbols and social institutions other than the Oedipal family constellation associated with classical Freudianism.

Giddens accepts much of Erikson's sociological corrective to the more mythic and individualistic aspects of Freud. In so doing he takes on board a notion of the agent very much in line with Erikson's version of Freud's 'ego ideal', seen by Erikson as more flexible, more conscious and more bound to prevalent cultural values and susceptible to change than the more thoroughly internalized super-ego of Freud (Erikson, 1968:210). There is thus an interesting consistency in Giddens' work. This model of the rational agent fits well with Giddens' fascination with the extraordinary capacities of the skilful actor derived from Garfinkel and goes hand in hand with the tacit neo-liberal impulse in the theory that people's capacities to 'make a difference' should be maximized. To quote Hoffman on Erikson's concept of the 'ego ideal': 'This definition, more than Freud's, resembles the classical liberal notion of an "inner-directing" conscience and assumes that individuals are capable of participating in the direction of their own lives' (Hoffman, 1982:140).

In a word, structuration theory articulates, with an implicit normative stress, the dominant self-experience and public code of behaviour of highly self-controlled individuals in advanced industrialized societies. But it is unable to show how this kind of individual came to develop in the first place: for Giddens, people have, apparently, always been the same since the dawn of history. I am not denying the importance of ego-psychology, which provides, for example, a profound understanding of individual identity formation as a series of stages. Nor that the incorporation of concepts derived from it into research programmes will not illuminate at least a certain range of problems in sociology. My point is that if a theory embodying the model of the agent described is pursued exclusively, one pays a high price. It effectively closes the door to an understanding of the crucial role played in society by socially controlled and regulated instincts and drives. By its very conceptual structure and assumptions, structuration theory cannot address the *emotional* 'constitution of society'. Excluded is the study of social standards of affect-control and individual self-control. Alien to the theory is the changing social regulation of pleasure, desire and aggression through shame, embarrassment and revulsion. These emotions have been systematically ruled out in advance as unsociological.[9]

Systematics or sociogenesis?

Structuration theory is conceived as a metatheory of action relevant to all the social sciences, a conceptual effort of synthetic theory construction designed to consolidate current developments in theory and reconstruct the orthodox consensus. But, I have been arguing, it is more than this. It is also the pulling together into a more-or-less coherent sociological package of a particular selection of concepts, tenets, assumptions, emphases and normative elements, the unity of which can be seen to constitute a world-view. The selective principle underlying its component parts is its prescriptive force as a moral-political platform for the social criticism of modernity from the point of view of the freedom of the individual, seen as potentially self-directing and expressive. This evaluative stress, as well as rational, intellectual criteria, determines what is included within or excluded from the purview of the theory. The liberal strand is the most dominant, in a number of senses, as we have seen. The socialist current is represented by the appropriation of the Marxist economic ontology of labour and the stress on individual freedom is also compatible with forms of democratic socialism. Conservatism provides the *longue durée* of sedimented and reproduced institutions and the concept of existential contradiction, both of which have a lower profile in the theory.

I do not think it imposes too great a degree of coherence to represent the world-view implicit in structuration theory in general outline as follows. Sociology is seen as the 'critical' social science that deals with the class societies of the discontinuous 'modern' capitalist world. Its central concern is with examining which conditions of action will maximize the capacity of knowledgeable actors to make a difference in this society when they are differentially socially endowed with access to resources. Sociology needs to be open to philosophy because here we find apposite discussions of rationality and intentional action that are appropriate for understanding the kind of self-monitoring people characteristic of the rationalized world of modernity. We concentrate on knowledgeability, discursive and practical consciousness because in the modern internally pacified nation-states the personality formation of actors is such that the unconscious is not much implicated in their everyday action. Hence it can be bracketed out. The choice of Marx, Weber and Durkheim as the 'selective tradition' is appropriate because they were pre-eminently the sociologists of discontinuous modernity and its problems. They criticized respectively early capitalism, the later anomic aspects of economic life and increasing capitalistic rationalization. This version of the nature and role of sociology in the modern world is institutionally prominent in various forms. This is because it is self-evidently plausible to the highly self-controlled, self-monitoring people who participate in the sociological community and who find mirrored in the programme their most deeply felt moral obligations as social critics.

For the sake of contrast and in order to open up a dialogue with this way of doing sociology, I have counterposed a number of opposite principles. This tactic is employed in order to retrieve from the theoretical bathwater some conceptual babies hastily discarded. These recoveries will hopefully also ultimately transform the normative implications by reconstituting a more realistic balance. Instead of a narrow sociology of modernity, I counterposed a broader conception of sociology as the unifying social science applicable to all historical societies. Instead of discontinuism I opposed continuism. Instead of the knowledgeable actor I substituted changing patterns of figurational compulsion. Against interaction I pitted interdependence. Instead of embracing philosophy I suggested we pull away. Instead of agents as first-person 'positions' I advocated multiperspective relatedness. Against the rationalistic actor I counterposed a more complete model of people in the plural, which incorporates the changing regulation of affect and individual self-controls. And against 'hodie-centric' (today-centred) (Goudsblom, 1977:7ff., 78, 168) sociopolitical diagnosis, I opposed the study of the long-range sequential order of development to help discern the general shape of the future that leads from the present national and global condition.

I have expressed these oppositions starkly and pithily for effect and can only make a couple of the qualifications needed to avoid being misunderstood. I am not intending to create another set of

103

dualisms. Nor am I counterposing a rival world-view, because *initially*, I eschew normative considerations. My aim is simply to open up a different range of questions. The task, ultimately, is to achieve a more complete sociological picture of society than is possible via structuration theory, illuminating though it is for some purposes. For example, it would be foolish and misleading simply to counterpose another *a priori* of continuism against discontinuism. Only a conservative would see *only* continuities. Rather, it is the assessment of the balance of these and other dimensions in tandem with an accent on long-term social development that is the key. Similarly, it is clear that actors are indeed knowledgeable and to some extent rational in all societies, perhaps increasingly so in our own society. But this exclusive focus is an arbitrary emphasis coloured by the dominant rationality of our society that puts in brackets the massively important emotional bonding in social life. It also tends to assume that people have been the same throughout history, leaving out of account the study of the ways in which people *themselves* change during social transformations, even during the course of the short 'modern' phrase.

Giddens' appropriation of Hans-Georg Gadamer's version of hermeneutics (Gadamer, 1960) illustrates very well the nature of the particular set of emphases and assumptions of the structurationist programme. For Gadamer, understanding is not a special method of *Verstehen* but an ontological condition of humankind. In the interpretation of texts written in different periods, it is impossible to eliminate the prejudices or preunderstandings that we bring to them, because we cannot escape the tradition from which we enter into the subject matter of the text. Both the interpreter and the tradition being investigated through the text contain their own 'horizon' in Gadamer's terms, so the task of hermeneutic inquiry is a circular one of integrating one's own horizon with that of the tradition concerned in a 'fusion of horizons'. This is an unending process whereby we test out our preunderstandings, so changing our understanding of the past and ourselves in a continuous process. Thus the present is always formed through a constant contact and interchange with the past, which Gadamer calls our effective-history (*Wirkungsgeschichte*). Gadamer is not offering a methodology for the human sciences, but rather his work is a philosophical attempt 'to understand what the human sciences truly are, beyond their methodological self-consciousness, and what connects them with the totality of our experience of the world' (ibid:xiii).

As Outhwaite has pointed out, Gadamer's Heideggerian radicalization of the hermeneutic tradition has had a growing influence on the social sciences: 'It has become increasingly clear th scientists can no longer pass over the hermeneutic founda their practice, nor consign them to the domain of an o *verstehende* sociology' (Outhwaite, 1985:37). Like Habe Giddens takes hermeneutics seriously. Consistent with his ind ualistic sympathies, he criticizes Gadamer for overreacting against earlier empathetic versions of textual hermeneutics by eliminating the author's intentions entirely. (This is a similar criticism to the one Giddens directs at structuralism.) But most importantly, he incorporates Gadamer's ontological view of understanding as the fusion of horizons directly into his prescriptions for explanation in sociology in his conception of the 'double hermeneutic'. This duplex process is one whereby the sociologists mediate ordinary language meanings of actors, obtained from sociologists' immersion in forms of life, with the technical metalanguage of sociology (Giddens, 1976a:161–2).

So Giddens takes existential hermeneutics on board, but contrary to the whole intention of Gadamer he reframes its essence as a method, i.e. as an explanatory prescription for sociology. This move is consistent with his customary strategy of taking from philosophies and sociological schools only what he needs for reconstructing the sociological tradition, which takes priority. At the same time he is anxious to appropriate this kind of hermeneutics without leading sociology into epistemological relativism, a known danger in this field. Such a result would, of course, undermine his commitment to the efficacy of reliable sociological knowledge in the modern world. In the hermeneutic debates he therefore sides with Emilio Betti's insistence on keeping hold of the integrity and autonomy of the object, i.e. the text as a 'situated creation of its author' (Giddens, 1976a:63). And he seizes on the distinction made by philosophers between sense and reference in order to reconcile the respect for the authenticity of mediated frames of meaning with the question of the *validity* of knowledge. He sees hermeneutic understanding as a 'condition of' (ibid:145) validity, rather than something that excludes it. Although, as is Giddens's wont, for principled reasons (Giddens, 1984a:xx), he does not pursue this vexed epistemological question any further; for him these kinds of debates get in the way of sociological research. It is predictable, therefore, that he would have backed Betti, although to do so runs counter to the drift of recent more sceptical commentary. For example, Bleicher regards Betti's concern with salvaging some limited objectivity from hermeneutics as representing 'a residual of the scientistic approach to the non-natural sphere' (Bleicher, 1980:125).

Furthermore, Habermas has objected that Gadamer's hermeneutics cannot deal with emancipation from structures of domination and authority embedded in language and traditions. Bleicher, again, locates the true fulfilment of hermeneutics as lying in its emancipatory function. There is a 'critical-anticipatory moment in understanding' that cannot be envisaged by Gadamer: 'Ultimately, the possibility of critical hermeneutics depends on the framework that Habermas is attempting to construct out of a materialist theory of society and of social evolution in conjunction with a theory of ordinary language' (ibid:258). On the other hand, Giddens sees Habermas's contention that language is a medium of domination as conceding too much to hermeneutics because it transmutes power into ideologically deformed communication. At the same time Habermas concedes too little because for Giddens the mediation of frames of meaning must form a basis for ideology-critique as a human activity (Giddens, 1977c:153).

In a word, Giddens abandons the difficult epistemological issue of validity arising out of hermeneutics because he has a prior commitment to eschewing elaborate epistemological discussions. Thus, he is able to appropriate hermeneutics in a methodological manner and still sleep at night. And he is insensitive to the Habermas-Bleicher problem of reconciling Gadamer's persuasive hermeneutics with 'critique' because, as we saw earlier, he already regards sociology as an inherently 'critical' enterprise, borrowing the term's established resonances for his own purposes.

Finally, let us turn more explicitly to what I am calling Giddens' 'systematic' method and contrast it with a sociogenetic approach, in order to build up a picture of the comparative gains and losses of each for the task of sociological synthesis. The term systematic in the sense I am using it here is of Kantian origins and is one side of the distinction between systematic and historical inquiries, delineating a division of labour between philosophy and social scientific disciplines. Systematic refers to a range of reflections of a conceptual or transcendental kind arising from the factual sociohistorical data assembled by the social sciences.

The related sociological use – and this is the sense implicitly embodied in Giddens' method – was codified by R.K. Merton in his essay 'On the history and systematics of sociological theory' (Merton, 1968b). By systematics he referred to the substance of theories, i.e. the generalizable conceptual yield derivable independently from their history or origins. His analysis went along with a plea for not merging or blurring the distinction which sociologists, far more than physicists or chemists, tend to do. (As will be clear later on, I accept this general advice but, because of various drawbacks to the analytic systematics of Giddens' approach, I advocate a 'historical systematics'.)

Giddens only involves himself in developmental thinking marginally in his discussions of institutions and various empirical areas in his work the *Nation-State and Violence* (1985a). He is generally uninterested in the study of long-term processes at the level of his metatheory in *The Constitution of Society* (1984a). Both works embody the equation: development equals evolution. And his summary dismissal of the sociology of knowledge blocks off access to the usefulness of this tradition not only for establishing the hidden interests of opponents' utterances, but also for aiding adequate concept formation itself in a developmental and historical way. There is more to the sociology of knowledge than debunking. Furthermore, his use of hermeneutics recommends the mediation of meaning frames or forms of life with the metalanguages of social science. But it is a method that seems to be geared only to the mediations between the west and other cultures, between forms of life in the society of the here-and-now or between the present and past forms of life in the shorter run *within* the 'modern' world. Giddens' hermeneutic programme excludes the project of securing a deeper and more long-range historical understanding of human-kind by recovering the forgotten distant developments that have shaped our world and ourselves.

Methodologically, moving in this direction means embracing (without teleology and with other modifications) the principle encapsulated in Marx's dictum that the 'anatomy of man contains the key to the anatomy of the ape', i.e. that the structure of a later stage of development enables us potentially better to grasp earlier ones, traces of which are found embedded in the later stage. This thrust is also embodied in various forms in Hegel, writers in the German tradition of historicism, various western Marxists, including Gramsci, Collingwood and Sartre in his *Question of Method* (Kilminster, 1979, pt. III and Ch. 15; Collingwood, 1946). Lacking a historical consciousness in this sense, Giddens is ill-versed in these traditions.[10] He significantly takes out of Marx only the appeal to the 'discontinuous' aspects of capitalism, disregarding entirely his equally central historical-genetic orientation, the so-called dialectical method. Not surprisingly, therefore, Giddens tends to assume that concepts in general are simply abstract in relation to the concrete, or empirical. He has no conception of concepts as synthetic, i.e. as having embedded within them traces of earlier stages of social and scientific development.

Giddens' systematic strategy treats the different schools of philosophy and sociology discussed as equipollent and hence as abstractly comparable. Each is assumed to provide a substantive yield irrespective of its nature and origins. The project has been made possible by the institutionalization of sociology in recent times in which, in Edward Shils' words, institutions 'foster the production of works' and 'create a resonant and echoing intellectual environment' (Shils, 1970:272). In this resonating intellectual world Giddens (skilfully and intelligently to be sure) discovers convergences between the schools and he finds ready-to-hand and side by side in curricula, journals and publications, but takes for granted their specificity and how they came to achieve their salience. The danger of overabstraction is compounded by the lack of acknowledgement of the potentially differing status and cognitive value of each school's contribution. As Shils warns: 'Institutionalization is not a guarantee of truthfulness: it only renders more probable the consolidation, elaboration and diffusion of a set of ideas' (ibid:277). Of course, it is possible to produce syntheses at a certain level of abstraction, as Parsons and Giddens have shown, and these may be of a certain heuristic value. But each takes too much for granted. However, following Elias and the sociology of knowledge tradition, I would advocate injecting into the process of theory formation a historical, sociogenetic way of controlling for the validity or cognitive value of synthesized components to supplement the logical criteria employed by Giddens. Perhaps this method could be called 'historical systematics'. Set out on the theory stall of contemporary sociology is a variety of theoretical products, their origins largely forgotten, some of which are philosophical and some sociological or various hybrids of the two. Structuration theory synthesizes a selection of the theoretical results of a complex social and institutional development that has thrown up the paradigms and placed them side by side. The point is that lacking a developmental theory both of society and of scientific development (which must in principle go hand in hand), Giddens has no way of sorting them out from the point of view of whether any one theory or concept among them is an advance over a previous stage of more-or-less adequate elaboration. Only with such a benchmark can we reliably judge which of the contemporary theories and concepts that we find available and disseminated:

1. are reworkings of theoretical ground already gained in the past;
2. are rehashes of what were dead ends even at a previous stage;

3. are based on philosophical abstractions; or
4. are genuine innovations in sociological theory.

Theories and concepts within all four of these categories may be institutionally consolidated, mixed up together and available for scrutiny, so they need to be differentiated. Giddens, on the other hand, working systematically, fuses many concepts and insights at a certain level of abstraction, but does not make his selection criteria explicit. The problem is, though, what is the cognitive value of the synthesis if it contains concepts or assumptions themselves of dubious cognitive value or sociological relevance? A sociogenetic approach, on the other hand, could in principle provide criteria for rejecting or ignoring theories under (2) or (3) as unserviceable. Hence a sociogenetic synthesis would take a different form and hopefully be of a more robust kind to inform empirical, sociological inquiries because it would contain only components that have been sociologically established. It would thus comprise a different kind of abstraction.

I appreciate that this approach, which I can only adumbrate programmatically and schematically here, in advocating a theory of scientific development as part of a theory of social development, runs counter to the tenor of a good deal of the contemporary philosophy of science which talks of 'progress' only through changing research programmes, if at all. And I appreciate the magnitude of the task. My aim is to juxtapose a sociogenetic approach so as to open up the issues. From this point of view, I can see three further disadvantages of the systematic synthesis, particularly in the hands of Giddens, each of which brings out the contrasting standpoint. Again, these ideas are set out provisionally with the idea of starting a dialogue.

1. To repeat an important point: because concepts are discovered ready to hand within the highly institutionalized settings of sociology, then the assumption tends to be that, just because they are there in an articulated form as part of a school, they must be credible and valid. As Shils said, however, this cannot be assumed and *nor can their usefulness for sociological purposes.* For example, there are many concepts used in the theory of structuration that are originally of philosophical provenance – such as praxis, contradiction, presencing, historicity – that need scrutiny on this count. I will look briefly in more detail at one, Giddens' appropriation of the concept of structure from structuralism, in order to make the point.

The concept of structure is used in structuration theory in several senses and word combinations, but one – that of the timeless, paradigmatic, virtual structure – is particularly problematic. In the works of Lévi-Strauss, typically within the structuralist tradition (Lévi-Strauss, 1962; 1964, Overture), the concept of structure in this sense has a particular epistemological function. For him, and others, the structure is not an aggregate, nor a composite, nor an essence or *Zeitgeist* behind the appearances of the aggregate, but the cognitive laws of relation between the units concerned. The structure is present in the observable units in the relations between them in the network, and is generative of them, including absences as well as presences (Piaget, 1971, Chs I and VI). Lévi-Strauss has arrived at this complex conception within a philosophical discourse. The concept is informed by an attempt to resolve an epistemological (indeed metaphysical) issue in the philosophy of perception without falling into empiricism, idealism, essentialism or subjectivism. His implicit targets are positivism and phenomenology.

Now, Giddens incorporates this concept, in this sense, into his synthesis assuming that the logical-philosophical idea of the existence of non-essential paradigmatic structures is a way of conceptualizing data automatically applicable to the study of patterns of social life. But why should this be so, when the structuralists' concept of structure was tailored to the solution of a problem posed by the thought/reality dualism of traditional epistemology? This concept of structure is then *made* relevant by Giddens to patterns of social life as rules and resources instantiated in social practices and found in memory traces. But surely its use by Giddens in his theory is a contrivance, the uncritical importation into sociological theory of a philosophical way of looking at human perception and the problem of knowledge. It seems to have been brought in simply because it is there, available as part of an academically respectable paradigm within institutionalized sociology, crying out for integration into structuration theory. But its adequacy and appropriateness to the object of sociology seem to me to be questionable. Only theory formation alert to the status and origins of concepts, I am arguing, can prevent us from going down cul-de-sacs of this kind.

2. The basic argumentation technique of Giddens is to say that dualisms, say individual/society or subjectivism/objectivism, can be 'resolved' through reasoning. This procedure consists in saying that we know, rationally, that the two sides are not mutually exclusive and have been wrongly regarded as alternatives. Hence, they can be replaced by the dualities of agency/

structure and constraint/enablement. Their resolution through reasoning in this way is an attempt to resolve the dualisms in a philosophical manner, often undertaken by Giddens with, to be sure, great ingenuity and craft. Having done this philosophical work, the way is apparently then cleared for empirical investigation unencumbered by the dualisms, which have been neutralized. Another way, however, would be to undertake sociogenetic investigation to show first how the dualisms came into being and acquired their cognitive force; and second to test how far they actually do articulate two sides of real social relations in real cases. Some theoretical and conceptual work will be necessary in conjunction with this empirical research, but this is not the same thing as attempting resolution or neutralization of the dualisms by reasoning prior to empirical research. Put another way, this method establishes the validity and range of applicability of the dualisms empirically and genetically. It is a scientific as opposed to philosophical procedure.

3. The 'systematic' method embodied in structuration theory fails to grasp that the paradigms, tendencies and schools upon which it draws were also, following Karl Mannheim (1928), interpretations of the world. They were also, and to some extent still are, the banners behind which groups have marched in a competition to impose their definition of reality in the teeth of the dominant one – the one Giddens calls the orthodox consensus.

Giddens does have some conception of the extra-theoretical group life lying behind paradigms when he remarks that: 'Any generalized theoretical scheme in the natural or social sciences is in a certain sense a form of life in itself, the concepts of which have to be mastered as a mode of practical activity generating specific types of descriptions' (Giddens, 1976a:162). But this is an anodyne and bloodless view of group life. For Giddens, the hermeneutic mediation of divergent forms of life and the immersion of sociologists in alien cultures are essentially smooth and harmonious negotiations. Nor is there any conception that the metalanguages of social science – such as structuralism, ethnomethodology, Althusserianism or Theorizing – have been *fought* for, involving passion, commitment, clashes and conflict. This because they were also interpretations of the society, carried by conflicting groups whose social existence and identity were bound up with them. How else can one account for the passion of the challenges to epistemological authority in recent years, the zeal of the manifestos for new perspectives in sociology, the conflict and the strife of the *Sturm und Drang* period

111

of the war of the schools? All the emotion of these conflicts is lost in the analytic-systematic method of Giddens, in whose hands each paradigm becomes, in Hegel's famous words, 'a corpse which has left behind its living impulse' (Hegel, 1807:69) (translation slightly amended).

Conclusion

A theory of cognitive change based in the competition between groups for the public interpretation of reality can, with some modifications and extension, provide a starting point for a socio-genetic account that could yield a more realistic and appropriate synthesis. It also enables us to explain the conditions of possibility of the synthesis itself – something it is impossible to envisage structuration theory doing.

As a preliminary approximation, based on Mannheim's first formulation of the problem (Mannheim, 1928), we can see in the recent development of western sociology a *monopoly stage*, when the academic establishment had secured its advantage through its monopoly of interpretation as the structural–functionalist ortho-doxy, which was orthodox because it was dominant. From their position of relative disadvantage, opposing groups challenged this dominant orientation because it did not seem consonant with their life experience and aspirations as a generation, within and part of wider political polarizations. There then ensued a period of intense conflict as groups challenged the epistemological authority of the orthodoxy. During this *competitive stage*, schools competed fiercely to be heard and the orthodoxy fought back, sometimes conceding ground, which is an early sign of impending synthesis. In this phase doubts were expressed about universal truths, and hierarchies of value and relativism were the order of the day.

During the next *concentration stage*, groups were forced by the nature of their intertwined conflicts, as the power gradient between the competing groups flattened out and alliances and mergers occurred, to take over concepts from others and to concede their own. Debates then began to polarize around certain key antino-mies, which in the 1980s seem to be:

constructivism/realism
agency/structure
meaning/cause
subjectivism/objectivism

In the British case a basic polarization has jelled around the left and right sides of these antinomies. The left-hand side represents the residues of the emphasis of the radicals, activists and outsiders to the academic establishment who, through these concepts, expressed their conviction that there were in every field no limits to change because all culture was constructed by active meaning-endowing actors and hence could be changed by them. On the other side, this tendency represents the more cautious, realistic pole, emphasizing the limits to change within the realm of constraint. But traces of group allegiances have faded as group power differentials have lessened and concepts have become the common property of all and are increasingly seen as reconcilable. Concepts that were previously the subject of strife – for example, indexicality, reflexivity, meaning, lay actors and hermeneutics (from the phenomenologically inspired schools), or mode of production, class struggle, critique, praxis, labour power and alienation (from Marxism) – have become common currency, more-or-less accepted and unproblematic.

The conditions for successful synthesis are now ripe; a synthesis is what *all* parties want by the nature of their social existence. What is usually called the 'post-modern' sensibility in sociology at the present time is, I would venture to speculate, simply a product of the transition between the stage of concentration and the jelling of a new synthesis, ready to become a qualitatively new orthodoxy on another level. And then the cycle recommences as new groups come to challenge, and this process constitutes the way in which progress occurs in the social sciences. My approach adds a group-conflict dimension to Weber's insight that: 'The greatest advances in the sphere of the social sciences are substantively tied up with the shift in practical cultural problems and take the guise of a critique of concept-construction' (Weber, 1904:106).

It will be objected that this sociological approach to the construction and evaluation of theory formation devalues the role of the reasoning mind in the process of synthesis creation, it being apparently relegated to a reflex of interests and power. But my point, following Weber and Mannheim, is that it is through real processes of the kind outlined, which are only partially understood, that progress in the social sciences occurs. Moreover, only a sociogenetic method can do justice to this process and provide the basis for adequate concept formation in sociology. The issue of validity is not, I think, as serious a difficulty as philosophers have made it, and, in any case, can be reframed sociologically on another level. Clearly, I cannot substantiate this claim in a programmatic essay of this kind. The point is that the sociological approach to concept formation and synthesis advocated here can be accomplished in a detached, organized, scientific and 'rational' fashion,

Richard Kilminster

and is by no means a method that inevitably runs into the arms of 'irrationality'. There is something dubious about this antinomy. The alternative, analytic-systematic way of approaching synthesis, pursued exclusively, runs the risk of endowing the thinking mind with an autonomous power of rationality bordering on the mystical. To conclude with the words of Mannheim:

> Anyone who wants to drag in the irrational where the lucidity and acuity of reason still must rule by right merely shows that he is afraid to face the mystery at its legitimate place.
>
> (Mannheim, 1928:229)

Acknowledgements

I am very grateful to Zygmunt Bauman, Ian Burkitt and Terry Wassall for many stimulating discussions about the themes of this article and to Eric Dunning and Ian Varcoe for their incisive comments on an earlier draft. I have learned much from all of them.

Notes

1 Sanderson (1987) refers to many other prominent professed eclectics in sociology, including Ralf Dahrendorf, Arthur Stinchcombe, Jack Goody and Jonathan Turner. In Marxism, the word eclectic is used as a term of abuse. See, for example, the evaluation of Habermas in Therborn (1971). The term eclecticism referring to arbitrary borrowing became a pejorative term in the late eighteenth/early nineteenth centuries in philosophy and in painting. Romantics contrasted the stylistic borrowings of eclectics and plagiarists with the exalted power of imagination associated with genius. See Wittkower (1965).

2 Giddens acknowledges the stature of Comte's early work *Cours de philosophie positive*, but suggests that Comte's later *Religion of Humanity* constituted something of a decline from the 'cool rationalism' of the early work because of its 'passionate advocacy'. But as a whole, he claims, Comte's work is of little relevance to sociology today. It is noticeable, however, how much of the racy detail of Comte's controversial life (his relationship with a prostitute, his violent rages, his bouts of madness, his wife-beating) Giddens irrelevantly parades in his discussion of his work. Presumably this is done to discredit Comte's ideas by association (Giddens, 1975b). For a contrasting assessment see Elias, 1970, Ch. 1.

3 See also Giddens, 1982h:72, where he expands further on his view of the 'critical' nature of sociology.

4 I am not of course suggesting that the kind of sociological commitment that might enable someone to get into perspective the many

competing paradigms that arrived on the sociological scene in the 1960s and 1970s could *only* have come from the Leicester Department.

5 Giddens writes: 'Here I should declare *parti pris,* and say that my political sympathies lie of the Left' (Giddens, 1982g:227). See also Giddens, 1982h, *passim.*

6 The vision of capitalism as relentlessly pervading more and more areas of social life, as creating monopolies and spreading across the globe to form a world market, is most forcefully expressed by Marx in the *Communist Manifesto* of 1848, the content of which in this respect was heavily indebted to the French political economist, Constantin Pecquer. See Owen, 1951.

7 This tendency in Giddens' work is apparent particularly in the stated rationale behind the collection *Profiles and Critiques* (Giddens, 1982c, Preface and Ch. 15) and in his 1985a, Chs 1 and 11.

8 The classical statement by Max Weber is:

> 'Economically conditioned' power is not, of course, identical with 'power' as such. On the contrary, the emergence of economic power may be the consequence of power existing on other grounds. Man does not strive for power only in order to enrich himself economically.
>
> (Weber, 1922:926)

9 I am not of course suggesting that Giddens is denying that people have emotions, but rather that the study of their social regulation is excluded from structuration theory by its very nature. In a word, the theory is rationalistic. This is an issue about which Giddens is clearly aware, but he does not follow it through. In discussing the writings of Herbert Marcuse, he rightly points out the differing appropriations of Freud by Marcuse and Habermas:

> ... the conception of the ideal speech situation [in Habermas], interesting as it may be in its own right, remains on a peculiarly cognitive level. What of affect, of sexuality, love, hate and death? Whereas Marcuse's formulation of critical theory is founded upon an abiding concern with these phenomena, Habermas's account provides little way of coping with them conceptually.
>
> (Giddens, 1982j:158)

Et tu, Giddens!

10 In this genre there is a brief discussion of Michael Oakeshott in Giddens, 1984a:355–6.

Chapter five

'Society as time-traveller': Giddens on historical change, historical materialism and the nation-state in world society

David Jary

Introduction

In more senses than one, the scope of Giddens' aspirations for his structuration theory is utterly global. In *Central Problems in Social Theory* (1979a) and *The Constitution of Society* (1984a) the goal was no less than to provide a total framework for the union of interpretative and structuralist sociologies. In the two volumes that are the main focus of this chapter, *A Contemporary Critique of Historical Materialism* (1981a) and *The Nation-State and Violence* (1985a) (and in a promised further volume on socialist societies), his objective is to realize the possibilities of a comprehensive reassessment of historical change first sketched in *Central Problems*.[1] His aim is to provide a theoretical and empirically based analysis of past, present and possible future societies that can replace both historical materialism and social evolutionary theories, each of these being seen as possessing serious weaknesses, not least their dependence on functionalism. Others, like Parsons and Habermas, have attempted a synthesis of theoretical perspectives as sweeping as Giddens'. There have been historical sociologists recently – notably Perry Anderson (1974a, b) and Michael Mann (1986) – who have supplied accounts of the development of the state and society that in their range and depth of historical analysis obviously outstrip Giddens. But no one has quite matched Giddens' integration of historical analysis and attention to theoretical foundations. Giddens is at one with Abrams (1982) who has suggested that sociology and history are methodologically speaking ultimately one subject, and that a proper attention to theory is essential. Undoubtedly, considerable advantages flow from Giddens' attention to theoretical bases. The value to macro- and historical sociology of his subtle discussion of the interrelation of action and structure – the conception of a 'duality of structure' at the heart of his structurationist sociology – has been widely acknowledged,

116

even by those unable to accept all its aspects (e.g. Urry, 1982; Thrift, 1983; Callinicos, 1987). The craftsmanship and clarity of his perceptive and highly systematic reworking of many of historical and political sociology's main typological concepts – a synthesis of Marxian and non-Marxian approaches – has also been much admired (e.g. Wright, 1983). In addition, the relative novelty of his analysis of historical change in terms of the general concept of 'time-space distanciation' – the 'stretching of social relations across time and space' – brings interesting new insights. Finally, if Giddens is to be believed, this approach can also lead us not only to a better understanding, but also to some prospect of influence on a world that, as he puts it, at present 'totters on the edge of nuclear disaster' – a world in which the analysis of the role of nation-states within a worldwide nation-state system must be made central, alongside the more conventional analysis in sociology of unitary societies and economic forces.

Aims of this chapter

The aim of this chapter is twofold:

1. to outline the main elements of Giddens' structurationist account of historical change, no easy task when he himself covers much ground,
2. to confront a number of issues that can be raised about this approach, seeking to assess its strengths but also its possible limitations.

While I hope to show that room exists for suggesting that Giddens is sometimes overzealous in this repudiation of 'rival' approaches, and overassertive in advancing aspects of his own model of historical change, this will not be seen as detracting from the many virtues of his analysis in charting the terrain of macro-sociological analysis. Since he himself sometimes insists that structuration theory is an 'approach' rather than a tightly formulated theory, I would see my criticism as operating within the spirit of Giddens' own work, as an attempt to get the best from all existing approaches. My argument will be that efforts such as his should be seen as part of a broader 'reform' movement already well established in comparative historical sociology (cf. Tilly, 1981; Abrams, 1982; Anderson, 1974ab; Mann, 1986; Collins, 1986; Eisenstadt, 1987), and that it is far from clear that Giddens' version of theoretical bases or his substantive account of historical change should simply be accepted.[2]

David Jary

Focus and main themes of Giddens' historical argument

As Giddens expresses it in *The Constitution of Society*:

> the fundamental question of social theory – the 'problem of order' conceived in a way quite alien to Parsons' formulation when he coined the phrase – is to explicate how the limitations of individual 'presence' are transcended by the 'stretching' of social relations across space and time.

(Giddens, 1984a: 35)

If such a 'stretching across time and space' is a feature of all societies – i.e. is intrinsic to all social institutions – it reaches its greatest extent in contemporary societies, which truly can be said to exist as part of a 'world-system'. In pre-historical 'band societies' regularized transactions with (live) others who are physically absent occurred only rarely. But in modern societies not only have interconnections grown, transportation dramatically improved and distances been bridged, but communications across space have become instantaneous. Moreover an increased capacity to organize time and space might seem of the essence of the greatly increased economic and political power exhibited by modern societies. How has such a time-space distanciation of social relations come about? What organizations, what logics, has this process involved? These are Giddens' questions. If Giddens' questions are relatively simple, his answers are more complex and involve an amalgam of empirical, theoretical and epistemological and ontological arguments concerning the implications of human agency, time and space and political and economic power that it is not always easy to unravel. However, four key elements in his overall argument can perhaps be initially identified.

1. If historical change is marked above all by time-space distanciation, then the accumulation of political power, especially the administrative and military power of modern states, is at least as significant as economic forces, and may even be more decisive.
2. Accounts of historical change must recognize its multicausal basis, eshewing all attempts at monocausal explanations. In line with his D-D-L-S model of institutions (see Figure 5.3, p. 124), Giddens identifies four interrelated institutional bases of social order and social change.
3. It is essential that societies should be seen as connected by 'intersocietal systems' and influenced by their location in 'world-time', i.e. by the variety of social forms that cross-cut societal boundaries, and by particular geopolitical contexts and

118

particular historical conjunctures.

4. Partly because of the complexities arising from (1), (2) and (3), but more generally because of human knowledgeability and the 'reflexive nature of human social life', 'episodic characterizations' of historical change, in which change is recognized as 'discontinuous' and 'historically contingent', are the only ones appropriate. This is to say, that social change always consists of *non*-evolutionary 'historically located sequences of change', each having 'a specifiable opening, trend of events and outcome' but *not* a part of any necessary sequence of social development (Giddens, 1984a: 374). Giddens' reasoning here would seem to be that any simple law-like explanation of historical change is ruled out, first, by the existence of 'time-space edges' – i.e. connections between, rather than any simple linear sequence of societies of different structural types – and secondly by the 'reflexive monitoring' carried out in this context, particularly by state elites. More generally, as Giddens puts it: 'there is no mechanism of social organization or social reproduction identified by social analysts which lay actors cannot also get to know about and actively incorporate into what they do' (Giddens, 1984a: 284).

If the first and second of these four points are directed especially against historical materialism, the third and fourth count equally against both historical materialism and evolutionary theory (and also functionalism). It is in this context that Giddens speaks of his thinking as 'deconstructing' rather than reconstructing historical materialism and evolutionary theory (Giddens, 1984a: 243). 'We live in a world', he suggests, 'for which traditional sources of theory have left us unprepared' (Giddens, 1987a: 166). The alternative he proposes is a multidimensional, non-evolutionary and non-functionalist analysis of historical change that he believes can be grounded in structuration theory.

In what follows we first note aspects of the general location of Giddens' historical thinking within structuration theory, then trace in more detail the main lines of his historical account before concluding with a critical discussion.

The location of Giddens' account within structuration theory

Complaints are made that Giddens' books present increasing problems of internal self-reference (Friedland, 1987). The extent of recapitulation and sheer repetition can also be a source of irritation, although doubtless this is intended to help the reader who dips into only parts of the ever-expanding corpus. What this leaves in no doubt, however, is how strikingly cumulative has been the development of Giddens' structuration theory. The theories and empirical accounts of others are endlessly mined, concepts are added, but relatively little is given up. Though always stressing the uncompleted nature of the enterprise, Giddens is evidently well pleased with the cogency of the framework of concepts accumulated over more than a decade. Concepts, when added, only supplement or enlarge the framework, rarely if ever changing it in fundamental ways.

'Time-space' in the constitution of society and in historical change

The analysis of time and space, and historical change, is integral to structuration theory. Actions and structures must both be seen as continuously in process. As Giddens remarks, quoting Rilke, 'Our life passes in transformation' (1979a:3).

The emphasis on 'process' and 'transformation' in structuration theory may ease the transition between accounts of 'order' and accounts of 'change', (see Figure 5.1) but it would be a mistake to assume that 'process' and 'transformation' are simply *equivalent* to 'historical change' as conceived in Giddens' historical sociology.

	Structuralist or voluntarist theories	Giddens' structurationist alternative
Characterization of structure	structure *or* agency	'duality of structure' the interrelation of action and structure
Characterization of actor	agents as supports of structure ('cultural dopes') *or* as purely voluntaristic	knowledgeability of actors/ conscious intentionality – but in context of structure as medium and outcome of agency and interaction
Characterization of historicality	ahistorical structures: synchrony *versus* diachrony, statics *versus* dynamics	time (and space) and 'historicality' as integral to action and structure, with 'historicity' as an emergent feature leading to 'time-space distanciation' as intended but also unintended consequence

Figure 5.1 Structure, agency and historicality in Giddens' sociology

Plainly this is not so. 'Prehistorical' band societies, for example, though continuously 'in process' and obviously existing in time, do not because of this *automatically* undergo 'historical change'. Certainly, the 'two most essential characteristics of human social life', are: (a) what Giddens terms, the 'transformative capacity' – the 'could have done otherwise' – inherent in all human action, and (b) 'the variety of ways in which, in social systems, interaction is made possible across space and time'. However, Giddens makes a point of contrasting what he terms the 'historicality' – i.e. the potentiality for historical change – of all societies, and the actual historical change and conceptions of 'historicity' that occur only in some. What Giddens means by historicity in this context is the existence within a society of conceptions that involve 'the identification of history as progressive change', and coupled with this 'the cognitive utilization of such identification in order to further change' (Giddens, 1984a:374). In societies – such as many tribal societies – entirely pervaded by conceptions of 'reversible' rather than 'irreversible' time (see also Chapters One and Six, this volume) conceptions of historicity do not exist and do not readily develop. Only in some societies, principally for Giddens those societies that also become states, do such conceptions begin to appear and become associated with the stretching of societies across time and space.

This is *one* very general sense in which the development of human societies can be seen as 'episodic'. The existence of such a two-phase notion in Giddens' historical thinking has a similar force to Michael Mann's assertion that while general evolutionary theory may be applied to the Neolithic Revolution, 'general social evolution ceased (with) the emergence of civilization' (Mann, 1986:39), when distinctively 'historical' change takes over.

Giddens and time-geography

It is the time-geographer Stig Hägerstrand who suggests that the life of the individual might be represented as 'movement through time-space' (Giddens, 1981a:38). His work is also of value in 'identifying sources of constraint over human activity given by the nature of the body and the physical contexts in which activity occurs' (Giddens, 1984a:111). Another time-geographer, Donald Janelle, is credited with introducing the notion of 'time-space convergence', 'the shrinking of distance in terms of the time needed to travel between different locations' (Giddens, 1981a:38; 1984a:114).

Giddens is critical of the time-geographers, however, in four

121

key respects: (1) a tendency to view the constitution of the individual independently of social settings, a dualism of action and structure; (2) lack of reference to the 'essentially transformative character of human action'; (3) 'concentration solely on the constraining properties of the body'; (4) the lack of a well-developed theory of power (Giddens, 1984a:117).

One difference of significance between Giddens and the time-geographers is his replacement of the concept of 'place' with the concept of 'locale' – a concept of special importance subsequently because it leads on to the crucial notion of historically decisive 'power containers' (including cities and states) as special kinds of locale. Giddens prefers the term locale because it can be given more than a positional reference (Giddens, 1981a: 39). Locales 'refer to the use of space to provide the 'settings' of interaction, these settings in turn being seen as essential to specifying the 'contextuality' of action – in time and space – in a fully sociological way.

It is from Goffman that the concept of 'social setting' is drawn, and it is Goffman who also provides a further vital element in Giddens' thinking, specification of the 'profound difference' that exists 'between *face-to-face interaction and interaction with others who are physically absent*' (Giddens, 1979a:203, emphasis in original). This distinction possesses a multiple significance within Giddens' historical macro-sociology (as it does within structuration theory in general – see Figure 5.2), first, in underlining that 'the study of day-to-day life is integral to analysis of the reproduction of institutionalized practices' (Giddens, 1984a:282) and, second, in indicating how far-flung connections in social life should be understood as involving an interpenetration of 'social integration' and 'system integration'. More generally, it is found valuable in bringing an explicit focus on 'the extension of social systems in space and time' as 'an evident feature of the overall development of human society' (Giddens, 1979a:20). In general, Goffman's work is taken as showing how different kinds of social setting arrange time and space (including the body) differently. Finally, it is within this general conceptual framework centred on time and space that further key concepts such as 'time-space edges' or 'world-time' can be readily incorporated. The latter of these concepts derives from the historian Eberhard (1965).

'Power' and 'surveillance' in structuration theory

For Giddens:

'Power', along with 'agency' and 'structure', is an elementary

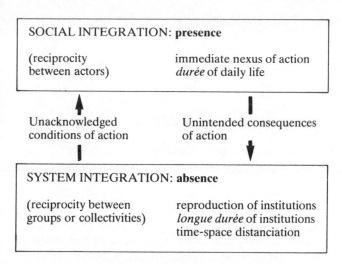

Figure 5.2 Social integration and system integration
Source: Adapted from Giddens, 1984a; Spybey, 1987

concept in social science. To be human is to be an agent –
although not all agents are human – and to be an agent is to
have power. 'Power' in this highly generalized sense means
'transformative capacity', the capability to intervene in a given
set of events so as in some way to change them. The logical
connection between agency and power is of the first importance
for social theory, but the 'universal' sense of power thus implied
needs considerable refinement if it is to be put to work in the
interests of substantive social research.

(Giddens, 1985a:7)

If power, is involved in all areas of action and institutions identified by Giddens (cf. Figure 1.3, p. 10), two conceptual refinements
can be seen as playing a pivotal role within his treatment of historical change: (1) the distinction between power based on 'allocative
resources' (domination over the material world, including material
facilities) and that based on 'authoritative resources' (domination
over human beings) (see Figure 5.3) and (2) his concept of 'surveillance', a term he borrows from Foucault (1975) but considerably reformulates. For Giddens, 'surveillance' refers to two aspects
of modern state power and the power of organizations that vastly
extend their effectiveness: (1) the collection and collation of information, greatly expanded in modern times by all manner of infor-

123

Signification (S)	Domination (D)		Legitimation (L)
Symbolic orders/ modes of discourse	D (auth) Political institutions	D (alloc) Economic institutions	Law/modes of sanction
[S-D-L]	[D(auth)-S-L]	[D(alloc)-S-L]	[L-D-S]

Figure 5.3 Giddens' D-D-L-S model of institutions

Source: Versions of this model appear in Giddens, 1981a and 1984a and elsewhere

mation technologies; and (2) the direct 'watching over' of human activities, made increasingly possible by the existence of many specialist 'bounded locales'. The latter include, as well as the state directly, the 'new ways of enforced regularizing of activities in time and space', including prisons and workplaces, referred to by Foucault as 'sequestration'.

Contrary to Foucault, Giddens stresses that the outcome of domination and surveillance is 'enabling' as well as 'constraining', and not only 'negative'. In addition, since it is always mediated by a 'dialectic of control', power is never 'absolute'. Giddens does not neglect the unacknowledged conditions or the unintended consequences of the exercise of power – as seen in Chapter One, this volume, he accepts that some of the most important tasks of social science are the investigation of the significance of these in system reproduction. Notwithstanding this, the main thrust of his general argument is that sociology has frequently overemphasized the decisiveness in history of allocative power, while underestimating the enormous significance, for good and ill, of authoritative power.

Giddens' historical account

It will not be possible to provide more than a sketch of Giddens' historical account. This is a pity, because he is often perceptive on historical points of detail, irrespective of how one may ultimately judge his overall theory. However, in order to make a general assessment of the applicability of structuration theory to historical analysis it is the broad lines of his account that it is important to grasp.

The 'city' and 'traditional empires' as 'power containers' and 'prime carriers' of the time-space distanciation of societies

The first step in Giddens' account, for which his analysis of both power and time-geography prepares the way, is the entry of the 'city' and of states on to the stage of history as new kinds of 'locale', as centres for the 'storage' of power, as 'power containers'. Although 'the storage of "material" or allocative resources' (for example, in grain stores or irrigation systems) may seem more obvious, in the end it is the storage of authoritative resources that Giddens categorically states as 'more significant' (Giddens, 1984a:94). While even the storage of material resources 'involves far more than *merely* the physical containment of material goods', what storage of authoritative resources crucially entails is *'the retention and control of information or knowledge'* (ibid: 94, emphasis in original). In this respect, writing is a 'decisive develop-ment', creating a storage 'container' beyond human memory. It is this that brings the capacity for time-space distanciation that is simply lacking in preliterate societies. First, listings and administra-tive records, and then 'recorded history' – and with this the possib-ility of 'historicity' – make their appearance in this way.

It is in these terms – here reviving the work of Lewis Mumford – that Giddens regards the 'city' as the first distinctive power container in modern history. Its role within early 'civilized' socie-ties in beginning the process of extensive time-space distanciation is crucial. When Spengler wrote, 'world history is city history', Giddens mainly agrees (Giddens, 1984a: 96). The city, in creating a new division (but also new relations) between an urban environ-ment and the countryside, becomes a 'crucible for the generation of power on a scale unthinkable in non-urban communities'. 'The enclosure of cities by walls' may enhance 'the metaphor of the "container"', but walls are only the physical expression of a more significant intramural power, the power of the city as a 'religious, ceremonial, and commercial centre' and as a centre of political power: the arrival of 'city-states'. The issue of whether the 'agricul-tural revolution' and the expansion of 'productive forces' is the underlying factor in the rise of cities and the chief mobilizer of social change is not ignored by Giddens. However, he dismisses Gordon Childe's longstanding thesis that a 'neolithic revolution' *preceded* the emergence of cities. Nor does he accept Jacobs' (1970) view that it was the purely 'economic' power generated by cities that was most significant (Giddens, 1981a:94–100).

The historical step that, according to Giddens, provides the next significant power container is 'the fusion of several cities to form

125

empires'. This again represents a 'qualitative break between two types of social organization' (Giddens, 1981a:100). Although limited developments in transport and communications restrict their power in comparison with modern states, empires constitute 'the only examples of large scale centralized societies before the establishment of capitalism'. They reflect the 'conscious attempts' of rulers to establish 'homogeneous modes of administration and political allegiance within particular territories' (ibid: 102). If military power (including developments in military technology) plays the decisive role in the creation and continuity of these new political forms, two further factors are also acknowledged as important: the legitimation of authority *within* the apparatus of government and the 'formation of economic ties of interdependence'. What Giddens insists, however, is that economic factors were the 'least important'. Again the message is clear, 'the first territorial states' become established *without* economic forces being decisive. Furthermore, Giddens goes on to assert that for all sorts of traditional state societies prior to capitalism the same is so, 'coordination of *authoritative* resources forms the determining axis of societal integration and *change*' (ibid: 4, emphasis added). Thus on Giddens' assessment, 'noncapitalist societies are definitely not modes of production, even if modes of production are obviously involved'. Nor do these societies possess any obvious inherent tendency to evolve.

If such statements as these would appear to conflict with historical materialism this, of course, is exactly what Giddens intends. However, as he is well aware, they do not conflict in the same way with much that Marx actually wrote, in the *Formen* and elsewhere, about 'pre-capitalist' forms of society. It is clear that Marx entertained many doubts about the 'dynamic' character of economic forces and class relations in these forms of society. What Giddens concludes about pre-capitalist agrarian states is that although they can appropriately be described as 'class-divided societies' – in contrast with earlier 'tribal societies' – they are not 'class societies' in that their central dynamic is not class. Above all, their subordinate classes, while remaining in control of the means of production as immediate producers possess insufficient 'spatial stretch' to sustain class organizations or class conflict. In Giddens' view, therefore, these forms of society must be sharply contrasted with modern forms of capitalist 'class society' (see Figure 5.4), in which class is the central axis of order and change.

What Giddens suggests about Marx's work at this point is summed up by him in the following way:

	CLASS-DIVIDED SOCIETIES	CLASS SOCIETIES (Capitalist societies)
	'Symbiosis of the city and countryside'	Commercially created 'built environment'
		Formal separation of economic and political spheres
MODES OF DOMINATION/ PREDOMINANT SANCTIONS	Local, relatively autonomous communal production – 'allocative power'	Private ownership of capital; 'asymmetrical' capitalist labour contract – 'allocative power'
	Centralized political and military power – 'authoritative power'	State surveillance – 'authoritative power' and violence extruded from the labour contract
	Predominant sanction: control of means of violence	Predominant sanction: economic necessity of employment
ROLE OF CLASS AND CLASS CONFLICT	Class divisions but not class conflict not the central dynamic – peasant rebellions, but only dominant class possess spatial stretch	Class divisions and class conflict a central dynamic (although not alone decisive)

Figure 5.4 Class-divided societies and class societies

that it is the themes of the *Formen* which are worthy of further elaboration rather than those involved in Marx's evolutionary interpretation of history. The forces/relations of production dialectic is not a miraculous device that somehow holds the answer to disclosing the underlying sources of social change in general. Nor can the contradictory character of social formations be understood in these terms – except in the case of capitalism.

(Giddens, 1981a:89)

David Jary

Giddens' non-evolutionary societal typology

Unlike some critics, Giddens writes about Marxism neither as an 'inplacable opponent or a disillusioned ex-believer' (Giddens, 1981a:1). Instead, though making plain that he is not a Marxist, he is eloquent in his 'belief' that 'Marx's analysis of the mechanism of capitalist production ... remains the necessary core of any attempt to come to terms with the massive transformations that have swept through the world since the eighteenth century' (ibid.). Elements of Marx's analysis of human *Praxis* are also accorded considerable value. Marx's 'evolutionary scheme', however, remains fatally flawed.

Reduced to essentials, Giddens' critique of historical materialism – a relatively conventional one – has two aspects. First, the focus of historical materialism on *Praxis* and human agency is undermined by an unjustifiable 'elision' of 'praxis in general' with 'labour' in particular (Giddens, 1981a:54) – the reduction of the 'transformative capacity' of human agents ultimately to merely economic agency. Second, evolutionary and functionalist arguments – Marxist and non-Marxist versions of these – are rejected so long as they continue to invoke untenable explanatory conceptions of 'societal needs' and societal 'adaptation'. What this second criticism boils down to is that there exists no 'evolutionary' operation of social contradictions and no functionalist 'autoproduction' of social systems (though 'counterfactual' forms of functionalist argument, asserting what would be required for a particular system to exist or reproduce, are accepted as legitimate by Giddens). For Giddens, such biologically derived concepts as 'adaptation' or 'need' are too lacking in precise content to possess any useful purchase faced with the complexities of social development. In any case, Giddens agrees with Gellner (1964) – from whom he also borrows the term 'episode' – that: 'Human history is not ... a "world-growth story"', in that it is a record that involves neither the continuous nor the unilinear development implied by historical materialism or social evolutionism (Giddens, 1984a:237 *et seq.*).

In these circumstances, Giddens' own typology of main types of society – Figure 5.5 – is a typology only of historically existing societies, not intended as an evolutionary scheme. Its focus is on the extent and kind of differentiation exhibited by different forms of society, as well as on the time-space distanciation of societies, but as an uneven historical sequence not a necessary evolutionary progression. Thus first there is 'tribal society', in which political and economic institutions remain undifferentiated and where the time-space is severely limited. Second, there is 'class-divided

128

(i) **Tribal society** (oral culture):
— Tradition (communal   [Fusion of social and
   practices)   system integration]
— Kinship
— Group sanction
Dominant locale organization: band groups or villages

(ii) **Class-divided society:**
— Tradition (communal   [Differentiation of social
   practices)   and system integration]
— Kinship
— Politics/military power
— Economic interdependence   } STATE
   (low lateral and vertical
   integration)
Dominant locale organization: symbiosis of society and countryside

(iii) **Class society:**
— Routinization   [Differentiation of
— Kinship (family)   social and system]
— Surveillance
— Politics/military power   } STATE
— Economic interdependence
   (high lateral and vertical
   interdependence)
Dominant locale organization: the 'created environment'

Figure 5.5 Typology of societies
Source: A modified version of figures that appear in Giddens, 1981a and 1984a
Note: In the 1984 version of this figure politics/military power is a feature of 'class society'; in the 1981 version it is absent.

society', in which the differentiation of political and economic institutions takes the form of a 'symbiosis of city and countryside', and where social integration and system integration also become separated and the time-space stretch of society begins. And third, there is 'class society' (and 'nation-state') with its far more formal separation of political and economic 'spheres', and highly extended distanciation and lateral and horizontal interdependence. The historical and 'non-evolutionary' nature of this sequence of societal development is also underlined by Figure 5.6, which indicates the intersocietal systems and time-space edges existing in world-time. What such a world-historical context for individual societies reinforces, according to Giddens, is that, though societal typologies have their uses, there can be no question of a simple sequence of 'endogenous' societal development.

David Jary

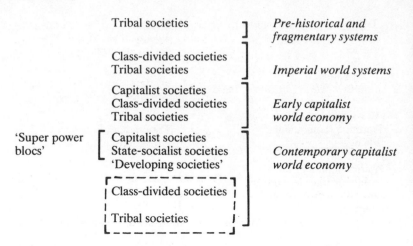

Figure 5.6 Intersocietal systems in 'world-time'
Source: Giddens, 1981a: 161

Capitalism, absolutism and the nation-state

As clear both from his remarks and his typologies, Giddens does not dispute the very great importance of capitalism in the time-space distanciation of societies. However, in line with his rejection of the evolutionary monism of historical materialism and his view of social change as episodic, he insists: (1) that the development of capitalism and the nation-state (and also industrialism) must be seen as interrelated phenomena with no one determining factor; (2) that these interrelated developments were historically contingent and *distinctively European*, leading to an ascendancy of the west finally confirmed only in the latter half of the seventeenth century; and (3) that this happened only in a geopolitical context in which, for the first time, Europe was no longer threatened militarily from the east and when its naval technology had also achieved a worldwide supremacy. That there was much that was not inevitable or 'evolutionary' about these developments, Giddens declares, is confirmed by noting how very different history might have been, for example, had Charlemagne succeeded in his goal of a new European empire or if the European powers had suffered lasting defeat at the hands of the Ottoman Turks in the seventeenth century.

For Giddens, the undoubted historical significance of western capitalism is that it involves the commodification of land, labour-

130

power and the means of production, as well as the abstraction of surplus value by capitalists, 'on an altogether new scale'. This in turn led on to the commodification of time and space generally in modern societies. If as is widely recognized, money, including new means of credit and accounting, plays a particularly vital role in 'disembodying social relations, in detaching these from time and space', then:

> Marx has to be given very great credit for first showing that it is the *commodification of time* that forms the underlying connecting link between the massive expansion of the commodity form in the production of goods, on the one hand, and the commodification of labour (as labour power) on the other.
>
> (Giddens, 1981a:130, emphasis in original)

Thus, to this extent in a manner broadly consistent with Marxism itself, Giddens sees the entire process of commodification in modern societies as a systematic outcome of the dispossession of workers from the means of production and the 'extrusion' of violence from the labour contract.

This said, however, it is a decisive element of Giddens' argument that the capitalist extraction of surplus value could not have occurred without the part played by the 'coterminous' emergence of new state forms in pacifying populations and enforcing the rule of law, or without new means of surveillance in the workplace – forms of authoritative rather than merely allocative power. Giddens quotes from Foucault as follows:

> If the economic take-off of the West began with the technique that made possible the accumulation of capital, it might perhaps be said that the methods for the accumulation of men made possible a political take-off in relation to traditional ritual, costly, violent forms of power, which soon fell into disuse and were superseded by a subtle, calculated technology of subjection.
>
> (Foucault, 1975:220–1)

Among the new methods in the workplace, of course, were the co-ordination of machinery and labour power by 'clock-time' and more general control over the labour process, described so vividly by E.P. Thompson (1967) and Braverman (1974). These replaced the self-control and more natural rhythms that had previously governed work in traditional societies. Thus, as Giddens puts it, 'struggle over time becomes the most direct expression of class conflict in the capitalist economy' (Giddens, 1981a:120), and the 'policing' of society a crucial factor in the effectiveness of capitalism.

For Giddens, however, the new state forms involve far more than the policing of civil society envisaged by orthodox Marxism or by liberal thought. Crucially in Giddens' view, the modern European nation-state is a 'bordered power container', enclosing far greater administrative intensity than traditional states. It can be sharply distinguished from its predecessors by its clearly demarcated borders and its existence within a state-system of similarly constituted states in which warfare and the preparation for war plays a fundamental constitutive role. In Giddens' own summary:

> Nation-states only exist in systematic relations with other nation-states. The internal administrative coordination of nation-states from their very beginnings depends upon reflexively monitored conditions of an international nature. 'International relations' is coeval with the origins of nation-states.
>
> (Giddens, 1985a:4)

Figure 5.7, indicates in outline the overall developments considered important by Giddens, who particularly criticizes Weber and other theorists for not stating more clearly the sharpness of division between traditional and modern states and the distinctiveness this gives to modern societies – their more unitary character than previous state societies.

In these developments it is the transitional 'absolutist' states of the fifteenth- and sixteenth-century Europe as well as the fully fledged nation-states of modern times that, according to Giddens, must be regarded as an integral part of capitalist development, providing both 'some of the conditions for its early development' as well as the means of its later expansion. Essential to this view is that capitalist *societies* came into being as territorially bounded states and as part of a *state-system*. Central to absolutism is the idea of 'sovereignty', first as personal power but later as impersonal administrative power. In Giddens' view, it was the successful institutionalization of new concepts of sovereignty that did much to ensure 'the dissolution of the city/countryside relations' that characterized the traditional state. In a heterodox but not unMarxist way, Giddens presents the development of absolutism as an alliance of traditional local and state elites in which traditional feudal power was reorganized rather than entirely replaced (cf. Anderson, 1974b). Thus, it is not strictly true to say, as does Friedland (1987:41), that for Giddens, the 'ruling ideas are not those of the ruling class, they are the ideas of rule'. However, contrary to historical materialism (at least as he sees it), Giddens' portrayal of the relation between capitalism and the new state forms is one that emphasizes reciprocal causation, so that in neither origins nor outcomes can the role of the state be reduced to economic factors.

At one level, for example, the suggestion is that the process of state development can be seen as driven in large measure by the demands of ever-changing modes of warfare. If, as Clausewitz the famous theoretician of modern warfare suggested, 'war is politics by other means', then for Giddens, economics must often be recognized as driven in large part by politics and by warfare. Thus, it is the geopolitical conflicts of states, first on a European scale and subsequently on a world stage, that he presents as frequently uppermost in influencing economic developments. In this way, for instance, the monetization of the economy arises as much from the fiscal demands posed by the ever-escalating costs of warfare as from the more general requirements of production and exchange. Likewise, many innovations in administration can be seen as having occurred first in connection with military needs, for example, the new forms of military discipline, that Giddens refers to as the 'Taylorism of this sphere'. Innovations in military technology also frequently predated advances in civilian technology. Giddens goes so far as to suggest that capitalism may even have become the dominant world mode of production *primarily* because of the military power possessed by the nation-states with which it was associated. For, while the imperial power of traditional empires might have resisted capitalism, these empires were unable to match the military power – more specifically perhaps the naval power – of the west. In more general terms, many of the technical inventions usually thought distinctive to modernity and often associated particularly with capitalism – improvements in transportation by sea, road, rail and air, and advances in communications and information technology such as telegraphy and computers – are as much driven by the strategic (and reflexive) requirements of state power, particularly the requirements of warfare, as than by any logic of capitalism (or industrialism) alone. It would be a wrong to suggest, as does Hall (1984), that internal relations play only an unimportant part in Giddens' analysis. But Giddens does insist that an economic- or a class-reductionist account of state power can only mislead as to the true role of the state in shaping both the internal and external relations of modern societies. Even nationalism, as Thrift (1984: 141) puts it, is seen as a 'psychological outproduct' of state power. Rather than the initial cause of the rise of nation-states, nationalism involves the state creation of new 'traditions'.

	TRADITIONAL STATE	ABSOLUTIST STATE (a transitional form)	MODERN NATION-STATE
CHARACTER OF BOUNDARIES OF STATES	No clear boundaries: frontiers not borders	Forerunner of modern nation-state	Clearly defined and highly administered borders
	State and society not coextensive: multisocietal states	Concept of 'sovereignty', at first 'personal' then linked to nationalism	State and society coextensive: the 'nation-state'
		State system in which war and preparation for war central	Existence (and definition) as part of a well-defined 'state-system' of nation-states
MONOPOLY AND ROLE OF VIOLENCE	*Internal:* violence as a routine feature of administration; limited pacification	*Internal:* obsolescence of city walls symbolic of new state power and unification of town and country	*Internal:* internal pacification largely accomplished, with the threat of violence mainly in the background
	External: military force and military technology as the basis of territorial domination	*External:* warfare and preparation for warfare central to state formation	*External:* industrialization of warfare – application of technology; standing armies; conscription, etc. – leading to 'total war'
		Naval superiority over non-European states	

SCOPE AND INTENSITY OF ADMINISTRATIVE REACH	Wide territorial control but low administrative intensity and limited penetration of many areas of life	Increasing administrative control – especially fiscal and in relation to needs of military. New legal order	High administrative intensity; surveillance – control of information and sequestration
CENTRAL INTERNAL CONFLICTS	Intra-elite conflicts (dynastic change) Peasant revolts, but no centrality of class conflict	Varying alliances between state and traditional and emerging elites	Class conflict between capital and labour and class conflict a central dynamic, but class conflict not alone decisive Polyarchy; citizen rights

Figure 5.7 Traditional, absolutist and modern nation-states

Giddens sums up his own view of the importance of state power when he describes the nation-state as the *'preeminent* modern power container'. While there are historians (notably Tilly, 1975) who claim that the association of capitalism and the nation-state is largely fortuitous (e.g. that the Hanseatic League had no association with a major state, that Spain and Portugal, though major powers, were not capitalist states), Giddens' reply is that this is true only of the earliest forms of capitalism, that thereafter the nation-state and capitalism require each other to survive and expand. Thus, the core of Giddens' argument would seem in fact to relate relatively little to the origins of capitalism. On the matter of such origins Giddens in fact says surprisingly little – a possible weakness of his argument *vis-à-vis* historical materialism we take up subsequently. Rather his argument is that it is in the establishment of capitalist societies that the role of the state must *certainly* be seen as crucial. In line with his multidimensional conception of historical causation, what Giddens concludes about modern societies is that in all four interdependent 'institutional clusterings' must be seen as associated with modernity: 'heightened surveillance, capitalistic enterprise, industrial production and the consolidation and centralized control of the means of violence'. Moreover, 'none of these is wholly reducible to any of the others' (Giddens, 1985a:5).

Contemporary 'world-society' and the 'world capitalist system'

The multidimensional, contingent and non-evolutionary, character of social development, with politics and the state playing a central role, is no less in evidence in Giddens' thinking when he brings his story up to date and turns his attention to the twentieth century and the contemporary world-system. So much is indicated by his assertion that: 'We live in what Wallerstein has called a "world capitalist economy", in which capitalist economic relations pertain on a world scale. *Even more important,* we live in a *world nation-state system* that has no precedent in history' (Giddens, 1987a:166, emphasis added). For Giddens, it is a decisive feature of the modern world-system that 'From the state system that was once one of the peculiarities of Europe there has developed a system of nation-states covering the globe in a network of national communities' (Giddens, 1985a:255) and that in this process: 'the military involvement of states also strongly influences the developments of ... other features of societal organization, in ways that can be fairly readily traced out, even if they are missing from most sociological discussions' (ibid: 233).

The multiple developments that Giddens regards as significant in this process include:

1. the 'industralization of warfare' – new weapons of destruction, the impact of new forms of communication and transportation – and 'total war'; in which both the old constraints of social convention and time and space have progressively diminished and in which entire populations are engaged either as conscripted participants or as targets;
2. the triumph of 'sentiments of nationalism' over internationalism in this process, signalling the new importance 'that the connection of sovereignty and citizenship had assumed and which would, henceforth, dominate the global community' (Giddens, 1985a:232);
3. the aftermath, in particular, of two World Wars, in which the concept of the 'independent unity of each state' finally replaces both the 'older type of imperial system' and the more recent forms of European colonialism.

That the contingent nature of these developments remains emphasized by Giddens, however, is indicated by his insistence, for example, that:

If the course of events in the Great War, including the participation of the USA in the hostilities and the peace settlement, had not taken the shape they did, the nation-state in its current form might not have become the dominant political entity in the world system.

(Giddens, 1985a:234–5)

Given his focus on the time-space distanciation of societies, it is no surprise to find that Giddens is strongly influenced by theorists of the 'world-system' such as Wallerstein. He praises especially the latter's strong emphasis on the 'regionalization of political and economic systems (and) upon spatial features of social organizations and change' (Giddens, 1985a:166). However, the 'ever-increasing abundance of global connections' and international organizations, Giddens insists, 'should not be regarded as intrinsically diminishing the sovereignty' of states, but rather seen as 'in substantial part the chief condition of the worldwide extension of the nation-state system in current times' (ibid: 5). Moreover, within this state-system warfare and the threat of war remains a significant factor; indeed its importance is in many ways increased by the arrival of nuclear weapons. Reflecting the continued importance of Marx's thinking within his overall analysis, Giddens does sometimes refer to the world-system in general as a 'world capitalist economy' (e.g. Figure 5.6, p. 130). Thus, Wallerstein's account of the origins of 'core' and 'peripheral' national economies – explained by him in terms of the presence or absence of strong states – is obviously accepted by Giddens. As often with Giddens' appropriation of the work of others, however, Wallerstein's account – seen as marred by functionalism as well as economic reductionism – becomes the butt of criticism, clearing the way for Giddens' own preferred model, which is that the contemporary world system will be fully understood only if it is seen as made up of four interrelated systems, corresponding to his D-D-L-S model of social institutions (see Figure 5.3, p. 124):

1. *world capitalist economy* (corresponding to D alloc);
2. *nation-state system* (corresponding to D auth);
3. *world military order* (corresponding to L);
4. *global information system* (corresponding to S).

A critic might suggest that many of Giddens' formulations made using this framework – e.g. 'a military order that substantially cross-cuts the division between the First, Second and Third worlds of the world capitalist economy' – amount to little more than a loosely textured synthesis of much that is already accepted within the disciplines of political science, international relations and sociology. But Giddens appears content that such distinctions make apparent the relative complexity – and unpredictability – of the forces operating in the current world-system compared with the picture that emerges from more reductionist and more determinate models. Giddens presents as his 'main emphasis' in *Nation-State and Violence* the provision of 'an interpretation of the development of the nation-state in its original, i.e. "Western, habitat"', and a tracing out of 'why this form has become generalized across the globe'. He states clearly that he makes 'no claim to offering an exhaustive analysis of variations among states in today's world' (ibid: 5).

Contemporary western societies

In characterizing contemporary western capitalist societies, Giddens' account is fuller, though it still depends heavily on the application of general categories. Again, it is the contingent character and the political dimensions of development – including the effects of war – that Giddens points to as relatively neglected and misunderstood by sociologists. For example, it was not the endogenous development of industrialism but war 'that dissolved the power of traditional elites in Germany and Japan, and it was not internal processes of political change that resulted in liberal democracy in these states' (Giddens, 1985a:243). In addition, Giddens' insistence on a multidimensional account is underlined by his rejection of the idea, much favoured in modern sociology, that western societies must nowadays be seen either as 'capitalist societies' or as 'industrial (or 'post-industrial') societies', that these can be characterized by a single determining dialectic or dynamic (Bleicher and Featherstone, 1982).

For all this, one important 'generic' feature of modern western nation-states is stressed by Giddens: power is 'double-edged'. The 'polyarchic character' of modern states derives from 'administrative concentration' ('achieved via the expansion of surveillance') and from the 'altered nature of the dialectic of control that this produces' (Giddens 1985a:5). Thus if the routine penetration of political power into the daily lives of citizens is increasingly evident in western societies – a tendency sometimes leading also to 'totalitarianism' – the other side of the coin, according to Giddens, has been a steady expansion of the arena for public discourse and political participation. Commentators such as Hall (1984) or Smith and Turner (1986) who categorize Giddens as only repeating a 'neo-Nietzschean' thesis about modern surveillance are therefore wide of the mark. Instead, seeking strenuously to steer a course between a view of modern societies as involving either a 'primacy of class interests over civil rights' ('the Marxian view'), or a 'primacy of civil rights over class' (cf. Bendix, 1978, or Marshall, 1973) Giddens proposes that the 'generic association' that exists between the modern nation-state and polyarchy – the rule of the many – provides increasing scope for *various* forms of agency, but the primacy for none. This discussion of 'rights' and 'social movements' in modern societies can be seen as a particularly crucial part of Giddens' entire argument for it also leads on to the 'critical analysis' of the main dynamics and prospects for change in modern society with which he concludes his analysis.

First, Giddens follows T.H. Marshall (1973) in identifying three distinct categories of citizen rights within modern societies: (1) *civil rights*, including freedom of expression and organization; (2) *political rights*, including the right to vote and to run for office; and (3) *economic rights*, including the right to welfare and social security. But whereas for Marshall the expansion of rights in all three areas greatly reduced the intensity of class conflict, for Giddens class continues to have major significance within contemporary western societies as *one* pervasive basis of conflict as a consequence of the 'asymmetry' of the capitalist labour contract. 'Class conflict' remains a 'threat' to the 'integration' and 'governability' of modern

societies, given that 'class compromise', 'based firmly on an "effort
bargain" between the labour force and the state', depends upon
the continued 'delivery of adequate economic performance' (Giddens, 1985a:322). For Giddens, however, concentration on class
as the only basis of significant social movements, or on 'the tran-
scendence of capitalism by socialism as the sole objective of future
social transformations' (ibid: 5), can no more be justified than can
Marshall's view. Instead Giddens suggests that each of Marshall's
three categories of rights corresponds to a distinct arena of 'surveillance and contestation' in modern societies, as follows: (1) civil
rights, corresponding to 'surveillance as policing'; (2) political
rights, corresponding to 'surveillance as reflexive monitoring by
the state'; and (3) economic rights, corresponding to 'surveillance
as "management" of production'. Finally, reformulating these
distinctions in terms of his D-D-L-S model, Giddens suggests that
in all, four bases of social movements are significant: labour movements; democratic movements; peace movements, and ecological
movements (see Figure 5.8). (As well as these movements, in a
more *ad hoc* way, the importance of the women's movement and

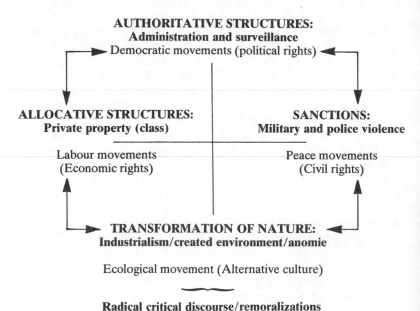

Figure 5.8 Modern social movements

Source: This combines a number of separate 'maps' provided by Giddens in *Nation-State and
Violence* (1985a), which he suggests can be superimposed

ethnic movements is also noted by Giddens.) Of these areas, the 'ecological' – although something of a mixed-bag, including debates about industrialism and all aspects of the 'created environment' – would appear crucial, for Giddens here locates the most general discursive and critical social debates about modern society – including sociology itself!

Some striking parallels exist between Giddens' thinking in these terms and the role seen for emancipatory discourse in the critical theory of Jürgen Habermas. But there are also important differences, for, as Giddens expresses it, Habermas's thinking remains bound up with the very evolutionary assumptions that must be avoided. Instead, in Giddens' view, critical theory today, while influenced by Marx, 'must be post-Marxist', recognizing that four main institutional axes of modernity are 'world-historical', and that stripped of 'historical guarantees, critical theory reenters the universe of contingency' (Giddens, 1985a:335–7).

In summary, then, the world revealed in Giddens' historical sociology is a world of competing social movements and competing nation-states as well as a world of capitalism, with no predictable outcomes. And not the least reason for this uncertainty – although plainly not the only reason – is a nation-state system: 'in which a fragile equality in weaponry of the two major superpowers is the only brake upon the political anarchy of the international order' (Giddens, 1987a:166). In these circumstances, Giddens restates his case for a structurationist historical sociology thus:

> Those who have wanted to model sociology upon natural science, hoping to discover universal laws of social conduct, have tended to sever sociology from history. In breaking, with such views, we have to go further than simply asserting that sociology and history – or more accurately the social sciences and history – are indistinguishable, provocative though such a claim may appear to be. We have to grasp how history is made through the active involvements and struggles of human beings, and yet at the same time both forms those human beings and produces outcomes which they neither intend nor foresee. As a theoretical background to the social sciences, nothing is more vital in an era suspending between extraordinary opportunity on the one hand and global catastrophe on the other.
>
> (Giddens, 1986c:156)

But how adequate is Giddens' view, and the scaling up of sociology's focus and the scaling down of sociological aspirations that this involves? More particularly, how far must this be seen as the only possible outcome of the adoption of a structurationist focus on structure and agency?

Commentary and evaluation

With so much ground covered by Giddens, the task facing any assessment of his work is no less daunting than its summary. Such an assessment is bound to be selective. I want first, therefore, to say something about the general orientation of what follows before passing on to a number of more particular points of criticism and evaluation.

Giddens' 'world-view'

A common criticism of Giddens' work (e.g. Urry, 1982; Gregson, 1986) is that many of his proposed additions to sociological theory, including crucially the concept of 'duality of structure', are conceptual and terminological only, although very interesting and valuable at this level. Other commentators (e.g. McClennan, 1984; Smith and Turner, 1986), while far from entirely hostile to Giddens' work, have suggested that some at least of his more specific conceptual and terminological additions – including many of his time-space concepts such as storage capacity or time-space edges – are merely metaphorical and analogical rather than making a truly original theoretical contribution. Regarding *Central Problems* and *Contemporary Critique*, the observation often voiced was that judgement must be suspended until the ideas therein had been more tried and tested in empirical inquiry (e.g. Gregson, 1986). Moreover, the publication of *Constitution of Society*, with its identification of preferred forms of research, did little to assuage such doubts since most of the examples of research accorded the structurationist seal of approval by Giddens were neither carried out under the auspices of structuration theory nor, equally importantly, did they always conspicuously *combine* accounts of structure and agency. *Nation-State and Violence* with its potentially more empirical focus might have been expected to resolve the issue. But not so. As Skocpol remarks:

> Those who might want pointed causal explanations or empirically grounded comparative historical generalizations must look elsewhere. Instead, this book offers a quintessential Giddensian exercise in macrosociological 'theorizing', spinning a *world-view* about modernization and a menu of concepts to characterize modern national states.
>
> (Skocpol, 1987: 295)

As in *Contemporary Critique* so in *Nation-State and Violence* what Giddens presents is an appraisal of the relevant literature in terms of the general principles of structuration theory, rather than any stricter testing of propositions. Both works, therefore, must be judged in this light. The central question about Giddens' historical theory, then, is how justified is this 'world-view'?

There are questions to raise in five main areas: (1) the value of the concept of time-space distanciation; (2) the interpretation and operational use of the conception of the duality of structure; (3) the distinction drawn between 'allocative' and 'authoritative' resources, and the cogency of Giddens' critique of historical materialism and evolutionary theory; (4) the character of Giddens' 'empirical' accounts; (5) problems associated with his approach to critical theory.

Time-space distanciation

Turning first to Giddens' reconceptualization of historical time-space, I do not intend to detract from its many sharp insights and considerable general interest. Undoubtedly, the concept of time-space distanciation illuminates Marx. As Gregson (1986:91) jokingly says, Marx's famous aphorism must now be rephrased to refer to: 'people making history in temporal and spatial contexts, but not in the conditions or in the time-space zones of their own chosing'.

The concept of time-space distanciation – with its focus on 'regions' in time-space and on 'intersocietal' relations – brings a fresh slant to the analysis of societal development. It is useful in synthesizing and integrating previously diverse accounts of social development and it has stimulated further research – especially perhaps in the new symbiotic relations this has established with geographers, although there are also reservations (see Thrift, 1983; 1985a; Gregory, 1984; Carlstein, 1981; and as well as Urry, this volume). As Thrift puts it, partly but not only as a result of Giddens' work, and 'even if the implications are only now being thought through',

> there is little doubt that it is becoming rare to find social action in space and time treated by social theorists as simply an after thought or as the mere imprint of social structure or as belonging, in some way, to an autonomous realm of existence.[3]
>
> (Thrift, 1983: 49)

The other side of the coin, however, is that many of Giddens' new concepts are metaphorical and analogical (cf. McLennan, 1984), often re-presenting the known facts about social development, even if to some extent in a new light. Thus, for instance, while the historical significance of the rise of cities and states is illuminated by their discussion within Giddens' time-space frame of reference – as specialist locales, and power containers, etc. – equally it is not the case that the significance of these is seen for the first time or in a wholly novel way using this framework. It is not the case therefore that Giddens can be said to have unequivocally established a decisively new theoretical perspective – still less the entirety of his historical theory – simply by his formulation of the concept of time-space distanciation.

Agency and structure in Giddens' 'world-view'

In order for him to be able to claim a decisive theoretical break-through for the entirety of his theoretical package, Giddens would need to establish unequivocally what I take to be the two most crucial aspects of his overall argument:

1. Theoretically, that his particular perspective on time-space distanciation – including its particular emphasis on historicity, 'episodic' transitions and the frequently decisive role of political agency – arises as a necessary outcome of the adoption of the basic tenets of a structurationist perspective with *no* alternative;
2. Empirically, that such an extended interpretation of structure and agency is also confirmed by the historical record.

A schematic reconstruction of what I see as the various elements in Giddens' argument in these terms is given in Figure 5.9.

Since Giddens, neither in whole or in part, subjects his overall historical theory to systematic comparative testing, and would at times even appear to find such systematic testing inappropriate, this would perhaps suggest that he does regard the justification of his historical sociology as more a matter of his having demonstrated its general theoretical basis in structuration theory and the general fertility of this in historical analysis, e.g. in providing 'sensitizing concepts'.

The first problem I see with Giddens' approach here, however, is that it is hard to escape the conclusion that a number of his decisive interpretative stances regarding historical change would appear to depend upon particular (i.e. contentious) interpretations of the interrelation of structure and agency. This problem we must sum up as a general ontological and epistemological 'bias' towards 'open agency' and against lasting lawlike structuration – an assumption that because agents construct and can and do *re*-construct social arrangements, the assumption must also be made that they always will reconstruct these in ways that cannot be

DUALITY OF STRUCTURE◄ – – ►DISTINCTIVELY HUMAN
TRANFORMATIVE CAPACITY
INTERRELATION OF
STRUCTURE AND ACTION   (i)   Historicality

(ii)   Contextual organization of
time and space

(iii) Historicity

(i)   Time-space distanciation as an
outcome

(ii)   Information and communication   CONTINGENT
as a major factor in time-space   SOCIAL REALITY
distanciation/convergence   AND 'EPISODIC'
CHANGE,
(iii) Reflexive monitoring (and   WITH POLITICS
storage of information) carried   AS A MAIN
out particularly within states   ELEMENT

(iv) 'Episodic' transformations rather
than evolutionary pattern, given
that individuals can always
behave differently and act with
an awareness of world-time

(v)   Potentiality for discursively
grounded social critique
informed by sociology, but a
'post-modern' world in which
there are no certainties, and
where social actors achieve
ontological security via 'routine'

Figure 5.9 Duality of structure in Giddens' 'world-view'

captured by lawlike propositions or general mechanisms (cf.
Layder, 1982, who suggests that in Giddens' work, structure 'col-
lapses into agency').[4] Thus, although in many places in his work
Giddens shows no reluctance to employ what, on the face of it, are
general models – e.g. his reference to 'axes of structuration', 'circuits
of capital', 'acceptable' forms of functionalist argument, etc. – in the
end an objection to 'vulgar' evolutionary or materialist developmental models often gets transmuted into the assertion of an
equally 'vulgar' assumption that sociological generalities and
general models *will* always be undermined.

David Jary

It is difficult to accept, however, that there is no alternative to such a simple dichotomous view as this, that this is not too sweeping and that it fails to do justice to the variety of forms in which general models and lawlike tendencies can be seen as central in both social and physical science (cf. Martins, 1974). Giddens does sometimes qualify his position, stating as the goal of sociology the generation of 'systematically coherent explanatory models' (Cohen, 1986:127). But in the event, his general concern to preserve agency – and contingency – usually means that he shows relatively little inclination to develop such models very fully or to explore systematically the range and possibilities of the many different kinds of general model, statements of general tendency, etc. that exist in the social sciences (cf. Turner, 1986b; Craib, 1986; Layder, 1981; Thrift, 1983; 1985a; Stinchcome, 1986; and McClennan, 1988 – who from their different perspectives, whether positivist, realist, or Marxist, agree on this and complain of the relatively weak sense of 'determination' in Giddens' work).

At times, Giddens has written perceptively on epistemological issues and is well aware of the highly contested character of discussions of the role and status of scientific laws in modern-day, 'post-empiricist' philosophy (e.g. Giddens, 1977j). At one level, therefore, it is surprising to find him apparently content to operate with so hard-and-fast a distinction between physical science 'laws' and social science 'contingency'. But this would appear to be the ontological and epistemological interpretation of the implications of agency often made by him. In this respect, Giddens declares himself mainly happy to follow Weber's lead on such general issues. Giddens is, of course, right that in key respects the difference between agents and physical objects does represent a distinction of kind. But, with so many controversies in the philosophy of science and social science, and such variety in the forms of lawlike tendencies, general 'mechanisms', etc. actually claimed within the physical as well as the social sciences, I cannot see that he can be regarded as having eliminated alternatives, or even that he could ever hope to do so in this manner. In today's ontological and epistemological climate – and in better keeping, I would argue, with the requirements of a structurationist focus on agency *and* structure more broadly viewed – it would seem to me that the question of what kinds of generalizations are possible is one better left open, to be settled only in particular cases, rather than in a once-and-for-all way.[5]

A further crucial reason for arguing thus is the general 'operational' problems of Giddens' formulation of a 'duality of structure' already alluded to (and well documented by Urry, 1982; Thrift,

1983; Gregson, 1986; Smith and Turner, 1986, among others), which is that this is above all a programmatic statement and *not* automatically an operational model or one from which a single set of answers can ever be expected.

One indication of this, of particular significance in relation to Giddens' emphasis on the state, is that on Giddens' own admission, accounts in terms of structure usually involve different methodological *épochés*. Thus, Friedland (1987:41–2) is able to complain that in *Nation-State and Violence* (Giddens 1985a) the 'human subject is barely visible ... the interpretative dimension is largely lost'. If this may seem paradoxical in view of my earlier claim of an 'agency bias', at one level the apparent paradox *can* be resolved by showing this particular structural bias arises from the combination of two sources. The first is the ontological assumption made by Giddens that 'individuals could always have acted differently'. The second is the difficulty of operationally accomplishing analysis in terms of both agency and structure, when these involve different *épochés*. Thus, the outcome of the combination of Giddens' ontological assumption with the inevitability at some point of providing a structural account would seem to be the assertion that it is state elites with their peculiar capacity for reflexive monitoring who must often possess the decisive historical role. It is significant in this respect that some commentators (e.g. Hall, 1984) have even suggested that Giddens' work, like that of Raymond Aron and others, can be viewed as part of a movement to *entirely* reverse the replacement of the political by the 'social' (and economic) that occurred in social theory with the rise of sociology. This allows, Hall suggests, in certain circumstances, even for an 'absolute autonomy of politics'. To a lesser degree, both Skocpol (1987) and Friedland (1987) reach a similar conclusion about the near primacy of the political within Giddens' historical sociology. Obviously, this is at odds with the more balanced approach that Giddens states as his goal. However, it is a reading of Giddens' work that at some points has some substance. And if we look for further explanations of the high profile of, and possible 'bias' towards, the political in his work, it is not hard to find these. The most prominent is the greater scope this leaves for human agency, but with paradoxical and questionable conclusions such as those indicated, which reference merely to the duality of structure cannot resolve.[6]

It is in such circumstances as these that alternative interpretations of the duality of structure seem bound to arise. Thus, Callinicos (1987) (cf. also Bhaskar, 1979; 1986), though attracted by Giddens' definition of 'structure': (1) as unanticipated conditions and unintended outcomes; and (2) as enabling and constraining, nevertheless wants to see this as leaving scope for analysis in terms of structural conditions and 'structural capacities' – including class locations – in excess of those seen by Giddens. None of this prevents Callinicos (or Bhaskar) from agreeing – in fact, an almost universal verdict among sociologists – that Giddens' discussion of structure and agency is of very great value. But this only underlines that valid alternative interpretations are bound to arise, and that Giddens goes too far in implying that any one set of implications necessarily follow from his structurationist view. Thus in terms of Figure 5.9 (p. 145), what can be suggested is that room exists for other world-views (cf. Kilminster, in this volume).[7]

'Allocative' and 'authoritative power' and the 'evolutionary' and the 'episodic'

More specific, but still significant, general questions concerning Giddens' overall historical world-view involve the cogency of his distinction between 'allocative' power and the role of this in establishing his 'non-evolutionary view' – a topic taken up with some élan especially by Wright (1983) and also by Thrift (1983) and Craib (1986). In this respect, Wright's position is of particular interest because, although a Marxist, he is fullsome in his praise of many aspects of Giddens' thinking – including the critique of historical materialism in its 'vulgar' forms – while dissenting from any acceptance that either historical materialism or evolutionary thinking are eliminated by Giddens' argument. In this context, at least two strong objections to Giddens' view arise:

1. that Giddens' use of his concepts of allocative and authoritative power leads to an unduly restrictive conception of the 'economic' (and of class), which would be simply unacceptable to many Marxists, and must therefore be seen as suspect in any claims to have eliminated historical materialism;

2. that whereas for most Marxists, class is defined – and 'economic primacy' claimed – in terms of the *overall* mechanism by which surplus products or surplus labour is appropriated, for Giddens, class is defined, and questions of economic primacy appraised in terms only of 'private property in the means of production'.

Thus, for example, when Giddens represents traditional agrarian empires as domination of authoritative power over allocative power, and as therefore inconsistent with historical materialism, such a conclusion is unacceptable to Marxists since, as Wright puts it, the 'appropriation of surplus value *always* involves specific combinations of economic and *political* mechanisms (i.e. relations to allocative and authoritative resources)' (Wright, 1983:21, emphasis added). And so, claims about the importance of class structures and class struggle – its presence or absence – which Marxists make central to social analysis are not seen as overturned by Giddens' attempt at 'elimination'.

In general, Giddens' category of allocative power is so narrowly drawn compared with authoritative power that finding a more decisive role for the latter would sometimes appear almost an inevitable outcome of the use of his terminology. I am not suggesting that this utterly overturns all of Giddens' claims about the relative importance of political power, merely that it raises questions about his claim to have eliminated historical materialism, and that once again he is far from establishing the overall superiority of his own view. As Wright stresses: 'When Giddens tries to explain the differences in the relationship between allocative and authoritative resources in capitalist and noncapitalist societies he relies heavily on differences in the system of property relations' (ibid: 20). Thus at one level there exists 'no *intrinsic* incompatibility between the substantive claims Marxists make about the importance of class structures and class struggle, and about the role of the state and ideology' (ibid: 34). Nor in a wider way does any overall incompatibility exist with 'Giddens' methodological stress on the knowledgeability of actors, the "duality of structure", the analysis of social processes in terms of the unacknowledged conditions of action, and so on' (ibid: 34).[8] In general, therefore, what Wright suggests, correctly in my view, is that:

> While Giddens' general theory of action may run counter to the mechanistic and functionalist reasoning in the Marxist tradition, it is largely compatible with most of the *substantive* claims of both classical and contemporary Marxism. Many of the criticisms of functionalism and class reductionism which Giddens makes from his methodological standpoint are also accepted by many, if by no means all, contemporary Marxist theorists.
>
> (ibid: 34)

The decisive difference, however, is that Wright along with many theorists like him (including other theorists generally quite sympathetic to Giddens, e.g. Thrift, 1983, 1984; 1985a, as well as leading Marxist historical sociologists such as Anderson): (1) retain a wider view of the 'economic' than Giddens' model of historical materialism, and (2) see no reason to give up an evolutionary or an historical materialist approach.

For a theory of society to be evolutionary, according to Wright (1983:26), three conditions must hold:

1. a typology of social forms 'which *potentially* has some kind of directionality';
2. 'the probability of staying at the same level' in terms of this typology is 'greater than the probability of regressing';
3. 'there is a positive probability of moving to the next higher level', although such a probability need 'not be greater than the probability of regressing'. However, once such a movement has occurred, 'the probability of staying there must be greater than the probability of moving back'; thus, 'however weak the tendency towards development', the typology is 'sticky downward'.

In terms of such a model, in Wright's view, not only has Giddens not succeeded in eliminating the possibility of an evolutionary theory, but his own framework with its 'clear quantitative ordering along the dimension of time-space distanciation' (ibid: 29) must also be seen as such a model. Thus, the situation we face, according to Wright, is one in which there must be seen to exist two 'contending' evolutionary theories! In Wright's estimation, historical materialism must still be seen as the stronger theory, in that: (1) 'the dynamics centred in *property relations* impose *fundamental limits* on the overall process of social change'; (2) 'capacity for control' *depends upon* 'control over material resources'; (3) the 'motivational' basis for such development of the forces of production is plausible, and more plausible than in connection with 'authoritative resources' (ibid: 32–3, emphasis added). Against such suggestions, Giddens' point remains well made that societal development is less easily captured by simple evolutionary principles and far more open-ended than often previously suggested, but this is altogether a different matter from unequivocally establishing his own view of the merely 'contingent' relation between political and economic factors or his overall 'episodic' view.

Thus none of Giddens' arguments would seem decisive in seeing-off the *real* alternatives to his own view. Certainly his point is well taken that political as well as economic factors play an important role, but this is not effective in eliminating Marxist – or broader – notions of primacy of material factors or the tendency of these to develop, as suggested by Wright, Thrift or Anderson.

Empirical historical issues

If the arguments by which Giddens claims to have eliminated methodological alternatives to his own view remain contentious, many of the more straightforwardly theoretical and empirical arguments within his historical account can also be challenged. Obviously, it is beyond the scope of this chapter to confront such detailed points of criticism very fully. However a number of specific empirical and theoretical points do merit consideration for the general light they throw on Giddens' overall historical project.

Critics – including historians, but not only these – have remarked about the *ex cathedra* character of many of Giddens' historical assertions (e.g. Hechter, 1987), his lack of respect for (ordinary) chronology (Friedland, 1987), his lumping together in his societal typologies of very different kinds of societies and states, and different eras (Hirst, 1982; Smith, 1982a) and so on. If any historical macro-sociology on Giddens' scale and generality is to be possible, a certain amount of criticism of this kind is, of course, only to be expected. In Giddens' case, however, rather more than the 'usual' level of concern has been registered about the corners that have been cut. Compared with Michael Mann or Perry Anderson, who cover broadly similar ground to Giddens, and often impress historians and other specialists by their generalists' grasp of the historical sources, Giddens can be said to skate over the surface.

A general indication of the problem here are the numerous 'caveats' of the following kind that punctuate Giddens' account:

> Nor is it my purpose (at any point in this book) to enter into endless debates about the weightings of contributory factors to the rise of capitalism.
>
> (Giddens, 1981a: 134)

> I have already commented briefly about absolutism, I do not wish to enter more than marginally upon such a contested terrain.
>
> (Giddens, 1981a: 184)

As well as omissions highlighted in this way, there is also surprisingly little reference to feudalism, or to ancient society and slavery, both areas where a fuller consideration might have been expected in any historical account, especially one so much couched in terms of a debate with historical materialism. Such purely empirical omissions in Giddens' work obviously raise with redoubled force the question of his entitlement to decide on such issues as the various forms of the primacy thesis or his 'episodic charac-

terization' of change. Thus, this lends weight to the earlier suggestion that he does regard such questions as decidable on
methodological grounds, and that his accounts are often 'illustrative' rather than involving decisive 'testing'.

Undoubtedly, Giddens' response would be that his assessment
is based, not only on methodological argument, but also on a
general examination of the historical record and the conspicuous
lack of clear-cut laws. But we have already seen that what counts
as 'primacy' or 'lawlike' regularity in such interpretations is also a
contested matter. Thus the absence of detailed examination of key
historical transitions can be taken to considerably weaken
Giddens' case – particularly so given that his emphasis is so much
on the relative uniqueness of historical episodes. Whatever the
view ultimately taken on such general methodological issues,
because of such empirical omissions in Giddens' account, ambiguities undoubtedly remain as to what Giddens is or is not
claiming about crucial periods of transition between societal types.
Thus, it is the overall symbiotic relationship between capitalism
and the nation-state that has pride of place rather than any
detailed unravelling of the complex causalities involved in the *rise*
of capitalism. Concerning the transition from traditional empires
to modern European society, for instance, Giddens would appear
to follow something like Anderson's (or for that matter Weber's or
Collins') account that a 'concatenation of antiquity and feudalism'
was decisive. Likewise, on the social basis of 'absolutism' Giddens
again follows Anderson. Yet in neither of these cases does he
make any sustained attempt to enter the complex debates that
surround such highly controversial accounts (cf. Fulbrook and
Skocpol, 1984; Hindess and Hirst, 1975) or to explore the implications of Anderson's own continued attachment to historical
materialism (cf. also Runciman, 1980).

In these matters the contrast between Mann and Giddens is
instructive. Mann's broadest rhetorical questions are substantially
the same as Giddens':

> Of all the issues raised by sociological theory over the last two
> centuries, the most basic yet elusive is that of ultimate primacy
> or determinacy. Are there one or more core, decisive, ultimately
> determining elements, or keystones, of society? Or are human
> societies seamless webs spun of endless multicausal interactions
> in which there are no overall patterns? What are the major
> dimensions of social stratification? What are the most important
> determinants of social change?
>
> (Mann, 1986:3)

His general answers to these questions also echo Giddens:

> Economic power relations do not assert themselves as 'finally necessary in the last instance' (to quote Engels); history is not 'a discontinuous succession of modes of production' (to quote Balibar); class struggle is not 'the motor of history' (to quote Marx and Engels). Economic power relations, modes of production and social classes come and go in the historical record. In occasional world historical moments they decisively reorganize social life; usually they are important in conjunction with other power sources; occasionally they are decisively reorganized by them. The same can be said of all power sources, coming and going, weaving in and out of the historical record.
>
> (ibid:523)

Mann's overall model of social change in terms of four main sources of social power (his IEMP model, Figure 5.10), though not identical with Giddens' own fourfold model, overlaps significantly with this. My own view for what it's worth, however, is that Mann's categories are framed in an empirically more straightforward manner than Giddens' equivalents. (Is this perhaps because they are unencumbered by the need to carry the more diffuse links with a general theory of structuration theory that are involved in Giddens' approach?) For whatever reasons, Mann's general categories are perhaps rather more unambiguously applied in historical analysis. But far more important – and in this he is perhaps more true to his episodic view than Giddens – Mann gives far more attention to detailed testing of his historical accounts (albeit usually *not* comparative testing, since he is wary of the implications of intersocietal connections, and claims that there are simply too few genuinely autonomous cases). It should also be noted in this respect that Anderson (1986: 1405) has much praise for Mann's 'comprehensive concern' with what he calls the 'exact infrastructures' of each kind of power. And there is little doubt but that Mann's general framework is one that is proving highly productive.

At best also, Giddens' kind of framework promises the same kind of results. However, the same can also be said of Anderson's own approach, which in developing more systematic comparisons between multiple European routes also goes further than either Giddens or Mann with their concentration mainly on a single Western European route. Furthermore, even if heterodox in the eyes of many Marxists, Anderson's approach remains materialistic, and he also wants to insist that Mann's study can be seen above all as amounting to an 'organizational materialism', in which possibi-

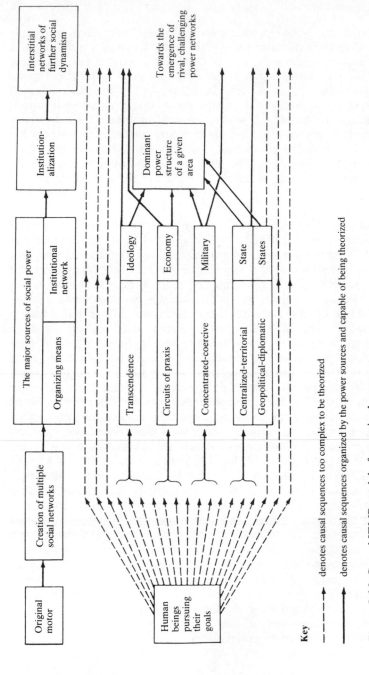

Figure 5.10 Causal IEMP model of organized power
Source: Mann, 1986: 29.

Key

- - - - - → denotes causal sequences too complex to be theorized

———→ denotes causal sequences organized by the power sources and capable of being theorized

lities of developmental models – substantially of Wright's kind – cannot be ruled out. Indeed, despite Mann's fondness, like Giddens', for portraying his own sociology – 'episodically' – as involving a 'radical break' with most previous approaches,[9] continuities, if some differences of emphasis, are also in evidence. Both Mann and Giddens offer more scope for rejection of a dichotomy between lawlike and non-lawlike accounts in sociology than they are prepared to admit. Thus, even if change occurs as the result of 'accidental conjectures', 'unevenly', or in a 'geographically shifty way', we find Mann asserting that:

1. stratification is the overall creation and distribution of power in society (Mann, 1986:10).
2. Human capacities for collective and distributive power have increased quantitatively throughout the historical period (ibid: 524).
3. Once invented, the major infrastructural techniques seem almost never to have disappeared from human practice, [resulting] in a broadly one-directional, one-dimensional development of power (ibid: 524).

Giddens as 'critical theory'

Where does all this leave Giddens' claim to have provided, as well as a new historical account, a new basis for 'critical theory'? Despite his different interpretation, Giddens' conception of 'historicity' draws on Marx. There are also obvious similarities between what Giddens refers to as his 'dialogical' model of critical theory and Habermas's more overtly neo-Marxian and evolutionary view of the implications of the inconstrained application of discursive will-formation in judgements of the effectiveness and legitimacy of economic and political institutions. For Habermas and Giddens alike a dialogical interaction between social science and lay actors in reaching such judgements is regarded as essential.[10] What Smith and Turner (1986) refer to as the 'moral seriousness' of Giddens' sociology is in no doubt. The difference is that for Giddens, there are no guarantees, only contingencies.

There is some truth in the comment that Giddens' overall account of the 'discursive constitution of territorial sovereignty and national historicity' (Friedland, 1987:41–2) provides no more than scant basis for any expectation that such a dialogic relation between social science and social movements might succeed when so much of that historical account suggests only a codified, malleable population. Thus, as Giddens puts it, 'the conditions of governability' may depend less on 'legitimacy', on the 'justifiability' of policies, than on mass acceptance of the daily routines shaped by administrative power, which he sees as replacing tradition within modern society (Giddens, 1985a: 322–3). For example, in this context 'anomie' (arising from widespread 'ontological insecurity' in modern societies) may be far more potent than class conflict in opening up the masses to social movements (e.g. nationalism or totalitarianism). However this is not to my mind the main problem since Giddens does not forget agency; on the contrary his model always retains the possibility of a two-way relation between dominators and those dominated, and in *Nation-State and Violence* and elsewhere he clearly wishes to be numbered among those who see very real gains from the existence of the 'new publics', that are one outcome of the spread of literacy and new forms of mass communications.

The more serious problem in my view arises from his reluctance to think through his 'developmental' models more systematically. Giddens suggests at one point that in many respects he is happy to be called a Weberian but states clearly that he wants to avoid Weber's relativism. Yet for all this, his restrictive view of a macrosociology, confined to analysis of episodes, would seem to leave his sociology in much the same boat as Weber's. As McClennan pointedly remarks:

> Giddens' wholesale dismissal of any version of social evolution and functional explanation thus chimes in well with postmodernist currents. Yet the very aspiration to provide a 'social theory' of any kind, especially one admitting of 'progressive' political implications, runs hard against deconstructionist logic.
> (McClennan, 1988: 117)

A related final point is that, although Giddens makes plain that a theory of 'the good life' ought to be a primary part of social theory (Giddens, 1981a: 248), and he is clearly prepared to use terms such as 'exploitation' and 'oppression', all this is undermined since he provides no normative theory 'capable of ordering the various goodness claims' that arise (Bertilsson, 1984: 352).

Conclusion

Notwithstanding the very great praise it has deservedly received, a central ambivalence exists in the reception of Giddens' work. A central ambivalence has also run through this commentary. On the one hand one might accept that in some respects approaches such as his point the way forward for historical sociology. This would be to recognize the undoubted value of:

- a focus on structure and agency;
- a multidimensional rather than a reductionist approach;
- an intersocietal and time-space perspective;
- aspects of his insistence on an 'episodic' characterization of historical change.

On the other hand, acceptance of the importance of accounts in terms of agency and structure, and characterization of historical change as 'multifactoral', requiring a time-space perspective for its analysis, and as, in part, 'episodic', 'uneven', etc. is far more widespread in sociology than Giddens suggests – including today many versions of Marxist and evolutionary theory. This is so, moreover, without such viewpoints leading to either the acceptance of a purely 'episodic' view of historical change or to an assumption that multifactoral causation must imply the rejection of all forms of theory that in any way continue to grant general primacy to one or more factors. Thus, Giddens can sometimes be accused of dealing in 'strawmen', of exaggerating the weaknesses of the approaches that he rejects while also hiding some of their potential strengths compared with his own. Nothing in my commentary has been intended as simply overturning Giddens' view, but rather as indicating that this is perhaps best regarded as representing only one significant view of historical change in structurationist terms. As suggested at the outset, I would see my critique as operating within the spirit of Giddens' work, but at the same time, as seeking to avoid a premature foreclosure on key issues. At a time when structuralism on the one hand and ethnomethodology and social phenomenology on the other threatened to lead to the fragmentation of sociology on a wholly new scale, Giddens' discussion of agency and structure was widely welcomed as a way of avoiding extremes. However, that it was received thus was more an indication of a prior acceptance within sociology of the general desirability of an explanatory mix of agency and structure than of any necessary acceptance of the entirety of Giddens' particular interpretation. Giddens' discussion of these issues must be seen as instructive rather than definitive. My suggestion has been that in his historical sociology, as elsewhere, Giddens has been perhaps overzealous in proposing the elimination of alternatives to his own approach. Much of his account of the method and empirical substance of structuration theory arises from 'debate' with the work of others and usually results in a fairly sharp distinction between this work and what can be incorporated within structuration theory. There is a widespread recognition that Giddens – a master in the distanciation of his work from the work of others in this respect – often proceeds by the construction of strawman of rival approaches to his own, employing in these matters, as Smith, 1982a, has put it, a 'ruthless dichotomous logic'. To have one's work singled out by Giddens has therefore often been something of a 'mixed blessing'. My critical comments have involved asking the question: Cannot a good deal of historical sociology, while operating in a broadly 'structurationist' way, be seen as justifiably reaching conclusions that are less restrictive than his? Whatever the verdict may be in this respect, however, the fact remains that the width of interpenetration of sociological theory and historical analysis achieved by Giddens is remarkable, and will continue to stimulate other sociologists, whether this be to develop his analysis or to take issue with him.

Notes

1 In Chapter Eight of the present volume Giddens indicates that he now also plans a fourth volume in his *Critique of Historical Materialism* (1981a), dealing with critical theory. Other relevant texts and articles by Giddens are: *Sociology, A Brief but Critical Introduction* (1982d), and his two volumes of collected essays, Giddens, 1982c; 1987a. His new general text *Sociology* (1989) arrived too late for any very full consideration.

2 For a fuller identification of the many works that might be considered part of such a broader 'reform movement' see Abrams, 1982; Skocpol, 1984; Eisenstadt, 1987.

3 A particularly perceptive paper, in many ways anticipating views such as Giddens', is Martins (1974). Apart from a discussion of the neglect of time in sociological theory, this article also stresses the importance of a focus on what Martins terms 'interphenomena', his term for inter-societal systems.

4 Whether, as suggested by Layder (1981), more integral features of Giddens' conception of 'structure' – e.g its formulation as a 'virtual' order, observable only in its instantiations – are the main problem in Giddens' approach cannot receive any very full treatment in this chapter (see also Chapter One). However, while the features identified by Layder are certainly related to an 'agency bias' in Giddens' work, and also inhibit the construction of more systematic institutional theories, the solution Layder proposes of a return to a 'dualism of structure and interaction' is, to my mind, to throw the baby out with the bathwater.

5 An important reason for suggesting this is that the 'duality of structure' is also a model of science, including both physical and social sciences. Thus, in post-empiricist terms, it can be argued that no ontological or epistemological argument can be decisive in prescribing the form in which accounts and theories may be advanced.

6 There are also complaints that there occurs 'a loss' in the treatment of

'the depth of human action as well' (Craib, 1986: 19; cf. Smith and Turner, 1986), a loss of depth in general in Giddens' work that Craib also sees as inherent in any attempt at synthesis such as Giddens'.

7   The generally restrictive viewpoint represented by Giddens' position can be further indicated by contrasting it with Martins' (1974) much more open-ended overview of the general implications of a new emphasis on 'time', or with the range of approaches that Abrams (1982) identifies as compatible with recognition of 'the mutual dependence of structure and agency'.

8   Bhaskar (1979), for example, regards Marx as quintessentially 'relational' in his treatment of agency and structure.

9   Not surprisingly, the major exception for Mann is Weber, whom he quotes with approval as follows:

> Even the assertion that social structures and the economy are 'functionally' related is a biased view, which cannot be justified as an historical generalization, if an unambiguous interdependence is assumed. For the forms of social action follow 'laws of their own' as we shall see time and time again, and even apart from this fact, they may in a given case always be co-determined by other than economic causes. However, at some point economic conditions tend to become causally important, and often decisive, for almost all social groups, and those which have major cultural significance; conversely, the economy is usually also influenced by the autonomous structure of social action within which it exists. *No significant generalization can be made as to when and how this will occur.*
>
> (Weber, 1922: 340, Mann's emphasis)

10 See also Bryant's discussion of Giddens' 'dialogical' model in the present volume, Chapter Seven.

159

Chapter six

Time and space in Giddens' social theory

John Urry

In this chapter it will be shown that Giddens has placed the analysis of time and space at the very heart of contemporary social theory. There is now a sense in which any such theory cannot be oblivious to the ways in which social activities are temporally and spatially organized. Giddens' various writings have authorized such a concern and provided some of the terms in which the debates are now cast. However, these concerns would probably have developed anyway since a wide variety of social processes would have forced the analyses of time and space onto the social theoretical agenda, in particular, through making clear just how historically and spatially specific is the concept of 'society'. It will be shown that Giddens' own formulations are highly frustrating, in the sense that they index some important issues but do not provide the basis for developing a really worked-out position. In particular, Giddens does not interrogate the concepts sufficiently. Time and space paradoxically remain for him as 'structural' concepts demonstrating not the duality of agency and structure but their dualism. No real account is provided as to how human agency is chronically implicated in the very structuring of time and space. They are viewed as essential to the context of human actions but as such they channel or structure such actions from the outside. By contrast, I shall argue that time and space should be seen as produced and producing, as contested and determined and as symbolically represented and structurally organized. Indeed, it will be argued that there are a variety of times and spaces, that they intrude at different levels within an adequate social theory and that Giddens' formulations do insufficient justice to the complexity of the resulting studies.

This chapter is organized into three sections. First, an exposition is provided of the key concepts that Giddens introduces to deal with the temporal and spatial ordering of human activity. Second, a number of deficiencies are outlined, particularly in relationship to the more general project to develop the theory of 'structuration'. Some claims are developed that attempt to remedy certain of the deficiencies in Giddens' study of time and space. Finally, there is a brief conclusion.

Exposition

Time and space first surfaced in Giddens' work in 1979 in a wide-ranging and innovative chapter in *Central Problems in Social Theory* (1979a, Ch. 6). In subsequent works many of the themes were to reappear, although the analysis of time rather than space has normally been more central. By the later 1980s he was devoting less explicit attention to matters of time and space. They were absolutely central themes in his writings in the early and mid-1980s, particularly within his major work *The Constitution of Society* (1984a). Detailed expositions of certain more specialized topics, such as Heidegger's philosophy of time, are also to be found in various chapters and articles written in the same period.

Thus, in a number of works Giddens attempts to demonstrate how time and space are absolutely central to social life. This has involved a quite profound attempt to redraw conventional academic boundaries, particularly between sociology, geography and history. Conventionally, sociology had been taken to be the study of social structures that are then seen as operating within the 'environments' of time and space. To the extent to which time was considered, this was something investigated *only* to the extent to which societies were thought to be undergoing change. By contrast, Giddens' theory of structuration treats time-space relations as constitutive features of social systems, implicated in the most stable as well as the rapidly changing aspects of social life (Giddens, 1981a: 30). Time-space is not, then, a contentless form in which objects exist but it expresses the very nature of what objects are (see Gregory, 1989: 7).

He is well aware that there is an extensive philosophical literature concerned with establishing just what can be understood by the notions of time and space. Surprisingly, he does not address the literature debated within geography, which has concerned itself with whether time and particularly space are to be viewed as absolutes, possessing their own natures or particularities, or whether they are merely relative, expressing the relations between objects or events (see Urry, 1985). Instead Heidegger is employed to demonstrate the irreducibly temporal character of human existence (Giddens, 1981a: 3ff). Heidegger (1978) repeatedly stressed in *Being and Time* that philosophy must return to the question of

'Being', something that had been obscured by the western preoccupation with epistemology. Central to Heidegger's ontology of Being was that of time, which expresses the nature of what subjects are. Human beings are fundamentally temporal; that they find their meaning in the temporal character of human existence. Being necessarily involves movement between or the 'mutual reaching out and opening up of future, past and present' (quoted in Giddens, 1981a: 32). However, the nature of time (and space) should not be confused with the ways in which it is conventionally measured, such as intervals or instants. Giddens' commentary on Heidegger ceases at this point and he sets out five ways in which, because of their temporal character, human subjects are different from material objects.

First, only humans live their lives in awareness of their own finitude, something reinforced by seeing the death of others and of how the dead make their influence felt upon the practices of the living. Second, the human agent is able to transcend the immediacy of sensory experience through both individual and collective forms of memory; through an immensely complex interpenetration of presence and absence. Third, human beings do not merely live in time but have an awareness of the passing of time, which is embodied within social institutions. Furthermore, some societies have developed an abstract concept of rational, measurable time, radically separable from the social activities that it appears to order (by contrast with the 'reversible time' of, say, the Nuer; discussed in Giddens, 1981a: 36). Fourth, the time-experience of humans cannot be grasped only at the level of the intentionality of consciousness but has also to be located within each person's unconscious in which past and present are indissolubly linked. And fifth, the movement of individuals through time (and space) is to be grasped via the interpenetration of presence and absence, which results from the location of the human body and the changing means of its interchange with the wider society. This particularly involves new communication and transportation technologies, such as writing, printing, telegraphs, telephones, railways, cars, jet planes, electronic transmitted information and so on. Each of these transform the intermingling of presence and absence, the forms by which memories are stored and weigh upon the present, and of the ways in which the long-term *durée* of major social institutions are drawn upon within contingent social acts. In order to investigate particularly these latter processes more fully, Giddens draws upon the work of Hägerstrand's 'time-geography'.

The starting point here is the routinized character of much daily life and the manner by which we can both characterize and explain it. Hägerstrand's approach is based upon identifying sources of constraint over human activity given by the nature of the body and of the physical contexts in which human action occurs (see Giddens, 1984a: 111ff.). There are six critical determinants here: the indivisibility and corporeality of the body; the movement of the life span towards death; time as a fundamentally scarce resource; the limited capability of human beings to participate in more than one task at once; the fact that movement in space is also movement in time; and the limited packing-capacity of time-space so that no two individuals can occupy the same point in space. These factors condition the webs of interaction formed by the trajectories of the daily, weekly, monthly and overall life paths of individuals in their interactions with each other. Individuals moving through time-space meet at 'stations' and comprise 'bundles'. Hägerstrand talks of individuals pursuing 'projects' that have to use the inherently limited resources of time and space. These consist of 'capability constraints', such as the need for regular sleep or food, and 'coupling constraints', which constrain activities that are undertaken with others at least for part of the time.

The result of these constraints is that daily conduct is not simply bounded by physical or geographical boundaries but by 'time-space walls on all sides' (quoted in Giddens, 1984a: 114). Obviously, though, there have been major changes in the character of such walls, particularly as a result of 'time-space convergence', namely the shrinking of distance in terms of the time taken to move from one location to another. The journey from the East Coast to the West Coast of the USA would take two years by foot, four months by stagecoach, four days by rail (in 1910) and five hours by air (ibid). Thus, at least for some people, the constraints on mobility and communication are much reduced, although Giddens also notes that such time-space convergence has a 'palpitating' character that may generate problems of appropriate 'coupling' (*sic*).

Giddens' reservations about the time-geography of Hägerstrand, that it has a defective conception of the individual, that it overly emphasizes constraint as opposed to enablement, and that it presents no developed theory of power, leads him to develop a partly alternative set of claims (see Giddens, 1984a:116-9; and Gregory, 1985 on Hägerstrand's work much more generally). These can best be understood through a number of novel concepts that present what Giddens terms 'sensitizing devices' (ibid: 326) by which to think through just how the life processes of individuals, including their daily, weekly and monthly paths, are linked to the *longue durée* of social institutions.

163

1. *Locale*: refers to the use of space to provide the settings within which interaction occurs. Locale is not to be described merely in terms of its physical properties but how it is used for human activities, how it provides for the contextuality of social life. Locales may range from a room, a house, a street corner, a shop floor, a town, a city, to the territory occupied by a nation-state.

2. *Regionalization*: locales are typically regionalized and these are critical in constituting contexts for interaction. Regionalization refers to the zoning of time-space in relationship to routinized social practices. Rooms in a house are, for example, zoned both spatially and temporally. There are obviously huge variations in such zoning between societies and over time. In the latter case, Giddens gives two examples: the development of powerful forms of artificial lighting that has dramatically expanded the potentialities of interaction settings within the 'night'-time; and the changing zoning of social activities as more 'specialized' rooms have developed in the houses occupied by the mass of the population (see Giddens, 1984a:119–22).

3. *Presence-availability*: the degree to which, and the forms through which, people are co-present within an individual's social milieu. Communities of high presence-availability include almost all societies up to a few hundred years ago. Necessary co-presence resulted from the corporeality of the agent, the limitations upon daily mobility because of existing transportation technology and the physical properties of space (see Giddens, 1984a:122–4). Presence-availability has been transformed in the past century or two. On the one hand, there has been the development of new transportation technologies and especially the separation of the media of communication from the media of transportation. The invention of the electromagnetic telegraph was a stunningly important invention that meant that communication between people who were spatially distant did not have to involve the literal mobility of the human body. And on the other hand, there has been an exceptional commodification of social life resulting from the development of money and its power to bridge distances and hence to bring about forms of interaction between people spatially distant.

4. *Front regions, back regions*: regionalization encloses zones of time-space that actors employ in the organizing the contextuality of action and the sustaining of ontological security. Contrary to Goffman, Giddens argues against the claim that it is only what happens backstage that is properly authentic (see Goffman, 1959; Giddens, 1984a:122–9). The sustaining of

ontological security could not be achieved if front regions were mere façades. Front regions are where much routinized daily life takes place, life in which people are often affectively involved. And backstage is not merely where the solitary individual prepares for his or her performance in a state of distracted anxiety, it is where people's basic security system is restored, particularly through dissipating the tensions derived from the demands of tight bodily and gestural control in other settings of day-to-day life.

5. *Time-space distanciation*: this refers to the processes by which societies are 'stretched' over shorter or longer spans of time and space. Such stretching reflects the fact that social activity increasingly depends upon interactions with those who are absent in time-space. From the eighteenth century onwards, society is increasingly organized via system integration rather than social integration through immediate presence-availability. Time-space stretching occurs via two sets of resources, the authoritative and the allocative and the particular forms and patterns in which power in each is stored (see Giddens, 1981a:92–7). Giddens emphasizes a number of factors that structure such patterns of time-space distanciation: the changing control of information, via the invention of writing, then printing and, recently, of electronic information, which separates presence in time from presence in space; the development of the city as a religious, ceremonial and commercial centre and power container; the development of the more modern urban form, as a created space through the commodification of land and the disruption of the ties of the city with nature; changes in transportation and communication technologies, especially the stagecoach system, the railway and particularly, the timetable, with its choreographing of activities in time-space, the car and lorry, the telegraph, the telephone, postal services and so on; the development of the territorially bounded nation-state with its expanded powers of documentation and surveillance; and the commodification of time so that it becomes separated from lived experience and actual social activities and appears like money as a universal and public measure (see Giddens, 1981a, Chs 4 and 6; 1985a, Ch. 7).

6. *Time-space edges*: this refers to the forms of contact or encounter between types of society organized according to different structural principles. This notion is part of a battery of concepts and arguments used by Giddens to emphasize the inadequacy of evolutionary theories based upon an endogenous or unfolding model of social change. Rather, it is essential to

investigate *inter*-societal systems, of the time-space edges by which, for example, a tribal society is confronted by a class-divided society. Episodes of social change also depend upon the emerging structures of world-time, that is the particular conjunctural phase of world development (see Giddens 1981a, Ch. 7; 1984a, Ch. 5).

7. *Power-containers*: time-span distanciation is integrally bound up with domination and power. There are, as we have seen, two types of resources, each of which is crucial to the possible forms of time-space distanciation and hence to the character of power in different types of society. Centrally important here is the storage capacity of different societies, particularly storage across time and space. In oral cultures human memory is virtually the sole repository of information storage. In class-divided societies it is, Giddens says, the city, especially with the development of writing, which becomes the primary crucible or container of power (see Giddens, 1981a, Ch. 5; 1984a, Ch. 6; Mumford, 1960). Particularly significant is how religious, military and administrative power is conjoined literally within the walls of the city to give physical shape to this crucible of power. By contrast, within capitalist societies it is the territorially bounded nation-state that is the dominant time-space container of power. The city loses its distinctiveness as such (as the walls come tumbling down!). A number of conditions have conspired to consolidate the unified administrative power of the nation-state: the mechanization of transportation and its separation from communication; the invention of printing and later of electronically recorded information, which expands the spatial power of the state; the enormous expansion of the documentary activities of the state, beginning with the keeping of official statistics; and the development of much more effective 'internal' pacification including in part the 'disciplinary power' of various total institutions (see Giddens, 1985a, Ch. 7).

These are, then, the array of concepts Giddens employs to make sense of time and space, concepts designed to problematize any easy assumption about the necessary coherence and closure of individual societies.

Critique

There is little doubt that Giddens' work represents a most important contribution to constructing a sociology of time. Less impressive is his contribution to current writing on space, to the degree to which the two topics can be separated. In the following I shall consider initially the limitations of his attempt to construct a sociology of time. I shall not here present an alternative formulation since this can be found in part elsewhere (Urry, 1985; 1987). Nor shall I say much about how these concerns relate to the rest of his theory since that is covered elsewhere in this book (and see the reviews in Thrift, 1985a; Gregory, 1989).

First of all, the status of time-geography in his argument is not made clear (for discussion, see Gregory, 1989). Once he has introduced some key notions it drops out of subsequent discussion. The analysis of time-space edges/distanciation is not obviously dependent upon time-geography. Indeed, such studies have been most significant in the analysis of 'place' (see, for example, Pred, 1985). And yet Giddens systematically avoids any analysis of place as such. This seems to be because, as we shall see later, the processes of time-space distanciation are seen as gradually over time eroding the importance of separate places, and indeed, contains a covert evolutionism (see Bagguley, 1984). Thus while many of the substantive analyses within time-geography have involved showing how changes in the structuring of time have affected the geography of place, this is precisely what Giddens does not examine. He implicitly operates with a modernization thesis couched in terms of a variety of time-saving processes that erode distance and transform presence-availability. As he says: 'Position upon an evolutionary scale becomes replaced by distance or proximity in time-space' (Giddens, 1981a:91; see also Bagguley, 1984, especially pp. 20–1).

Curiously though, not only does Giddens not consider the time-space organization of particular places, he also does not analyse the varying organization of time within different societies, except in two rather limited respects. These are, first, the reversible time of the Nuer, and second, the way in which in modern societies a rational and abstract time ('clock time') has developed through, especially, the generalization of the timetable. However, what he does not examine is how and especially why a different structuring of time is found in some industrial countries rather than others (for extensive discussion of such changes at the turn of the century see Kern, 1983). For example, the weekend is a time-zone implying also a particular organization of space (in, for example, the family home, or at church, or at sports events). It is more important as a time-zone in some countries than others. For example, in New Zealand until recently, shops did not open on Saturday or Sunday, much of the industrial labour force worked a set five-day week, and the weekend was mainly spent in the space of one's home with one's family. Two factors that appear to have produced such a zoning were the considerable strength of the labour movement to prevent the temporal flexibilization of the labour force; and the power of the churches to protect the sanctity of the weekend (that is, the family) from commercialization. One should also note the importance of the Judaic tradition in the artificial construction of the 'week' in the first place, this being the only important time-zone that is not derived from nature (see Colson, 1926).

Giddens seems to regard the organization of time as given, somehow embedded within the structuring of rules and resources that characterize modern societies in general. The organization of time is not seen to vary greatly between modern societies or to stem from the particular powers of social forces concerned to 'produce' different ways in which time may be zoned. In Britain the attempt in 1987 to transform the traditional Sunday by allowing all shops to open was met by furious opposition that was successful in sustaining Sunday as a distinct time-zone. The production and reproduction of zones of time, as with the production and reproduction of spaces or places, is unanalysed in Giddens' work. There is in effect what Mouzelis (1989) terms the dualism rather than the duality of structure.

A further aspect of time that is curiously absent is any serious examination of travel. Giddens does discuss some of the changes associated with new forms of transportation technology. But there is no examination of why people travel and hence why saving 'time', or covering more 'space', might be of 'interest' to people. One obvious reason for travel is for pleasure. It is a kind of liminal zone where some of the rules and restrictions of routine life are relaxed and replaced by different norms of behaviour, appropriate to being in the company of strangers. Travel is also pleasurable because it enables one to visit other places and people. Giddens' conception of human activity is too routinized, too boring, and it is difficult in his framework to conceptualize pleasure-producing activities such as travel, leisure, holiday-making, sightseeing, shopping, playing sport, visiting friends and so on. Much social activity indeed involves semi-routines in which travel is an important element. What are involved are disruptions to everyday patterns that are nevertheless recognizably acceptable. In travel and related activities, the maximizing of time-space distanciation may often be irrelevant. People want to transcend particular distances via specific forms of transportation. And often there are well-established connections between certain forms of travel and resulting social activities (travelling by train to English seaside resorts, by air to European holiday destinations, by car to theme parks and so on). Travel is an irreducibly social phenomenon rather than merely a means of transcending distance.

This can be seen by briefly considering the nineteenth-century development of the railway, certain aspects of which Giddens rightly stresses. However, his emphasis is all upon how the railway permitted phenomenal increase in time-space distanciation in mid- to late-nineteenth-century Britain. As a commentator at the time wrote: 'As distances were thus annihilated, the surface of our country would, as it were, shrivel in size until it became not much bigger than one immense city' (quoted Schivelbusch, 1986:34). But what this ignores is a whole series of further changes that the railway generated in transforming social practice and consciousness (see Schivelbusch, 1986; Mackenzie and Richards, 1986). These included: the bringing of machinery into the foreground of people's everyday experience outside the factory; new methods of building that were not mimetic of nature but involved its flattening and subduing; the perception of landscape as a swiftly passing series of framed panorama; the development of new public areas, the stations, which were a partially liminal space; the potential heightening of new forms of worker organization and consciousness; the provision of the basis for the growth of mass holidays; and the development of new ways of maintaining social distance as a result of people finding themselves with large numbers of strangers in the enclosed space of the railway carriage.

Thus, the effects of particular modes of overcoming what geographers term the 'friction of distance' are complex and by no means reducible to the *extension* of time-space distanciation. Giddens does not examine in any detail how time-space changes will often have the consequence, not merely of heightening distanciation, but also of helping to encourage resistance, opposition, pleasure, autonomy or a sense of deprivation. Giddens views many of these developments in a rather one-dimensional fashion, as in effect 'modernization' through distanciation. This he sees as becoming more and more extensive and is, first, making people more oriented to the future and to the further progressive extension of such distanciation; and second, gradually dissolving the significance of specific spaces or places as people are able to move through time and space in increasingly rapid fashion. On the first point, it is curious that Giddens barely addresses the concept of post-modernism and the way in which it involves a re-evaluation of past, present and future. In particular, there is a 'panic' about the future and a collapse of social historical projects and narratives that bound together the past, present and future (see Kroker and

Cook, 1986). Jameson talks of the headlong rush into pastiche rather than parody – a fragmented, arbitrary and wide-ranging juxtaposition of various kinds of signs that have little or no connection with anything substantive or real; time is fragmented into a series of 'perpetual presents' (see Jameson, 1984; Lash and Urry, 1987, Ch. 9). In this free-floating economy of the sign, those from the past have become exceptionally highly valued, constructing various kinds of nostalgia for a range of historical images (see Stauth and Turner, 1988). Post-modernism thus involves the disruption of the relationships between past and future in which signs from the former have become widespread, a process involving a 'new nostalgia', including the heritage industry, which poses immense problems for, amongst others, socialist parties that were organized around a particular historical project and narrative (see Edgar, 1987; Hewison, 1987). Frampton summarizes: 'We live in a paradoxical moment when, while we are perhaps more obsessed with history than ever before, we have, simultaneously, the feeling that a certain historical trajectory, or even for some, history itself, is coming to an end' (Frampton, 1988:51).

Thus, there are a number of features of contemporary western societies that involve transformed temporal relations that Giddens does not address, issues that involve treating time as more than a structural property of societies. I shall now consider some of the more spatial elements of his structurationist theory. Again it will be shown that these elements are not viewed in terms of their production and symbolization, but only in terms of the structural effects *upon* human action. This can be seen, first, by considering the notion of 'co-presence'. This often looks as though this is *the* most important element in his analysis of space and time. It seems essentially to consist of face-to-face interaction between people, albeit extended by letter, telegraph and telephone (and one may add answerphone; see, for example, Giddens, 1979a: 332ff.). Co-presence is thus viewed in a literal sense, of all those with whom actual interaction is or could take place. But what this ignores is what could be termed 'imaginary co-presence'. David Cooper once talked of one's 'imaginary family', the family that one carries around with one even when the actual members of it are geographically distant or even dead (Cooper, 1972). In terms of one's contemporary conduct it is often this imaginary family, its likes and dislikes, its jealousies and hostilities, its warmth and passions, that are of great emotional significance. Giddens, as we noted, talks of each person's unconscious linking together past and present. But he does not tie this together with his more general analysis of time-space relations, which are viewed in a resolutely literal manner. Indeed, in the case of space this seems to involve, as Gregory (1989) points out, his reconstruction of the programmatics of a spatial science.

Some related problems with his 'spatial' analyses can be seen with respect to a number of key distinctions employed, namely, frontstage/backstage, time-space regionalization between home and work and core/periphery. On the first of these some such separation conceived of at least in a partly spatial sense is treated as ontologically necessary for human existence and the main question is taken to be the way in which such a distinction enables human activity to be sustained. However, what this ignores are the more interesting sociological questions, namely: how such a division between front- and backstage varies within and between societies; how such a division is set up and sustained and the *degree* to which it depends upon a spatial separateness; how the resulting pattern may involve complex interconnections between a number of determinants, viz capital accumulation, land markets, regimes of surveillance, regimes of pleasure and so on; and how such a division may be struggled for or struggled against by individuals or larger-scale social forces. Elsewhere it has been shown how the mass media has served to undermine the information systems that are specific to particular social groups. Such systems had, in a sense, constituted a repository of meanings 'backstage' and they were separate from how that group acted 'frontstage'. Television has, however, made all backstages public property and hence served to undermine such a demarcation (see for further detail, Lash and Urry, 1987:297–8).

Similar points can also be made with regard to the process of time-space regionalization between 'home' and 'work'. Giddens treats this as a factual or structural characteristic of certain types of society. Such a division and the resulting allocation of women to the former and men to the latter is seen as being inscribed within the structuring of capitalist societies. However, this is not an appropriate way of understanding such a division. Rather, the pattern should be seen as resulting from the intersection between new forms of social organization, viz factories and large urban settlements, *and* collective struggles, especially by male workers to exclude women from the workplace and force them back *into* a much more domesticated sphere of the home (see Walby, 1986, for extensive documentation of this). After all, the earliest factory workers were women textile workers and there was a considerable intermingling of the relations of paid work and of domestic/familial organization. Time-space regionalization is not something that should be taken as fixed and given.

171

This can also be clearly seen in the main distinction Giddens employs to characterize larger-scale time-space regionalization, namely, that of core and periphery. He seems to regard this division as given, fixed and structural (paralleling what he says about the south/north divide). It is not something that historically changes, nor is the division viewed as being more-or-less important depending upon a number of complex determinants. What is particularly strange is that there is no discussion of the literature that has particularly addressed and confronted the notion of a fixed, ahistorical and functional core/periphery, namely that of 'restructuring' (see for the clearest account, Massey, 1984; Bagguley *et al.*, 1989). In this alternative approach it is argued, first, that there are a number of patterns by which industries come to be sociospatially reorganized and core/periphery is most definitely not the only pattern. Second, it is shown that the pattern actually adopted within a given industrial sector is the result of complex determinants, including in part at least the role of the organization of labour as a collective agent. Third, the resulting social and spatial organization within a given society is highly complex, since it depends upon the overlapping effect of the spatial division of labour found within each of the industrial sectors that have been present. And finally, in more recent restructuring literature, it is demonstrated that there are forms of organization within civil society, particularly those of gender relations, which are not reducible to the patterns of industrial restructuring but nevertheless are centrally important to the structuring of social relations within particular places (see, for much more detail, Bagguley *et al.*, 1989).

And that brings us back to the point noted earlier, namely that Giddens really says nothing about place as opposed to space. When he talks of place as such it is seen as given or fixed rather than socially constructed and contested. Locale is viewed as the context for action rather than as the outcome of action, particularly that resulting from what one can term 'collective knowledgeability'. Giddens' argument is, if anything, reductionist (as well as partly evolutionist) since he emphasizes with particular force the commodification of space, that space becomes entirely 'created' through the commodification of time. As Marx argued, the development of capitalist relations had the effect of overcoming spatial barriers. However, what both Marx and Giddens ignore is that this annihilation can only be achieved through the production of new, fixed and relatively immobile spatial configurations. As Harvey says: 'spatial organisation is necessary in order to overcome space' (Harvey, 1985: 145). There are a number of important points to note about such old and new forms of spatial organization. First, people are highly attached to different spaces – the threatened destruction of which is often bitterly resisted. Much politics is, in effect, a defence of existing spatial arrangements, such as a particular neighbourhood, a given town centre, a factory located within a community, an unspoilt landscape and so on. Such a politics stems from the fact that 'space' comprises a set of physical and built forms that conveys a plethora of signs and meanings to observers. Such meanings although often ambiguous are none the less important in their effects. Spaces thus are redolent with signs and a variety of possible meanings. There is to put it simply a politics of landscapes and townscapes – a politics of space (see Daniels and Cosgrove 1988:7).

Second, even the apparently simple, two-dimensional spaces found on maps are social. This is so both in the sense that they 'speak' about the social world and because they result from particular social and political forces. Maps are thus to be seen, not primarily as inert records of townscapes or landscapes, but as discourses, as ways of conceiving, articulating and structuring the human world that are biased towards, promoted by and exert influence upon particular sets of social relations (see Harley, 1988: especially pp. 278–80). Maps may be almost as important as timetables, as involving forms of control, surveillance and the determination of property through space, central in fact to the extension of time-space distanciation. Harley talks of maps contributing to the development of 'space-discipline', which parallels the development of capitalist 'time-discipline' (see Harley, 1988:285; Landes, 1983). Maps, moreover, have the effect of 'desocializing' territory, fostering the notion of a socially empty space when in fact they are discourses about the social and involve the language of social power.

Third, one crucial point about places is that they are often symbolized by particular features of the built environment. They stand for that particular place (such as King's College Chapel in Cambridge, Canterbury Cathedral, the Royal Pavilion in Brighton, the Ford works in Dagenham and so on). Such individual buildings connote a range of social, historical and spatial features. Buildings stand for that particular place – they are in a sense *the* place and help to construct what people feel and think about it. Such buildings are almost sacred (even when they are not literally so), so that it would be unimaginable for them to be destroyed. To demolish such a building would be, symbolically, to demolish the whole place.

Fourth, places are important as repositories of knowledge. It is important to consider the changing availability of knowledge and the manner in which certain kinds of place either limit what can be known or permit knowledge to be enhanced. There are a number of senses though in which a social group can be said not to have 'knowledge': first, the knowledge that is literally unknown because of the group's position in time and space; second, there is that knowledge that a group cannot understand; third, there is knowledge that is undiscussed because the social world is taken for granted; and fourth, there is knowledge that is concealed or hidden because of the distorted character of dominant social relations (see Thrift, 1985b). In order to decipher the 'geography of knowledge', what needs to be undertaken is an analysis of just how different places affect these different forms of 'unknowing'. And this involves two breaks with Giddens' project. On the one hand, knowledge is not seen simply in terms of surveillance but also in terms of its capacity to empower social groups. And on the other hand, cities are to be seen as not simply constraining but as also enabling, to use Giddens' terminology. Cities may permit the rapid diffusion of all sorts of knowledge often of a quite disruptive sort, including new technologies (see Gregory, 1989: 12), new social and political beliefs (see Lane, 1982), or new forms of professionalization strategy (see Lash and Urry, 1987, Ch. 6).

Conclusion

There are therefore a range of issues concerned with the analysis of, especially, space that Giddens fails to address. Without considering the more philosophical issues involved here (see Urry, 1985, for my views thereon), it should be noted that there is really no 'space' as such – only different spaces. This is because there are at least three different levels at which space (and time) can be seen as intruding into social analysis. First, empirical events are distributed in space and time. Second, social entities are built around particular spatial and temporal structures, including the forms of stretching across space and time. And third, social entities are temporally and spatially interrelated with each other, interrelationships of immense complexity over time and across space. Giddens' principal concept of 'time-space distanciation' is too blunt an instrument to capture the temporal and spatial interdependencies between social entities, which possess immense and yet historically and spatially contingent causal powers.

Giddens' thesis also fails to capture important features of contemporary social development. It will be remembered that he maintains that in each type of society there is a single power container, the city in class-divided societies and the nation-state in capitalist societies. Both of these raise problems. On the first, although he correctly notes how cities in different kinds of society differ, he seems to treat them entirely in terms of their power-containing capacity. So although he also asserts that the analysis of urbanism should occupy a central position in any empirical programme deriving from 'structurationism', he in fact ignores such research that has been undertaken on the changing functions of the city. Recently, it has been asserted that many cities have become not centres of production but increasingly centres of consumption (see Zukin, 1988). As such they may be centres of important resources, but not the authoritative or allocative resources that Giddens concentrates upon, but of what could be called symbolic resources of 'distinction' or 'status' (see Bourdieu, 1984; Turner, B., 1988; Zukin, 1988).

On the second point, he does not show just why the nation-state will continue to be the dominant power container in the future. He notes after all extraordinary increases in time-space distanciation of a *supra*-national sort which would seem on the face of it to suggest that the power container of the nation-state has perhaps had its day. Elsewhere I have argued more generally that contemporary capitalist national societies are being dislocated or disorganized, from 'above' via internationalization, from 'below' via decentralization and from 'within' via the growth of a powerful middle class (see Lash and Urry, 1987). In such a dramatic transformation of the previously organized capitalist societies, it is hard to see why the organization of time and space means that the nation-state will remain as *the* dominant power container in disorganized capitalist societies.

Giddens' opening up of the issues of time and space within social research has thus revealed a veritable Pandora's box of topics of investigation. But his own formulations are too blunt and insufficiently integrated with the other supposed characteristics of structurationism to provide that much assistance in unravelling the paths of time and space travelled by knowledgeable social actors.

Chapter seven

The dialogical model of applied sociology

Christopher G.A. Bryant

Introduction

One one thing at least, all commentators on Giddens can agree; viz, that he is an extraordinarily prolific writer. This being so it may seem perverse to devote a chapter to a dimension of his work, the applied, that he has never seen fit to develop systematically himself. This omission is itself surprising. Giddens began his theoretical formation by critically appropriating the 'classical' contributions of Marx, Durkheim, Weber, Simmel and others. For the most part these writers intended their social science to be of practical relevance to the issues of the age. Indeed a great deal of what they are about can be brought out by discussing them under the heading of 'sociology in action' (Bryant, 1976). But where the author of *The Rules of Sociological Method* asks rhetorically, 'Why strive for knowledge of reality, if this knowledge cannot serve us in life?', the author of *The New Rules of Sociological Method* seems unwilling to put so direct a question (Durkheim, 1895:48). This is unfortunate because the problem of how to make sociology apply is very much a live one and Giddens' version of a critical sociology is highly relevant to it.

On both sides of the Atlantic, the 1960s and 1970s saw a big expansion of social research funded from public sources in general expectations of an applied pay-off. In the mid- to late 1970s expansive hopes gave way, as Giddens himself acknowledges, to disappointment, disillusionment, even recriminations, at the apparently limited application, actual and potential, of much of the research completed (Giddens, 1987b:45). Analysis and empirical research in America have related this to the inadequacies of the research and the inadequacies of the users – but also to the multiple inputs to most decision making and policy formation of which research is but one, and the limited tractability of many of the problems addressed. Out of this reassessment a new way forward is

176

emerging. The deficiencies of one erstwhile popular model for applied research, the social engineering model, are now widely recognized, and the deficiencies of perhaps its most trumpeted successor, the enlightenment model, are also becoming plainer. What seems now to be required is what could be called the interactive model. In America, Scott and Shore (1979), Lindblom and Cohen (1979), Weiss with Bucuvalas (1980) and others have done enough to suggest that development of an interactive model is both necessary and possible. One of the as yet unremarked, but potentially very valuable, features of Giddens' theory of structuration is the support it can lend it. In particular, Giddens' theory of structuration is allied to a model of social science that is consistent with interactive application in a way in which the model of science favoured by those who first identified interactive application is not. He has a consistency that they do not have.

I shall proceed first by outlining the characteristics of the social engineering and enlightenment models and then by indicating how and why the interactive model overcomes some of their deficiencies. This is a journey already taken by Bulmer (1982) but my route departs from his not just in detail and nuance but also in its approach to enlightenment and interaction. I shall then point up the consistency between Giddens' theory of structuration and the interactive model of applied sociology and I shall draw attention to a number of texts in which he offers relevant comment including one in which he advocates a 'dialogical model' of the practical implications of sociology (Giddens, 1987d:46–7).

Engineering and enlightenment

The social engineering model depends upon sharp distinctions between pure and applied research and between existential and normative statements. It also lends itself to what the 1971 Rothschild report on government research and development in the natural sciences called the customer–contractor principle (Rothschild, 1971). The customer or client wants information about, or an analysis of, something, and the sociologist is contracted to provide it. The customer has an objective and the sociologist helps to engineer it by using expertise in research design and techniques to obtain relevant information and by drawing upon the stock of sociological knowledge in order to advise how it might best be achieved. Third parties, perhaps even the public at large, are just there to be manipulated. This model sometimes works in practice. Durkheim's contributions to teacher training served the cause of the French Third Republic and represent a kind of cultural engineering. The Hawthorne experiments, conducted in the early 1930s by Mayo and his colleagues for the Western Electric Company in Cicero, near Chicago, in order to help the company raise worker productivity, provide another much-discussed example (Roethlisburger and Dickson, 1939). But then again the engineering model often does not work. In particular, the client-users of research are often inadequately specified; where they are specified, or have indeed contracted the research, they often do not know what they want (they may even have commissioned the research to avoid having to decide what they want); sociological research is never incontestable in the way the engineering model supposes in so far as values are built into all terminologies and methodologies: and third parties seldom prove totally predictable. At best the engineering model is managerialist: at worst it is irrelevant.

Given the limitations of the engineering model, it is not surprising that many sociologists have preferred the enlightenment model. This is how Janowitz describes it:

> The enlightenment model assumes the overriding importance of the social context, and focuses on developing various types of knowledge that can be utilized by policy-makers and professions. While it seeks specific answers its emphasis is on creating the intellectual conditions for problem solving ... The consequence of effective sociological inquiry is to contribute to political freedom and social voluntarism by weakening myths, refuting distortions, and preventing an imbalanced view of social reality from dominating collective decisions.
>
> (Janowitz, 1972: 5–6)

Despite its name, which calls to mind the negative philosophy of the eighteenth century, the enlightenment model repeats some of the features of the positive philosophy of nineteenth-century France. The sociologist brings order where there was confusion, provides scientific knowledge where there was myth, shows the need to adjust to changed circumstances where there was resistance. This model, too, sometimes works in practice. Wherever shifts in public opinion occur, sociological studies have usually made some contribution. Attitudes towards minorities – ethnic, religious, sexual or whatever – as well as the latter's own estimations of their place and prospects, are a case in point. The same is true of at least one majority – women. The attractive aspect of the enlightenment model is that it promises service to all, not just those in positions of authority or management; the unattractive features are the touch of elitism – the sociologist brings light to the benighted – and the conceit – the sociologist announces and the world responds. Well, maybe sometimes it does; but all too often it does not – and the problem of how to make sociology apply still remains.

Interaction

The attraction of the interactive model is not that it guarantees success in circumstances in which the engineering and enlightenment models lead to failure, but rather that it provides a much more sophisticated account of what is involved in making sociology apply, regard for which can only be to the benefit of all parties. Although its development has been largely an American affair, Carol Weiss, one of the key figures involved, acknowledges a seminal paper by a Briton, Donnison, on 'Research for Policy' (1972). (Donnison, interestingly, begins with a reference to a classic study by Hägerstrand (1953), the Swedish geographer who remained largely unknown to social scientists in Britain and America until Giddens took him up (Donnison, 1972:45).)

Donnison argues that the linear model of science application favoured by Rothschild, which posits a movement from pure research to applied research and development, oversimplifies even when used in connection with the natural sciences and technology for which it was intended, and is of no help at all when used with the social sciences and social policy. Instead of this 'lazy-minded' dichotomy, Dainton (1971) used the trichotomy of basic, strategic and tactical research, but this, Donnison continues, is still grossly insensitive to the complexities of application in the social sciences. Using the examples of income maintenance and distribution, town and country planning and rent regulation, Donnison shows how policy-oriented research impacts depend on the interpenetration of four fields.

> The four fields are: that of *politics* where new policies are approved, major resource allocations made, powers conferred and decisions formally registered; the field of relevant *technologies*, mechanical and social; the field of relevant professional, commercial and administrative *practice* where present policies and programmes are carried out, and new ones are formulated and tried out, and the field of *research* in which – as in the other three – the people interested in social security, education (or whatever it may be) are part of a much larger community concerned with other things. Meanwhile those engaged in all four of these fields participate in the larger universe of voters,

179

taxpayers, clients of the policies in question and members of
political movements, which together constitutes public opinion.

(Donnison, 1972: 52)

How the four fields connect will vary from case to case. This is
Donnison's briefest example:

> in response to demands coming mainly from *practitioners* in
> central and local government, a Planning Advisory Group was
> appointed to reappraise British town and country planning
> practice, and its recommendations, published in 1965, were
> later incorporated by the *politicians* in the Town and Country
> Planning Act of 1968. This measure introduced new concepts
> and procedures – 'structure plans', 'action plans', 'subject
> plans', and so on – calling for new work and skills in the field of
> *practice* which coincided with the dissemination of computers,
> contributed by the *technologists*, and consequential improve-
> ments in the gathering and analysis of data. These demands and
> opportunities promoted new *research* on the analysis of urban
> and regional development which, drawing on other technolo-
> gies, furnished *practitioners* with new ideas and analytical
> methods.

(ibid: 53)

Donnison concludes that 'Things go better once it is understood
that in policy studies, people from each of these fields (politics,
technology, practice and research) should meet on an equal
footing. Each has different skills and experience to offer, and each
can learn more than he teaches' (ibid: 66). Pieties apart, it is not
hard to see why Weiss should have regarded Donnison as a source
for the development of the interactive model.

Before turning to Weiss's version of the interactive model, it is
worth considering briefly books by Scott and Shore and by Lindblom and Cohen, both published in 1979. Scott and Shore give
their book the disturbing title *Why Sociology Does Not Apply*. It is
based on an examination of the use made of sociology in the formation at the federal level of public policy on domestic affairs in the
United States. The examples they discuss include recent Presi-
dential Commissions on Law Enforcement and Criminal Justice
(1968), the Causes and Prevention of Violence (1969), Obscenity
and Pornography (1970) and Population Growth and the
American Future (1972). From these and many other cases they
conclude that:

> First, a great deal of sociological research done for application
> carries no discernible policy implications of any kind; second, in

instances where it does, sociology has served as the basis for formulating policy recommendations, less often the basis of enacted policy; and third, most of the recommendations ... were rejected by policy-making bodies of government as *impractical or politically unfeasible.*

(Scott and Shore, 1979: 33)

One reason for this is the determination of most 'applied' researchers first to locate their work within disciplinary concerns and only afterwards to cast around for applications. Another is their subscription to a conception of scientific planning, which is respected in the academy but inappropriate in the national polity. This conception involves:

a commitment to rationality, a willingness to be persuaded by scientific fact and to be guided by reason, a basic commitment to devise policies based upon scientific determination of what is expedient, [and] a conscious decision to undertake regular assessment and evaluation of programs and to agree to be guided by the results.

(ibid: 63)

It leads to two difficulties. First, sociologists encounter technical problems in the determination of rational policy that they cannot always overcome. Second, policy making in America at the national level is about the ability of politicians to get re-elected and that in turn depends upon the satisfaction of constituencies with different, and sometimes incompatible, interests and expectations. There is, then, a basic contradiction between sociologists who strive to make their argumentation as rational, coherent and systematic as possible and a society in which reason, coherence and systematicity have only a limited currency or relevance.

What should sociologists do about this? In the name of political realism, Scott and Shore propose that they should concentrate on politically tractable variables that have a bearing on possible marginal additions or revisions to policy, incrementalism being the political rule except in moments of national crisis. This proposal has the drawback, however, that its open adoption would threaten a drastic reduction, not only in the massive public funding of social research, which is largely dispensed in the mistaken belief that it will lead to knowledge usable in policy formation, but also in the accompanying university postgraduate programmes, which tend to render their products insensitive to the only kinds of social research that public policy makers are capable of using.

Scott and Shore's idea of making sociology apply is confined to expert advice to the policy maker. Perhaps a better response to the failures they uncover would be to worry less about Washington and more about everywhere else, less about influencing policy directly through the policy makers and more about influencing it indirectly through the constituencies to which politicians look for votes, and less about exerting their influence from the top down and more about building it from the bottom up.

Scott and Shore conclude that sociology does not apply, or at least has not applied, because sociologists are naive about what is involved in making it apply. They are less sanguine than Donnison, however, that greater awareness of what is involved will enable them to do better. Their weariness is easier to understand in the face of Lindblom and Cohen's crudely pragmatic account of usable knowledge. Lindblom and Cohen are interested in social problem solving. 'By social problem solving, [they] mean processes that are thought to eventuate in outcomes that by some standard are an improvement on the previously existing situation, or are presumed so to eventuate, or are conceived of as offering some possibility to so eventuate' (Lindblom and Cohen, 1979:40). Any individual or collective subject having to do something has a problem in so far as some kind, any kind, of improvement in a previously existing situation is sought. What the subject does constitutes a solution. All kinds of processes, from general elections to consulting *Which?* or tossing a coin, yield solutions; all kinds of acts from discovering America to inventing co-ops or inviting the mayor to open the fête constitute solutions. In the social construction of problems and solutions ('interactive problem solving'), what place is there for professional social inquiry ('PSI') or professional social inquirers ('pPSI')? Lindblom and Cohen are not sure. Inputs to the interactive problem-solving process are only authoritative in so far as they are deemed to warrant action to get something done, getting it done being a solution. Unfortunately, PSI seldom warrants anything, at least on its own, such are the awkward ways of both social science and the social world, but they do suggest that pPSI might learn how better to insinuate themselves (improve the PSI input) in interactive problem solving by elaborating their own relationship to it into a research agenda.

Lindblom and Cohen are hard to take in so far as they ignore the special claims to knowledge that social scientists make in doing social science. Instead they place decision takers and policy makers at the centre of their analysis. Usable knowledge is the knowledge the latter use, and PSI is but a minor contributant to it. No doubt the rarity with which social scientists speak with one voice about anything only reinforces the inclination of decision takers and policy makers to pick and choose what they heed. In sum, Lindblom and Cohen seem to condone a sort of take-it-or-leave-it approach to social science that few social scientists could ever accept. Certainly Donnison, largely looking forward, does not expect it, and Scott and Shore, largely looking back, never submit to it. But Lindblom and Cohen can also be read as trying to force social scientists to consider realistically both their place in interactive problem solving, and the place of social scientific knowledge in what we would now call practical reasoning. Certainly less extreme writers, like Weiss and Bucuvalas (1980), agree with their suggestion that:

> the principal impact of policy-oriented studies, say, on inflation, race conflict, deviance, or foreign policy – including those specifically designed to advise a specific policy maker at a particular time – is through their contribution to a cumulating set of incentives for a general reconsideration by policy makers of their decision-making framework, their operating political or social philosophy, or their ideology.
>
> (Lindblom and Cohen, 1979:5–6)

Donnison, Scott and Shore, and Lindblom and Cohen have paved the way for an interactive model of applied sociology. It is Weiss who has done most to set out what it consists of. The basic idea was first introduced, albeit briefly, in a paper in 1979. Like Lindblom and Cohen, she places decision takers and policy makers at the centre of her account:

> Those engaged in developing policy seek information not only from social scientists but from a variety of sources – administrators, practitioners, politicians, planners, journalists, clients, interest groups, aides, friends, and social scientists, too. The process is not one of linear order from social research to decision but a disorderly set of interconnections and back-and-forthness that defies neat diagrams.
>
> (Weiss, 1979: 35)

Two key subsequent publications suggest possibilities of order where first there has seemed only disorder. One is a large empirical study; the other a paper on 'Ideology, interests and information' (Weiss and Bucuvalas, 1980; Weiss, 1983).

Social Science Research and Decision-Making (Weiss with Bucuvalas, 1980) reports a major empirical study of the usefulness of social researches on mental health as perceived by 51 officers of the federal Alcohol, Drug Abuse and Mental Health Administration and three bodies responsible to it, and 104 senior officers in state and local mental health agencies. The authors recognized that their respondents have to contend with three sets of expectations; first, as managers they must respect executive norms for getting things done; second, as professionals in fields that lay claim to a scientific basis, they have to keep abreast of relevant research; third, as senior members of bureaucratic organizations, they have to remain alert to the political need to protect and promote their agencies, programmes, budgets and careers. Against this background, Weiss with Bucuvalas: 'hypothesised that decision makers would consider social science research studies more useful to the extent that studies (a) provided implementable conclusions; (b) were methodologically competent; and (c) conformed with users' beliefs and agency policy' (Weiss with Bucuvalas, 1980:69).

Each respondent was assigned two abstracts of researches on topics of relevance to his or her responsibilities. Respondents rated the abstracts on 129 descriptors. Factor analysis of the ratings yielded three types of factor.

> First, there is relevance to issues being considered by one's office (and its related items of priority of the topic and timeliness). Second, there are two factors that provide a basis for trust in a research study. These are Research Quality, which gauges the soundness of a study according to the canons of science, and Conformity with User Expectations, which subjects study results to the test of experience. Third, there are two factors that provide direction. Action Orientation, with its characteristics of explicitness and practicality, offers guidance for incremental change within existing programs. Challenge to the Status Quo, which questions intellectual, organizational, and political perspectives, points towards fundamental change.
>
> (ibid: 80)

Weiss with Bucuvalas then used multiple regression: 'To test the effects of the research characteristics on decision makers' judgments of the usefulness of research studies' (ibid: 83). They found that the multiple demands upon decision makers do indeed prompt them to apply multiple standards in their assessment of research usefulness. First, of course, studies have to be relevant. Of the other four factors involved, however, it is notable that the two scientific merit factors count for more than the two practical utility factors. In connection with practical utility, it proved necessary to distinguish between the value and policy positions preferred by the decision makers and those adopted by their agencies – the former often welcoming challenges to a status quo with which they disagreed.

The authors also set up 100 interviews with researchers who had

184

been funded by the federal agencies concerned and members of their research review committees. Both groups made judgements of the usefulness of research broadly similar to those made by the decision makers, although the researchers expressed doubt as to whether decision makers really take much notice of research. Finally Weiss *cum al.* invited respondents in all five groups to comment on selected hypotheses about obstacles to the use of research. Obstacles identified included the unwillingness of decision makers to rely on research that runs counter to their own beliefs or the philosophies of their agencies, the political nature of decision making, the insensitivity of scientists (partly because of different, disciplinary, career imperatives in the universities), inadequate communication between decision makers and researchers (despite the best efforts of government research programme officers) and the inability of decision makers to define and specify their research needs.

In conclusion, Weiss with Bucuvalas emphasize that decision makers look to research as much for perspectives, generalizations and concepts that afford them help in defining what it is they are doing as they do for data; diffuse gains in understanding are often as important to them as the acquisition of specific, immediately implementable, findings. In consequence, 'Social science research formulated and carried out by external investigators seems likely to have its effects by modifying the climate of informed opinion' (Weiss with Bucuvalas, 1980:264).

Interestingly, Tijssen (1988), using a research design explicitly derived from Weiss with Bucuvalas, reached broadly similar conclusions in her inquiry into how central and local board members of the Royal Dutch Medical Association assess the usefulness of social science research.

In one way, health professionals may be atypical research utilizers. Given that their practice is supposed to have a scientific basis, one would expect them to be more attentive to research than are decision makers in fields for which no such claims are made. In another respect, however, they may be more typical. It is to technical proficiency in research design and execution, and in data analysis, that they look when establishing the scientific credentials of researchers, but it is not to research findings as such but rather to theoretical perspectives and concepts that they turn when revising their practice and their understanding of that practice, and these theories and concepts, as often as not, owe nothing in their formation to the technical skills of those who convey them. It is the display of technique that wins the confidence of the research user; it is theories and concepts that the user most often uses.

In a subsequent paper, Weiss introduces further elements of order into a process she had formerly described as disorderly. She holds 'that the public policy positions taken by policy actors are the resultant of three sets of forces: their ideologies, their interests (e.g., in power, reputation, financial reward) and the information they have' and of these the third, to which social science is but one contributant, is usually outweighed by the first two, which 'carry higher emotional loadings' (Weiss, 1983: 221, 220). She outlines the interaction of ideology, interests and information within what she calls the 'I-I-I framework': interaction is deemed to be 'constant and iterative, and policy makers work out the specification of their ideologies and interests in conjunction with their processing of information' (ibid: 229). She discusses relations between research and prior information, ideology and interests; and between ideology and interests; and she stresses that '*The distribution of power determines WHOSE ideology, interests and information will be dominant*' (ibid: 239; original italics).

The 'organizing construct' of the I-I-I framework enables Weiss to treat systematically matters that hitherto had seemed haphazard. Its adoption also promises to help social scientists identify more effectively appropriate points of entry into relations between the three Is whatever the circumstances they have to contend with. Yet for all that, her conclusions are both low key and shrewd. She warns researchers to be modest in their expectations of influence and she offers advice to all concerned on research choice, which goes against the grain of Thatcherite thinking about the value of academic research.

> One suggestion to those who propose, fund, and do policy relevant research is not to spend a heavy share of research money and time on studies designed to answer immediate policy problems. To do such work usefully usually requires accepting the conceptual and practical constraints of government sponsors – that is, limiting research to the variables that the funding bureau has the authority to manipulate and adopting the premises that currently guide the agency's action. If, in fact, even such practically oriented research is likely to run into entanglements with interests and ideologies both inside and outside the bureau, we may serve government better by broadening the scope of the research we do and contributing more critical perspectives on agency activities. Although such research will not have immediate impact, it probably represents a wiser investment of social science resources. And when alignments of ideology and interests make the information relevant

to policy making, the contribution may prove to be significant.
(Weiss, 1983: 241–2)

This may sound like a return to the enlightenment model but it is not. Weiss has abandoned use of the elevated term 'enlightenment' in favour of a modification of Shapley's rather less dignified 'knowledge creep' (ibid: 220). She has no illusions about the capacity of social scientists to enlighten anyone.

Scott and Shore claimed that sociology has not applied because sociologists have failed to place decision takers and policy makers at the centre of their analyses. I have suggested (p. 182) that Scott and Shore were wrong to identify application with influence upon top people; relations between sociologists and anyone other than top people seem hardly to have entered their thinking, yet they can be significant even in the public policy arena. Be that as it may, Weiss does exactly what Scott and Shore ask – but still concludes that social scientists are unlikely to have impacts upon decision takers and policy makers of the kind Scott and Shore desire. There are a number of reasons for this, but one in particular is worth stressing. Social scientists find it hard to give government departments and agencies what they say they want because, by the time they deliver their reports, the latter's perception of what it is they do want has all too often moved on in response to more-or-less subtle shifts in the ideological, interest and informational factors to which they are subject. In short, and contrary to Tijssen, there is often little point in exhorting social scientists to keep up with the actualities of the organizations that commission their research. To my: 'Consider your interaction with all manner of groups and constituencies, not just people in positions of authority', can now be added Weiss's (implicit): 'Stick to the theoretical perspectives and the long-term views which are the forte of social science'.

En route to dialogue

Giddens' equivalent to the interaction of which Weiss and others speak is dialogue. He did not formally announce the dialogical model of social science application until a lecture in New York in 1986 entitled 'Nine theses on the future of sociology'; the model is, however, but a formalization of something that has been clearly in the making since the *New Rules of Sociological Method* a decade earlier. I will say something about that making before looking at both the 'Nine theses' and two other essays included in *Social Theory and Modern Sociology* (1987a).

Rule D1 of *The New Rules*, which refers to the double hermeneutic, includes the germ of the dialogical model:

there is a continual 'slippage' of the concepts constructed in sociology, whereby these are appropriated by those whose condition they were originally coined to analyse, and hence tend to become integral features of that condition (thereby in fact potentially compromising their original usage within the technical vocabulary of social science).

(Giddens, 1976a: 162)

The term 'dialogue' itself is taken from Gadamer. In the essay on 'Ideology and consciousness' in *Central Problems in Social Theory* (1979a), Giddens discusses Habermas's response to Gadamer; 'Hermeneutics, according to Gadamer, can be regarded as concerned with the creation of dialogue from the encounter of traditions' (p. 176). Later in the same volume, in the essay on 'The prospects for social theory', Giddens repeats the point that:

There is a two-way relation involved between lay language and the language of social science, because any of the concepts introduced by sociological observers can in principle be appropriated by lay actors themselves, and applied as part of 'ordinary language' discourse.

(ibid: 248)

Variations on how what can happen in principle happens in practice are not spelled out, but Giddens does introduce the important distinction between mutual knowledge, which is incorrigible, and common sense, which is corrigible. Mutual knowledge refers to the mediation of frames of meaning, including the mediation by social scientists of lay frames; it 'brackets the factual status of the tacit and discursive understandings shared by an observer with those whose conduct he or she seeks to characterise' (ibid: 251). Common sense, by contrast, refers to the 'un-bracketing of mutual knowledge: the consideration of the logical and empirical status of belief-claims involved (tacitly and discursively) in forms of life' (ibid: 252). The first respects the authenticity of belief; the second allows critical evaluation of the justification of belief, including the critique of ideology, in terms of natural and social science knowledge claims. Here Giddens comments that Winch (1964) was right to insist that Zande witchcraft beliefs and practices are rational in so far as there exist internally coherent frames that sociologists and the Azande can draw upon in generating descriptions of witchcraft, but wrong in supposing that recognition of the authenticity of Zande beliefs and practices precludes their critical evaluation. Mutual knowledge establishes what is going on, but it does not rule out critical examination of the empirical grounding of beliefs or their ideological ramifications. What Giddens omits, however, is any reference to those features of natural and social knowledge claims that make their use in critical evaluation distinctive and something that parties other than their authors should attend to. (Adoption of the term 'common sense' to refer to the unbracketing of beliefs also jars.)

Three essays in *Profiles and Critiques in Social Theory* (1982c) add further points of relevance. In 'Hermeneutics and social theory' (1982i), Giddens returns to the two-way tie between social science and lay concepts, and to the double hermeneutic; and again he uses Gadamer's term 'dialogical' to refer to 'relations between the social sciences and the lives of the human beings whose behaviour is analysed' (p. 14). That those analysed can take up social science 'findings' is 'the hinge connecting two possible modes in which the social sciences connect to their involvement in society itself: as contributing to forms of exploitative domination, or as promoting emancipation' (ibid). He does not enlarge on which is more likely in what circumstances. Giddens goes on to stress that human agents are 'knowledgeable' about their society and 'capable' of acting in it (and in speaking of 'action' he alludes to the ineliminable possibility of their acting otherwise). Moreover, this guarantees that social theory is inevitably critical theory. 'Human beings ... are not merely inert objects of knowledge, but agents able to – and prone to – incorporate social theory and research within their own action' (ibid: 16). Then in 'Action, structure and power' (1982l) and 'Power, the dialectic of control and class structuration' (1982m), Giddens uses 'dialectic of control' to refer to the knowledgeability and capability that enables even the subordinated to act. Interestingly, he here complains that Braverman exaggerates the helplessness of the workers in his classic *Labor and Monopoly Capital* (1974).

All these ideas recur in *The Constitution of Society* (1984a) where there is also an extended discussion of social science application. Once again Giddens starts by rejecting transfer of the 'revelatory model' of natural science to social science. He then builds upon his distinction between mutual knowledge and common sense. 'The first refers to the authenticity of belief or the hermeneutic *entrée* into the description of social life' (Giddens, 1984a: 336). The second refers to 'the propositional beliefs implicated in the conduct of day-to-day activities' (ibid: 337). Contrary to empiricism and objectivism: 'Common-sense beliefs, as incorporated in day-to-day language use and action, cannot be treated as mere impediments to a valid or veridical characterization of social life' because they are part constitutive of it (ibid: 336). But that does not make them incorrigible. To suppose it does is to succumb to 'a paralysis of the critical will' that has claimed many interpretivists (ibid: 336); 'common sense is mutual knowledge treated not as knowledge but as fallible belief' (ibid: 337).

At this point the distinction between 'credibility criteria' and 'validity criteria' comes into play.

> Credibility criteria refer to criteria, hermeneutic in character, used to indicate how the grasping of actors' reasons illuminates what exactly they are doing in the light of those reasons. Validity criteria concern criteria of factual evidence and theoretical understanding employed by the social sciences in the assessment of reasons as good reasons.
>
> (ibid: 339)

Validity criteria are integral to social science; they play a part in constituting what it is.

> The main role of the social sciences in respect of the critique of common sense is the assessment of reasons as good reasons in terms of knowledge either simply unavailable to lay agents or construed by them in a fashion different from that formulated in the metalanguages of social theory.
>
> (ibid: 339)

This presumes that social science can demonstrate that some beliefs are false and others true. Giddens chooses not to try to justify that presumption, a major evasion if ever there was one.

The next step in Giddens' argument is very simple. If one assumes, as he does, that action flows from beliefs, then demonstration that a belief is false carries with it practical implications for the transformation of action.

> Criticizing a belief means (logically) criticizing whatever activity or practice is carried on in terms of that belief, and has compelling force (motivationally) in so far as it is a reason for action ... Now social beliefs, unlike those to do with nature, are constitutive elements of what it is they are about. From this it follows that criticism of false belief (*ceteris paribus*) is a *practical intervention* in society, a political phenomenon in a broad sense of that term.
>
> (ibid: 340)

In addition, social science cannot but be political wherever action descriptions are contested by agents themselves. For a social scientist to choose one terminology is to reject others – an act that is at once critical and political.

From all of this, Giddens draws the confident conclusion that 'new knowledge developed in the social sciences will ordinarily have immediate transformational implications for the existing social world' (ibid: 341). There are, however, the following exceptions: (1) when new knowledge has to do with past events and social conditions that no longer obtain; (2) when the conduct in question depends upon motives and reasons that remain unaltered by new information; (3) when new knowledge sustains existing conditions; (4) when those who seek to apply new knowledge cannot do so for whatever reason (for example lack of resources); (5) when new knowledge turns out to be false; and (6) when new knowledge is trivial or uninteresting.

In his *A Contemporary Critique of Historical Materialism* (1981a), Giddens had already argued that there are no universal laws of society (or economy) of the kind often (if contestably) attributed to the natural sciences, i.e. laws which state invariable relations of constant conjunction and temporal succession: 'In social theory laws involve causal connections that are capable of being modified in terms of what social actors know (believe) about the conditions of production and reproduction of the social system they constitute in their action' (Giddens, 1981a:233).

The point is developed further in *The Constitution of Society*: 'causal mechanisms in social scientific generalizations depend upon actors' reasons, in the context of a "mesh" of intended and unintended consequences of action' (Giddens, 1984a:345). Social science generalizations are, then, unlikely ever to be invariant and universal because 'the content of agents' knowledgeability, the question of how "situated" it is and the validity of the propositional content of that knowledge' all influence the circumstances in which they hold (ibid). In Giddens' own terminology:

> the rationalization of action is causally implicated, in a chronic manner, in the continuation of day-to-day actions. The rationalization of action, in other words, is a major element of the range of causal powers that an individual, *qua* agent, displays.
>
> (ibid)

There are, however, two types of 'causal factors that influence action without operating through its rationalization ... unconscious influences and influences that affect the circumstances within which individuals carry on their conduct' (ibid: 346). The latter provide the enabling and constraining features of contexts of action and include material and social phenomena.

Generalizations that pertain to outcomes that actors make happen are liable to change. 'Since agents' knowledge about conditions influencing the generalization is causally relevant to that generalization, these conditions can be altered by changes in such knowledge' (ibid). The causal mechanisms at work are inherently unstable, 'the degree of instability depending upon how far those beings to whom the generalization refers are likely to display standard patterns of reasoning in such a way as to produce standard sorts of unintended consequence' (ibid: 347). Propositions can prove self-fulfilling and self-invalidating. In sum, generalizations in the social sciences hold only within limits of time and place because they depend upon mixes of intended and unintended consequences of action. They 'may directly reflect maxims of action which are knowingly applied by agents' and they may wittingly or unwittingly feed back into those maxims (ibid).

Giddens stresses that natural science enjoys a 'technological' relation to its object world 'in which accumulated knowledge is "applied" to an independently constituted set of phenomena' (ibid: 348). By contrast, in the social sciences – and here Giddens quotes Taylor – 'the practice is the object of the theory. Theory in this domain transforms its own object' (Taylor, 1983:74). With this in mind, Giddens uses the example of Machiavelli to illustrate the transformative impact of social science. He also gives as an example coroners and court officials whose reading of the social science literature on suicide informs the practices to which suicide statistics refer. In general:

> 'Discoveries' of social science, if they are at all interesting, cannot remain discoveries for long; the more illuminating they are, in fact, the more likely they are to be incorporated into action and thereby to become familiar principles of social life.
>
> (Giddens, 1981a: 351)

But if 'technological' describes the relation of natural science to its object world, what term should be used to describe the relation of the social sciences to their world? In *The Constitution of Society*, Giddens does not tell us. Subsequently, he has adopted 'dialogical'.

Dialogue

It is following mention of Weiss's work that Giddens first proposes a 'dialogical' model of applied sociology. The location is his 'Nine theses on the future of sociology' (1987d); these were first offered at a conference in New York in 1986 but it is the version published a year later to which I shall refer. Early in this essay he sets the context.

Sociology does not, and cannot, consist of a body of theory and research built up and kept insulated from its 'subject-matter' – the social conduct of human agents. There is only a 'single hermeneutic' in natural science. Scientists construct theories about a 'given world', however much the technological applications of their theories allow us to change and control the world. The social sciences operate within a double hermeneutic, involving two-way ties with the actions and institutions of those they study. Sociological observers depend upon lay concepts to generate accurate descriptions of social processes; and agents regularly appropriate theories and concepts of social science within their behaviour, thus potentially changing its character. This introduces an instability into sociological theorizing which inevitably takes it some distance from the 'cumulative and uncontested' model that naturalistically-inclined sociologists have in mind. There is more, however. The social world is an internally contested one, in which dissensus between actors and groups of actors – in relation to divergent world-views or clashes of interest – is pervasive. The ties which connect the social sciences constitutively to the social world inevitably mean that these divisions tend to shape strongly the theoretical perspectives sociological observers assume (this is not merely a matter of deficiencies in their 'objectivity'). If all this is seen in conjunction with the traditional difficulties of replication and control of variables in the empirical testing of theories, we surely must be sceptical of the ambition to achieve a professionally agreed-upon schema of theories and concepts in sociology.

(Giddens, 1987c: 30–1)

Giddens rejects the idea that such a position amounts to anything goes. 'Different theoretical frameworks can be assessed in terms of their fruitfulness and accuracy; and theories can always be in some degree evaluated in terms of observations generated by empirical research' (ibid: 31). Some limit to theoretical diversity is possible; indeed, the outline of a new synthesis is visible.

In discarding naturalism, [this new synthesis] will accept that sociology is not a purely 'interpretative' endeavour, but involves the formulation of accounts of social life which differ from those offered by social agents themselves. Generalizations suggested by social research have to be validated by reference to detailed empirical observation, but such generalizations are in principle capable of being modified by their incorporation within the tissue of social life itself. The new synthesis will reject all forms of explanation which suggest that human behaviour is in a direct sense the result of social causes ... At the same time, it will acknowledge the significance of institutional constraints and parameters forming both the condition and outcome of individual action. All this will alter the self-perception of sociology, because in this emergent standpoint emphasis is placed upon a relation between social science and the subjects of its study. The concepts, theories and findings generated by sociology 'spiral in and out' of social life, they do not form an ever-growing corpus of knowledge.

(Giddens, 1987c: 31-2)

This and later passages do take us a little nearer to identifying what it is that social science can contribute to the corrigibility of common sense.

Giddens argues that much of the post-war development of sociology has been accompanied by a belief that it would underpin better policy making in government and administration, and that much of the present disillusionment with sociology stems from recognition that all too often it has failed to do so. American analysts of research implementation, among whom Weiss is particularly worthy of note, have shown why. But the research that failed has, for the most part, conformed to a model of social science that Giddens believes to be increasingly rejected. (This may be wishful thinking; whether all sociologists have taken to post-empiricism as readily as have some theorists and philosophers of social science is open to question (cf. Bryant, 1989).) This model is based on what natural science is assumed to be like. It aims at a unified conceptual structure, universal laws and ever-increasing incontrovertible knowledge, and it believes objectivity to be indispensable to their achievement. By contrast, Giddens' 'new synthesis' rules out the possibility both of a unified conceptual structure and of causal laws that directly determine human behaviour; instead it stresses the double hermeneutic and the ineliminably contestable character of social science.

Giddens calls his version of interactive application the dialogical model, thereby alluding to 'the notion that the most effective forms of connection between social research and policy making are forged through an extended process of communication between researchers, policy makers and those affected by whatever issues are under consideration' (Giddens, 1987c: 47). Instead of policy objectives determining the research which gets done, the process of research helps to generate the policy objectives. Three suppositions underlie the dialogical model.

First, social research cannot just be 'applied' to an independently given subject matter, but has to be linked to the potentiality of persuading actors to expand or modify the forms of knowledge or belief they draw upon in organizing their contexts of action. ...

Second, ... 'the mediation of cultural settings', coupled with conceptual innovation, are at least as significant for the practical outcomes of social research as is the establishing of generalizations.

(ibid: 47)

The mediation of cultural contexts refers to the 'communication, via social research, of what it is like to live in one cultural setting to those in another' (ibid: 47). It is coupled to conceptual innovation inasmuch as 'the will to change things for the better involves positing "possible worlds" of what might become the case via programmes of social reforms' (ibid: 47–8). Conceptual innovation is important because: 'Novel conceptual frameworks open up possible fields of action previously unperceived either by policy makers or by the agents involved' (ibid: 47–8).

Third, the practical implications of the double-hermeneutic should be underscored. The most far-reaching practical consequences of social science do not involve the creation of sets of generalizations that can be used to generate instrumental control over the social world. They concern instead the constant absorption of concepts and theories into that 'subject-matter' they seek to analyse, constituting and reconstituting what the 'subject-matter' is. Nothing confirms more completely the importance of a dialogical model, for only such a model incorporates the attention to reflexivity thus entailed.

(ibid: 48)

Given this approach to social science and to sociological application, it is not surprising that Giddens should go on to refer to organizations and social movements as 'the two ways in which reflexive appropriation of knowledge about the social world is mobilized in the modern world', or that he should be attracted to the greater dynamism of social movements (ibid: 48).

Finally, I want to refer to two more of the essays in *Social Theory and Modern Sociology*. In his Cambridge inaugural lecture, 'What do sociologists do?' (1987k), Giddens extends the point about suicide and other social statistics first made in *The Constitution of Society*. Population statistics might appear unlikely candidates for incorporation in the phenomena they describe; on the face of it they are quantified analyses of objectively given sets of

195

phenomena. But this is deceptive; the gathering of social statistics has entered into the constitution of modern societies: 'Modern societies could not exist were their demographic characteristics not regularly charted and analysed. In the study of class divisions, bureaucracy, urbanism, and many other areas, sociological concepts regularly enter our lives and redefine them' (Giddens, 1987k: 21). He might have added that this property of statistics is always a more-or-less political one; Mrs Thatcher, overseeing repeated changes in what counts, and what is counted, as unemployment has understood this better than many social scientists.

Giddens also argues that every time he uses a passport he demonstrates his practical grasp of the concept of sovereignty – a concept that originated in political theory. In this and countless other instances, 'the achievements of the social sciences tend to become submerged from view by their very success' (ibid). But it is this process that moves him to insist that 'the social sciences have influenced "their" world – the universe of human social activity – much more strongly than the natural scientists have influenced "theirs"' (ibid). The social sciences, for Giddens, have quite literally been part of the making of modernity – and their future value is inestimable.

> Only societies reflexively capable of modifying their institutions in the face of accelerated social change will be able to confront that future with any confidence. Sociology is the prime medium of such reflexivity. The degree, therefore, to which a society fosters an active and imaginative sociological culture will be a measure of its flexibility and openness.
>
> (Giddens, 1987k: 21)

How will Britain do, one wonders, compared with America, other western European societies or Japan (cf. Bryant and Becker, 1990, chs 8–13)?

The absorption of social science into the universe it describes occurs with economics as much as any other social science. In 'Social theory and problems of macroeconomics' (1987h), Giddens criticizes the very notion of positive economics and seizes instead upon aspects of rational expectations theory which are consistent with the double-hermeneutic. (On positive economics he refers to the innovative work of Friedman (1953); a better indication of its pervasiveness might be Lipsey's best-selling textbook *Positive Economics*, which went through seven editions between 1963 and 1989.) In a way he treats the development of rational expectations theory over the last twenty years as a recovery of what economics was originally about.

When the discourse of what has come to be 'modern economics' developed in the eighteenth and nineteenth centuries the concepts involved did not merely serve to describe independently-given changes leading to modern industrialized societies; they helped constitute the very nature of those societies. Economics (like all the social sciences) is reflexively tied to what it is about.

(Giddens, 1987l: 198)

This point has been made before (cf. Louch, 1967); the simplest reminder of it is the word 'economize'. What rational expectations theory does is assume that the information available to economists is also available to economic agents. Both 'share an "environment of information" which helps define in fact what that environment becomes' (ibid: 193). Giddens has a number of criticisms of rational expectations theory. Two are relevant to the concerns of this chapter. First, it operates with an unwarranted dichotomy between the wholly predictable and the wholly unpredictable; as the first belongs only to the 'artificial world of virtual time-space' and the second to the real world, the constitution of regularity in the real world remains obscure (ibid: 199). Second, its proponents might do better to think in terms of the knowledgeability of actors rather than their rationality. Despite these and other criticisms, rational expectations theory interests Giddens because it holds out the possibility of a rapprochement between economists and other social scientists.

Conclusions

Social theorists and applied sociologists and social-policy analysts form two distinct groupings with minimal overlap. There is therefore some risk that the relevance of Giddens' model of social science to applied sociology will go unnoticed – particularly as he has not made social science application, as distinct from critical sociology, one of his major concerns. This risk has been increased in Britain by the failure of Bulmer, one of the foremost sociologists working on social policy, to make the connection. This is particularly unfortunate in so far as Bulmer has himself written about interaction albeit within his own framework of patterns of influence (Bulmer, 1982, Ch. 7). Bulmer accuses Giddens of disparaging applied research and quotes in evidence a passage from 'Nine theses on the future of sociology' in which the latter discusses instrumentalism in the relation between research and policy (Bulmer, 1990: 121–2). Instrumentalism treats research as a means to a practical end – the effective control of social organization and social change. 'From this point of view', Giddens says, 'research does not play a significant part in shaping the ends of policy making, but serves to provide efficient means by pursuing already formulated objectives' (Giddens, 1987c: 45–6). Bulmer comments that 'Such a handmaiden function is, by implication, very much of a second order of importance', and he goes on to include Giddens among those who have obstructed sociology's applied role (Bulmer, 1990: 122). In so doing he seriously misrepresents Giddens' position. Giddens acknowledges that the instrumental approach may sometimes have paid off; but all too often it has not – hence the disillusionment with applied social research in many quarters. His remedy is to abandon the handmaiden function for dialogue; that way sociological research and analysis will have their impacts on the formation of practical social policies and reforms and not just their implementation. Giddens' questioning of the handmaiden function is a prelude, not to disengagement from applied research, but rather to identification of a more effective model of social science application.

For dévotés of the quasi-natural science model – such as Scott and Shore – the interactive model of applied sociology is a disappointment; for subscribers to Giddens' version of post-empiricism it is all one could ever expect and all one should ever want. Giddens' importance to applied sociology, then, lies not in empirical research on the applications of sociology that adds to the conclusions reached by writers from Donnison to Weiss – for he has not done any; rather it has to do with his promotion of a model of social science in which applications can only be constituted interactively in contrast to the model of social science favoured by the American writers on interactive application in which interaction is at best something imposed on it from outside and at worst a distortion to be fought.

It is this model that also sets Giddens apart from others who have noted the transfer of ideas from sociological to natural discourse, such as Abrams (1981) with his echoes of Marx or Laeyendecker (1990) whose position is nearer that of Weiss. Abrams also makes the additional point that sociology runs the continual risk of association with bad or useless ideas in the eyes of wider publics because the sociological provenance of good or useful ideas appropriated by society is quickly forgotten. Sociologists have a responsibility, then, to resist this social amnesia.

It was Abrams who came up with the aphorism that: 'Once it is realised that the truth of true pictures does not change the world, the sociologist is either a dilettante, a pedant, or a polemicist'

(Abrams, 1981:61). Giddens would reply, I think, that dilettantes and pedants can never be certain that they will be ignored; on the contrary, they may end up polemicists inspite of themselves. Nevertheless, precisely because dialogue does flow naturally from Giddens' conception of social science, there is a danger that he will reinforce the old conceit that sociologists have only to publish on topics of social concern for their work to apply. The danger of monologue puffed up as dialogue can be averted, however, so long as they remember that they have to make their sociology apply. Exactly how they should go about this they have to decide for themselves case by case. They could do worse than to take into account the factors that influence 'the level and nature of the "penetration" actors have of the conditions of system reproduction' (Giddens, 1984a:91). These are listed in the section on 'positioning' in *The Constitution of Society* – a section quite separate from the chapter on 'Structuration theory, empirical research and social critique' – as:

1. the means of access actors have to knowledge in virtue of their social location;
2. the modes of articulation of knowledge;
3. circumstances relating to the validity of the belief-claims taken as 'knowledge';
4. factors to do with the means of dissemination of available knowledge.

(Giddens, 1984a:91)

The largely American literature on interactive application also provides a valuable resource upon which they can draw.

Giddens' dialogical model of applied sociology flows from elements of structuration theory – the knowledgeability and capability of actors, the dialectic of control and the double hermeneutic – which are of universal relevance. Together they make up a philosophical anthropology that presents men and woman as the same at all times and places. By contrast, Giddens adopts a discontinuist view of history. It is the discontinuities, not the continuities, between tribal, class-divided and class societies – his three main categories – that stand out. And within each category, case by case differences are large. Now as societies are not everywhere the same, the balance between enablement and constraint which their social structures afford may also be expected to vary. But instead of homing in on variations in human capacity for transformative action, Giddens continually prefers to assert a noble, almost Promethean, characterization of the species-being of *homo sapiens*. It is, I submit, central to his version of a critical sociology.

This insistence upon human transformative capacity is coupled with a 'libertarian socialism' (Giddens, 1981a:175) that seems so natural to Giddens as hardly to require justification:

> If Marx's project be regarded as the furthering, through the conjunction of social analysis and political activity, of forms of human society in which the mass of human beings can attain freedoms and modes of self-realisation in excess of any they may have enjoyed before, who can dissent from it?
>
> (Giddens, 1981a:24)

In their engagement with society, sociologists should not, then, be afraid to combine their sociology where appropriate with philosophy – including normative theory. Indeed he endorses the device of the normative counterfactual theory – 'A counterfactual theory of exploitation would recognise that, notwithstanding revolutions and reforms that might take place, there is always room for further advancement' – and he commends for our attention, whatever their shortcomings, Rawls' theory of justice and Habermas's conception of the 'ideal speech situation' as the basis for a critique of asymmetries of power (Giddens, 1981a: 247; Rawls, 1971; Habermas, 1976). Even so Bernstein (1986a) has a legitimate complaint that Giddens does not use any such device himself to warrant his own critical judgements – or what I would call his ahistorical philosophical anthropology.

As ever it is the synthetic character of Giddens' work – the integration of structuration theory with a particular conception of social science, a particular model of application and gestures towards a particular mode of philosophizing – that impresses most. The critical dimension of the dialogical model, however, is incomplete. Structuration theory is critical in a minimal sense in so far as it suggests that human agents can always act otherwise than they do; but it will not be critical in a fuller sense until a normative counterfactual theory is supplied to warrant either the philosophical anthropology that currently informs it or some more historical successor.

Acknowledgement

I presented an earlier version of this paper to a seminar in the Social Sciences Faculty of the University of Utrecht in May 1989. I am grateful to colleagues in Utrecht, and to Rob Flynn in Salford, for comments on that draft.

Chapter eight

Structuration theory: past, present and future

Anthony Giddens

I shall not seek to reply to the various critiques contained in the preceding pages of this volume. I am grateful to the contributors for the careful and positive way in which they have developed their various appraisals of my work, and I feel I have learned something from all of them. Naturally, I have reservations about some of the criticisms offered, but I will not analyse these in this context (but see Giddens, 1989c). I shall attempt instead to meet the brief suggested by the editors, who asked me to write about the following issues: the origins and development of structuration theory; the directions I propose to take in my writings in the future; the uses – and abuses – of structuration theory, as I would see these, in the hands of writers who have used it as a framework for their own researches; and the thoughts I have about the current state of, and future prospects for sociology in general. Since these are all fairly large topics, my remarks about them will be far from complete; however, the interview carried out by the editors should help fill in some of the gaps.

The development of structuration theory

I regard structuration theory as only one part of my writings as a whole. Specifically, it is the label I attach to my concern to develop an ontological framework for the study of human social activities. By 'ontology' here, I mean a conceptual investigation of the nature of human action, social institutions and the interrelations between action and institutions. I came to these concerns from an early preoccupation with the development of classical social theory. In that early work, I wanted to provide a new approach to categorizing and interpreting classical social thought. When *Capitalism and Modern Social Theory* (1971a) was published, not far off twenty years ago now, some reviewers wondered why I had not set out to subject the ideas of the writers discussed therein to more systematic critique. The reason was that I was not interested in offering a critical analysis of the figures involved in terms of their own standpoints; nor did I aim to demonstrate that their work tended towards a grand synthesis of social theory in the manner in which Parsons argued in his celebrated study, *The Structure of Social Action* (1937). I wanted to develop a much more 'extended' critique of classical social theory by means of projects that either took over from where the classical founders of sociology had left off, or developed lines of thought distinctively different from theirs.

I would still hold today to the words with which I closed *Capitalism and Modern Social Theory*: that we have to seek, in the late twentieth century, to break away from the formulations which the classical social thinkers made. What I eventually came to call 'structuration theory' forms one way in which in my own writings, I tried to follow this precept. My first attempts to amplify themes signalled in *Capitalism and Modern Social Theory* were more in the area of substantive discussion than methodological analysis, and concentrated especially on problems of class structure. The book I wrote on this subject, *The Class Structure of the Advanced Societies* (1973), is perhaps the one with which I feel least happy when looking back over the period of the intervening years to my early body of writings. I would continue to support some of the main arguments of the book today – in particular, the claim that class division is a fundamental feature of a capitalistic social order – but would alter many other parts substantially. In *Class Structure* I first introduced the term 'structuration', but without at that time reflecting upon its likely importance as a general concept in social theory. The term appears quite often in the writings of French-speaking authors, but to my knowledge had rarely been used in English previously – unsurprisingly, perhaps, since while it sounds elegant enough when used in French, it has a somewhat unattractive ring in English! I introduced the notion in *Class Structure* to emphasize the complicated and variable nature of class relations in different societies. Classes, I thought, had too often been thought of as entities or groups; a more apt way of understanding class, it seemed to me, was to analyse the ways in which class relations became bases for group formation. Classes as such are neither groups nor communities, but various features of class systems can provide the 'structuring' basis of group affiliations.

The study of class systems raises in acute form the question of the relation between agency and structure. Since at least the time of Marx it has been well established that class relations are 'objective' – that is, institutionalized – elements of social systems. On the

202

other hand, the study of class also raises the vexed issue of the nature of class consciousness and its connection to these 'objective' social circumstances. In *Class Structure*, instead of operating with simply a notion of 'class consciousness', I introduced the notion of 'class awareness'. By this I meant to indicate that there is more to the 'subjective' side of class relations than simply whether or not people are directly conscious of which class they belong to, or whether they actually employ class terminology in day-to-day talk. Class awareness refers to forms of cognition that express class divisions without as such using the language of class. It seemed to be plausible to suppose, for example, that the 'individualism' frequently found among those in economic positions allowing for career mobility and personal economic advancement could be seen as a form of class awareness. The distinction between class consciousness and class awareness may or may not be a useful one. But it was a factor which led me to think further about how one might best conceptualize the 'subjective' aspects of social relationships without identifying this subjectivity simply with knowledge 'about' those relationships. In other words, knowledge is somehow incorporated in social relations in a constitutive fashion without being in any simple sense opposed to their 'objectivity'.

From then on I began to take the notion of 'structuration' seriously in its own right and sought to use it to work out an abstract interpretation of the nature of social reproduction. *New Rules of Sociological Method* (1976a) portrayed in outline fashion the basis of an account that I was able to then flesh out in subsequent publications. The theory of structuration, of course, is more than just an exploration of the idea of 'structuration' itself. I came to see that an 'ontology of social life' must supply a detailed understanding of the nature of action, together with what in post-structuralism is described as a 'theory of the subject'; and that, likewise, the notion of 'structure' itself is a complicated and difficult one. The pre-existing debate about the relation between 'the individual' and 'society', which overlapped with the controversy between methodological individualists and their opponents, seemed to me misleading in its terms of reference. According to the structurationist approach, social theory does not 'begin' either with the individual or with society, both of which are notions that need to be reconstructed through other concepts. In structuration theory, the core concern of the social sciences is with recurrent social practices and their transformations.

Whereas in the title of *Class Structure* and at various points in its text, 'structure' is used in a very conventional and casual way, in formulating structuration theory I endeavoured to give the notion a more abstract and technical sense. The notion that structure, in its most elemental guise, should be regarded as rules and resources involved in the instantiation of social systems has been widely criticized. However, I see no reason to alter this standpoint. Social systems have structural properties, including that institutional 'fixity' so beloved of Durkheimian sociologists, but they are not, as such, structures. 'Structure' presumes continuity of social reproduction across time and space, but it is the medium of such reproduction as well as its outcome. The theorem of the duality of structure occupies a central place in structuration theory precisely because it encapsulates the recursive elements of social life so fundamental to social organization and change. In the sense in which I use it – to refer to the way in which social activities regularly reconstitute the circumstances that generated them in the first place – recursiveness has only a tenuous connection with the mathematical sense of that term, and I was more influenced by theories of autopoiesis (i.e. of self-reproducing systems) in biology than by the mathematical concept.

Structuration theory is not intended to be a theory 'of' anything, in the sense of advancing generalizations about social reality. While this emphasis has infuriated some critics, it is quite necessary to any attempt to provide an ontology of social activity in the sense noted previously. In seeking to come to grips with problems of action and structure, structuration theory offers a conceptual scheme that allows one to understand both how actors are at the same time the creators of social systems yet created by them. Critics who argue either that structuration theory provides too little space for free action or, alternatively, underestimates the influence of structural constraint (both types of criticism have been made) miss the point. The theory of structuration is not a series of generalizations about how far 'free action' is possible in respect of 'social constraint'. Rather, it is an attempt to provide the conceptual means of analyzing the often delicate and subtle interlacings of reflexively organized action and institutional constraint.

I see *The Constitution of Society* (1984a) as the fullest exposition of structuration theory that I have attempted to provide, but I do not think it merely supplants my previous writings on the issue. I regard earlier books, especially *New Rules* and *Central Problems in Social Theory* (1979a), as complementary to it. *New Rules* concentrated, as the subtitle of the book indicates, upon a critical dissection of interpretative sociologies, trying to forge a position that recognizes the centrality of the interpretation of meaning – on various levels – in social analysis, but at the same time showing why sociology cannot be wholly 'interpretative'. In *Central Problems* I was more concerned with the critique of structuralist and post-structuralist thought, as well as considering themes brought to the fore by Marxism. While I have been influenced in various ways by each of these traditions, I was particularly concerned to juxtapose them to elements drawn from Wittgensteinian philosophy – or my version of it. Post-structuralist thought is now beginning to exert a strong influence in English-speaking sociology, particularly as filtered through debates about modernity and post-modernity. But I believe Wittgenstein's work to be of more enduring importance. Wittgenstein's specification of 'differences', as mediated in the *Praxis* of language games, seems to me superior to that filtered through signifiers or 'discourse' as understood in post-structuralism.

Structuration theory is supposed to be something that can be put to use in concrete social scientific work – although by this I do not mean simply 'applied' in empirical research programmes. In developing the presuppositions of structuration theory, I have consistently kept in mind more empirical questions of social organization and development, especially in so far as these bear upon the trajectories of change of modern institutions. The various volumes of *A Contemporary Critique of Historical Materialism* (1981a, 1985a, etc.), actual and projected, form the main basis of my attempt to cope with these problems. Although these studies make use of some of the major concepts of structuration theory (and I hope do so fruitfully), most of the views they set out do not stand or fall in terms of the value of those concepts.

Structuration theory represents an effort to reconstruct some of the basic premises of social analysis; in my other, more substantive, work the element of 'deconstruction' is more marked. Although my main emphasis is upon the nature of modernity, I have been concerned in a general way with questions of history and social change. The social sciences, I think, are irremediably historical. However, 'history' is a complex notion, and not only because of the usual distinction between history as events and as the recounting or analysing of those events. Considering what history is, in either of these senses, brings us face to face with the need to theorize temporality, a notion at once banal and ineffable. I have sought to show how concepts of time – and space – might be brought into the core of social theory and what implications might follow for understanding history. This endeavour means in part writing a history *of* temporality – how time, or more accurately, time-space, is 'handled' within differing types of social system, thereby entering into their constitution. It also means breaking

205

sharply with the idea that history can be equated with social change – as though things that stay the same have no 'history'. The writing of history and events-as-history come together in a special form of temporal engagement into which human beings enter with their past and their prospective future: this is 'historicity'. Historicity enters 'history' with the very emergence of the forms of writing that make recorded history possible.

Such reflections on temporality and history form one part of my attempt to deconstruct some of the dominant types of theorizing about social change. In *A Contemporary Critique,* I focused particularly upon historical materialism and upon evolutionary theories in the social sciences. These approaches, I argued, are not only empirically dubious, but have logical limitations. They cannot be reconstructed, but have to be replaced with an approach of a different character. This assertion has received a certain battering from critics, particularly, of course, those who defend historical materialism or evolutionism. In fact, however, my deconstruction of theories of social change stretches well beyond either of these two traditions of thought.

In my view, generalizations about social change, and 'history' more widely, are both possible and worthwhile. Yet the scope, and sphere of application, of such generalizations is often much more restricted than is commonly recognized. The factor of human knowledgeability, when geared to historicity, alters the causal conditions under which otherwise comparable actions are undertaken. But this is not all. Whenever we analyse large swathes of history, we are liable to find ourselves with an aggregate of 'causal influences' rather than conclusive generalizations about why things 'had to happen' as they did. This has nothing to do with historical contingency; it expresses the necessarily incomplete nature of generalizing explanations in the social sciences. There are no patterns of universal causation in the social sciences – that is to say, conditions in which circumstance X will, and must, always be followed by circumstance Y – because all causal connections in human social life are mediated in one way or another by agents' knowledgeability and agents' reasons. In analyzing lengthy historical periods, and looking for overall dynamics of social change, we can rarely, if ever, have detailed knowledge of agents' reasoning processes. Although these can sometimes be inferred, and generalized about, our attempts at explaining general patterns of social change are liable always to remain fairly fragmentary (cf. Giddens, 1990e).

Current and future work

Modernity is the core concern of sociology. Sociology was established as an endeavour to understand the massive changes that,
from about the eighteenth century onwards, disrupted traditional
modes of life and introduced quite novel forms of social organization. While writing *The Constitution of Society* I came to see that
the connections between sociology and modernity were considerably more complicated than I had imagined previously. Sociological concepts, theories and findings are not simply ways of
analysing an independently given subject matter, but enter directly
into what modern institutions are. This constitutive involvement
with modernity characterizes all of the social sciences, and in some
part the humanities; but sociology has a peculiarly central position
in this regard because of its analytical focus upon modern social
life.

Sociological work is a core component of what I have come to
see as the intrinsic reflexivity of modernity. Human beings in all
societies routinely reflexively monitor their actions and thereby
processes of reproduction. However, in conditions of modernity,
marked by an intrusive historicity, the reflexive ordering and
reordering of the conditions of system reproduction is more or less
all-pervasive. In other words, modernity is marked by the tendency
routinely to incorporate new information about conditions of
action, as a means of altering or reorganizing those conditions. The
reflexivity of modernity connects directly with Enlightenment
thought, which seemed initially to be providing foundations for
knowledge, including sociological knowledge, rather than – as it
has turned out – corroding the very basis of foundationalism. The
'circularity' of sociology's involvement with modernity forms part
of a wider circularity of knowledge, based more upon the radicalizing of doubt than upon the securing of certainties. All claims to
knowledge are in principle open to revision in the light of further
information. The outlook of modernity is one in which literally
nothing is sacred, if this term refers to beliefs or principles that are
held to be 'above question'.

As in my earlier work, I am not particularly interested in the
epistemological aspects of this situation. I do not believe that they
imply relativism or the view, sometimes associated with post-
structuralism, that all knowledge, or even 'truth', are no more than
contextual. On the contrary, in my view, those who have taken
such a standpoint have misinterpreted what is essentially a set of
profound institutional changes (the development and radicalizing
of modernity) with the undermining of valid knowledge claims as

such. Their position is as much an expression of these institutional transformations as a means of adequately comprehending them. In my current writing, I am concerned to relate the theme of the inherent reflexivity of modernity to a concrete institutional analysis of modern social life.

I offered the outlines of such an account in the second volume of *A Contemporary Critique (The Nation-State and Violence)* (1985a) and I am currently extending – and I hope deepening – this analysis. In a forthcoming work (1990b), I try to account for the extreme dynamism of modernity – the way in which it has ripped our lives away from traditional orders of all kinds – and to trace out its implications on various levels. Developing the arguments of the concluding chapter of *The Nation-State and Violence,* I propose that modernity is multidimensional on the level of institutions. Some of the best-established sociological perspectives look for a single major institutional order in seeking to analyse the nature of modern societies. In particular, debates about this matter have centred upon the question: Are modern societies 'capitalistic' or are they 'industrial'? Many authors, especially those influenced by Marxism, have regarded capitalism as the pre-eminent moving force in modern history. For them, as for Marx, industrial production is to be understood primarily in terms of the prior emergence of capitalism, of which it is an adjunct. Other authors, by contrast, insist that industrialism is the primary dynamic force levering the modern world away from traditional cultures. In their view, capitalism is a subtype of industrialism, characteristic of an early period in the emergence of modern industrial orders. The debate between the two sides raises some real issues, but is in substantial part based upon false premises, since each tends to advocate a reductionism – either of industrialism to capitalism, or the other way around.

According to my standpoint, capitalism and industrialism are two partially independent dimensions of modernity – dimensions, for sure, that overlap with one another, but are analytically distinguishable and have divergent consequences. By 'capitalism' I mean a system of commodity production, involving competitive markets for both goods and labour-power. Industrialism, by contrast, refers to the use of inanimate sources of energy in production, conjoined to the central role of machinery in the production process. Each of these dimensions of modernity is in turn separable from control of information, or 'surveillance' as a medium of administrative power in modern societies. The administrative power that states and other organizations are able to generate is not simply a direct outcome of either capitalism or industrialism, but depends upon the co-ordinated supervision of subject populations. Surveillance in turn can be separated from a fourth dimension of modernity, which is control of the means of violence in the context of the industrialization of war. One of the objectives of *The Nation-State and Violence* was to help counter the neglect of military violence in the core traditions of social theory. Like surveillance capabilities, co-ordinated military power from the beginning has been associated with the development of states; but in the modern period, where government apparatuses for the most part successfully monopolize control of means of violence, and where industrial production is directly utilized in military organization, military power takes on certain very distinctive qualities.

The association of modernity with military power of enormous destructive potential is one of the main reasons why, as anyone today can see, modernity is a double-edged phenomenon. The development of modern institutions has opened up a vast gamut of opportunities for humankind; at the same time, modernity has many dark and threatening aspects. I do not think the sombre side of modernity has been adequately grasped in pre-existing forms of social theory. Consequently, I focus a substantial part of my discussion upon the themes of security and danger in the modern world, using concepts of trust and risk to seek to analyse these. The notion of trust connects directly to the concept of time-space distanciation, which I introduced in earlier writings. One of the key features of modern institutions, along each of the four dimensions distinguished, is that they 'disembed' social relations from local contexts of action. Disembedding means the 'lifting out' of social relations from local involvements and their recombination across large spans of time-space. The mechanisms of disembedding depend upon trust, where trust is defined as having 'faith' (of some sort) in the workings of systems, or processes, of which one possesses only limited knowledge.

Money is an example of a disembedding mechanism, as are forms of professional knowledge and expert systems of all kinds. Trust in disembedding mechanisms is vested not first and foremost in individuals, but in abstract capacities. Someone who uses a monetary token, for example, presumes that other people – who may be widely distant in time and space – will honour its value. But it is money as such that is 'trusted' rather than only, or even primarily, the persons involved in specific monetary transaction.

We can analyse feelings of security and danger in conditions of modernity by looking at how far disembedding mechanisms alter parameters of risk, both in respect of individual agents and larger social systems. In the balance between trust and risk can be located many of the contingencies which affect day-to-day life, but which also operate on a global scale. Modernity is inherently globalizing as a result of the capability of disembedding mechanisms to organize social connections across indefinite sectors of time-space. The globalizing influences of modernity, however, should not be understood simply as increasing unification of an emergent 'world society'. The intensifying of worldwide social relations sets up dialectical ties between the global and local, such that what happens in any particular milieu is an expression of, but also can often stand in contradistinction to, distanciated social forms. Thus the prosperity of one area in the international division of labour may be the very origin of the impoverishment of another.

The globalization of risk is plainly a fundamental aspect of globalization processes in general. The risk of nuclear war, or risks of environmental catastrophe, affect all human beings in the world. At the same time, however, such 'high-consequence' risks produce many forms of local experience and reaction. Everyone on earth has to live with the risk of nuclear war, but individuals in particular contexts may decide passively to accept such risk, hoping that political leaders and other experts will avoid going to war; others may attempt directly to influence political processes, or perhaps join peace movements.

One of the most characteristic features, therefore, of modernity is the connection between day-to-day life and far-flung global connections and events. A theory of daily life in conditions of modernity can be developed via the notions of trust and risk. Trust vested in disembedding mechanisms is associated with a 'deskilling' of day-to-day activity: many aspects of our everyday lives are filtered by the intrusion of expert knowledge. All of us have some kind of 'faith' in the systems that surround us and enter into the most intimate parts of our lives – the systems that provide water, generate food production, transport us from one place to another, interpret health and disease and a multitude of other things. It is misleading, however, to see this situation in Habermas's term, as 'the colonisation of the life world by expert systems'. Just as in the case of deskilling processes in the workplace, there is a constant tension between the appropriation of knowledge on the part of experts and other officials and its re-appropriation by lay actors in the contexts of day-to-day life. This is intrinsic to the very reflexivity of modernity. Thus, a person who contracts a particular illness might consult a doctor about it, but might also investigate the illness systematically via the popular accounts available, and may perhaps on this basis opt out of the official system of medicine, looking instead to alternative therapies, or perhaps rejecting specialist practitioners altogether. Of course, there are limits to how far any given individual can disengage from the whole range of expert systems that permeate modern life.

The 'extensional' and 'intensional' aspects of modernity intertwine to affect the nature of personal identity and the self in contemporary societies. Just as it is an error to speak of the colonization of the life-world, it is wrong to suppose that the impersonal increasingly swamps the personal. What happens is not just a diminishing of personal life in favour of the increasingly pervasive influence of impersonally organized systems; rather, what occurs is a genuine transformation of the nature of the personal itself. Trust relations between individuals on a personal level can no longer be sustained by the relatively fixed reference points of kinship or local community, as in the case of most pre-modern systems. Trust becomes something that has to be 'worked at', and demands the opening out of the individual to the other – a process of mutual self-disclosure that is also part of the phenomenon of 'finding oneself'. Like other aspects of life, the self in circumstances of modernity becomes a reflexive project.

The 'quest for self-identity' is not, as is often suggested, simply a defensive process whereby the person seeks to fight off the encroachments of an increasingly large-scale social world over which he or she has little or no influence. This relation is again a dialectical one, in which self-fulfilment or self-actualization takes on rich new forms. We can live 'in' the world of modernity much more comprehensively than was ever possible before the advent of modern systems of representation, transportation and communication. In many situations, conditions of modernity promote activism rather than privatism, because of modernity's inherent reflexivity, and because of the many opportunities for individual action and collective organization that are offered.

'Post-modernity', according to this standpoint, is a condition yet to be realized: it is a set of possible developments beyond modernity, rather than anything that exists in the here-and-now. A post-modern world could be a more benign social universe, in which certain kinds of high-consequence risks are minimized or eliminated, and the more 'positive' side of modernity is developed more completely. A critical theory that engages with the imminant possibilities of modernity must recognize that history provides no guarantees, and must balance realism with a utopian element. What is needed is the creation of models of what I call utopian realism – which is not as contradictory as it sounds. The connecting of realism and utopianism is fundamental in a world threatened with high-consequence risks. Utopian thinking taken on its own can be highly dangerous – if applied, say, to the politics of deterrence. Anyone concerned with weapons futures must be alert to the tactical and strategic issues involved in potential processes of demilitarization, not just impelled by pure moral conviction. On the other hand, if realism is not tempered by a utopian component, the radical transitions that are imperative to guarantee a stable and secure future will not materialize.

Utopian realism, I think, presumes two types of political engagement: one I call 'emancipatory politics', the other 'life politics', or the 'politics of self-actualization'. Emancipatory politics refers to political engagements concerned with liberation – with the alleviation of oppression. In emancipatory politics there are always 'others' – the rich versus the poor, white versus black, men versus women, and so forth. In the sphere of life politics there are no 'others'. Life politics concerns the development of a fulfilling and satisfying life for all, in the context of a world in which the local and the global are continuously bound up with one another. Questions such as the proper relation of human beings to nature, the legacy of present acts for future generations, control over the body and its reproductive capabilities, and the aesthetics of the built environment, all form part of life politics.

In the third volume of *A Contemporary Critique*, as yet incomplete, I examine some of these issues in more detail and connect them to current debates about the future of capitalism and socialism. Capitalism is part of modernity, and one of its great dynamic impulsions; but it exists in conjunction with the other institutional complexes previously mentioned. Even if socialism were in some sense the 'future' of capitalism, its influence would extend only to certain aspects of a post-modern order. Thus although in the third volume I discuss current dilemmas about socialism, the study as a whole is more concerned with analysing the overall contours of a post-modern system. The differentiation of emancipatory and life politics is fleshed out in some detail, and the work gives a good deal of attention to the problem of the self and self-actualization. I pursue the themes of ontological security and existential anxiety, which I introduced quite early on in my writings but have not so far managed to expand upon satisfactorily. If everyone is not by then too bored with this long-running enterprise, I would like to produce a fourth volume of *A Contemporary Critique*, concentrating upon the nature of critical theory, in particular the critique of ideology. I would also propose at some point to write a book on religion. The principle that 'nothing is sacred' –

including that principle itself – is one that continually creates friction. One source of such friction, although certainly not the only one, is the persistence or rediscovery of attitudes of religiosity. I aim to produce a theoretical interpretation of religion that takes this situation as its point of departure.

The uses of structuration theory

In the concluding chapter of *The Constitution of Society* I set out some of the connections, as I saw them, between structuration theory and social research. My aim was to explore the empirical relevance of some of the concepts discussed in the book in the light of research projects of various types. Some reviewers considered this approach inadequate. What I should have done, according to them, is to have shown how structuration theory generates distinctive research projects of its own. However, while structuration theory touches at many points upon the conduct of social research, it is not a research programme. As I have often remarked before, its concepts should be regarded as sensitizing devices, to be used in a selective way in thinking about research questions or interpreting findings. They do not furnish a distinctive research programme in the manner, for example, of Garfinkel's ethno-methodology, or identify a definite 'slice' of social life to be studied, like Erving Goffman's 'interaction order'.

Structuration theory, and concepts or ideas introduced in other parts of my writings, have been used in a great variety of research contexts. On the whole I like least those works in which authors have attempted to import structuration theory *in toto* into their given area of study. The overall framework of structuration theory, I hope, is relevant to anyone writing about very broad questions of social organization and transformation, as I tend myself to do. In many more confined arenas of empirical research it is not especially helpful to drag in a large apparatus of abstract concepts. I like most those usages in which concepts, either from the logical framework of structuration theory or other aspects of my writings, are used in a sparing and critical fashion. There are by now many such examples in the literature, but let me just mention a few that I would particularly endorse.

One is Patrick Burman's study of unemployment (Burman, 1988). The research concerned was carried out in an area of Canada in the years 1982–83, at a period when rates of unemployment were very high. Most previous work on unemployment, according to Burman, has taken what he calls an 'aerial view' of the phenomenon. That is to say, it has researched the issue in terms of large-scale studies of aggregates of people. The unemployed, as it were, are seen at a distance, reducing them, in Burman's words 'to a complex of functions and attributes within a socio-economic system' (ibid: 4). The unemployed individual does not appear in this research as a knowledgeable agent living through the various experiences that becoming unemployed involves. This is a sort of 'decentring of the subject', Burman argues, although obviously not in the usual sense in which this term is understood in post-structuralist theory. Such 'decentring' is not confined to the analytic level: many of the individuals interviewed in Burman's study found that becoming unemployed corroded their own sense of agency. As one remarked, 'I feel like I no longer have a life ... I am a participant in a script that someone else has taken over' (ibid: 5). Yet few of the individuals concerned in the study relapsed into a state of numbed acquiescence; virtually all made attempts to 'recentre' their lives, actively reordering their social relationships and material conditions of life.

Burman makes use of the notion of the duality of structure in setting up and interpreting the results of his research. The key units of analysis are recurrent social practices, and Burman seeks to analyse how the active mobilization of particular kinds of practice both draws upon larger systems and at the same time recast larger institutional orders. In particular, Burman shows how activities in what he calls the 'microsocial sphere' (individuals, families and groups, friends) intersect with those carried out in the 'intermediate community sphere' (unemployment organizations, union locals, local enterprises and social networks), and in the 'macrosocial sphere' of larger organizations, including state bureaucracies.

Burman devotes considerable attention to the temporal organization of day-to-day life, showing that unemployment alters both the experience of time and the modes in which the temporal conjunction of social practices is organized. For a person in full-time paid work or schooling, times of the day are structured in quite a fixed fashion, as is the temporal organization of weeks, months and years. The temporal perspective and situation of the unemployed person is quite different, involving large acres of 'inchoate time', separated from the regular practices in which the employed are caught up. While some people responded in a very intense way to being confronted with large stretches of 'poorly structured time', taking courses, doing volunteer work, carrying out various hobbies and doing work around the home, others quite often 'did nothing'. 'Doing nothing' is of course itself a form of time-management, and actually always does involve doing some-

214

thing: such as sleeping, watching TV or sitting in the park at regular periods. How far Burman's work would have been different if uninfluenced by structuration theory is difficult to say. However, he does take very seriously the subtle connections of modes of reproduction and transformation and the situated activities of individuals and groups.

As a second example, let me take R.W. Connell's *Gender and Power* (1987). The book is a major contribution to the understanding of gender relations, and draws upon various theoretical traditions in addition to structuration theory. Connell is critical of my approach and makes use of it only at a few junctures in his argument. Yet these seem to me pivotal to the overall claims of the work and result in a standpoint that I find persuasive. An adequate interpretation of gender, Connell asserts, depends upon a sophisticated account of the agency/structure relation. We need to grasp, as Connell puts it, the 'active presence of structure and practice, and the active constitution of structure by practice' (ibid: 94). He criticizes my particular formulations, but develops this perspective in telling fashion. Different types of what Connell calls 'gender regimes' are identified in various structured contexts of action. Consider, for example, the sexual division of labour. In any given work setting, the division of labour between the sexes sets structural constraints upon what any individual can achieve. Thus segregated labour markets set up constraints upon job advancement through the influence of differential skilling and other factors. Institutionalized discrimination tends to be perpetuated as a result of 'rational' choices in the allocation of labour made by employers in such circumstances. The intersection of paid employment with the domestic sphere, women being expected to shoulder most of the burden of housework and the raising of children, also influences gender inequalities. These factors do not only operate 'externally' but are incorporated within the various practices carried on in paid work and in the home. The sexual division of labour should not be seen as a structure in its own right, but part of a 'gendered system of production, consumption and distribution'. Gender, Connell suggests, is not a property of individual people but a phenomenon intrinsic to the organization of definite types of social practices. It is therefore not an overriding dichotomy, but a series of oppositions in terms of which forms of belief and social relationship are organized.

These emphases allow Connell to develop a subtle discussion of sexual ideologies, among other issues. It will not do, he points out, to analyse ideology solely in terms of 'discourses' treated as closed systems; syntactical and symbolic modes of expressing power differentials are deeply implicated in day-to-day practical activities, often of the most mundane kind. All these elements are fed into Connell's discussion of how 'hegemonic masculinity' is reproduced. 'Masculinity' and 'femininity' are not simply given, but are repeatedly reconstituted and reformed in the context of power differentials. The 'economic' relation between employer and secretary, for instance – given the sexual imbalance in the staffing of such positions – reproduces gender differentiations through the very unequal power it embodies. Hegemonic masculinity, in Connell's analysis, is quite different from older-established accounts of male and female 'roles'. The ideas or ideals whereby images of masculinity are reproduced do not necessarily conform to the actual personalities or actions of most men. Media images of masculinity, for instance, quite often involve fantasy figures, such as film characters, remote from everyday life but none the less sustaining an aura that influences ordinary contexts of action. While there is no femininity corresponding to hegemonic masculinity, feminine identities often have a very public form – Connell calls this 'emphasised femininity', as portrayed in a plethora of media programmes, articles and advertisements.

> Central to the maintenance of emphasised femininity is practice that prevents other models of femininity gaining cultural articulation.... What is hidden from it is the experience of spinsters, lesbians, unionists, prostitutes, mad women, rebels and maiden aunts, manual workers, midwives and witches. And what is involved in radical sexual politics, in one of its dimensions, is precisely the assertion and recovery of marginalised forms of femininity in the experience of groups like these.
>
> (Connell, 1987: 188)

Let me take as a third illustration a study quite different from the other two: Christopher Dandeker's recent discussion of surveillance, bureaucratic power and war (Dandeker, 1989). Dandeker's book makes use of notions from my more substantive writings, rather than those concerned with structuration theory as such. His book develops these notions in such a way as to provide a fresh account of the nature of administrative power in modern societies. The notion of surveillance, of course, derives primarily from Foucault, but Dandeker adopts my version of the notion and connects it to the fourfold institutional designation of modernity to which I have already referred. His book discusses the modes in which various major traditions of social theory have dealt with the issue of surveillance, and tries to specify the conditions under which the surveillance capabilities of different forms of organization are either advanced or inhibited. On this basis, Dandeker is able to cast new light upon long-standing debates about the characteristics of bureaucracy in modern societies.

I do not have the space here to represent Dandeker's arguments in detail. He has a good deal of interest to say about the development of the modern nation-state, its connection to capitalist enterprise, and the relation of both to military power. The armed forces, he points out, made up the most significant and developed branch of the early modern state in terms of organizational complexity, level of state expenditure and numbers of individuals involved. The bureaucratization of the military provides both a vital case study of expansion of bureaucratic power and offers lessons for the wider interpretation of bureaucratic mechanisms elsewhere. Developing a theme discussed in *The Nation-State and Violence*, Dandeker shows how the bureaucratization of the military was accompanied by a decline in the role of armed force as a means of sustaining internal political order. Surveillance mechanisms producing the rise of policing and the origins of legally defined 'deviance' form the counterpart to the 'military machines' that confront one another within the nation-state system.

An important contribution of Dandeker's book is that it documents in detail the argument that the modern state involves not just an insulation of political and economic power, but a separation of both of these from military organization. So far as the economic sphere is concerned, the burgeoning surveillance capabilities of the modern business enterprise form a fundamental element of the relative independence of economic activities from direct state supervision within capitalistic systems. The surveillance capacities of the modern business organization, Dandeker shows, are not just a means of consolidating the control of employers or managers over employees, but a means of co-ordinating market operations and monitoring relations with other organizations.

In general, Dandeker argues, when we consider the role of surveillance in bureaucratic systems we have to differentiate a number of major processes concerned. There is, as Weber claimed, a shift from personal relations of patronage to impersonal control based on formal-legal regulations, in terms of which rule is exercised and legitimated. However, such a shift has to be conceptually distinguished from changes in the nature of supervisory power and discipline. This is not marked by a unilinear transition from the personal towards the impersonal, but by new strategies of personal affiliation as means of exercising authority, such as in 'human relations' thinking of 'Japanese-style' management. These two processes are in turn separable from the development of

217

systems of collecting, storing and processing information used for the surveillance purposes. The organizational 'files' are not just retrievable records but enter constitutively into how the organization operates. Finally, we have to recognize the partially independent significance of the expertise that individuals at different levels in organizations possess. Dandeker argues that expertise (I would agree with this) is itself a form of surveillance, in which access to specialized knowledge forms a central element of systems of power in settings of modern societies – although as in all other aspects of surveillance many sorts of contestation of power differentials are found.

I would not endorse all the arguments made by the authors in the three studies mentioned, but they each make worthwhile contributions to the pre-existing literature. In no way do they exhaust what I would regard as interesting and worthwhile attempts to draw upon my ideas. Studies of comparable interest and appeal influenced by my perspective are to be found, for example, in media studies, urban analysis, communications, educational systems and international relations, among others. These are all fields in which I have a direct personal interest and to which I have already tried to contribute, or would like to do so in the future.

Sociology: current state and future prospects

Considered as an academic discipline, sociology has undoubtedly passed through a difficult period during the course of the last fifteen years or so, both in this country and internationally. In terms of student numbers, sociology today has limited appeal compared to the enthusiasm it once generated, although there are signs that the pendulum is swinging back. Has this period also been one of intellectual decline in the subject? Many probably see things in such a way. In the 1960s sociological thinkers seemed to be in the vanguard of public debates and (to alter the metaphor slightly) at the cutting-edge of new intellectual developments. On the face of things, this seems less true of the more recent period. Where are the figures now to compare to Parsons, Merton, Mills or Bell in their prime? The intellectual high-ground today seems to be occupied by thinkers in philosophy, cultural theory or history, such as Habermas, Foucault or Derrida.

The supposed intellectual diminishing of sociology, however, is more apparent than real. In some part, it expresses a movement away from a period in which American sociology was utterly dominant internationally, to one in which European influences have reasserted themselves – as is indicated by the fact that each of the thinkers mentioned in the second group are Europeans. Other factors are also important. Ideas and methods of research pioneered in sociology have become extremely influential in neighbouring social science disciplines: for instance, history, political science and human geography have changed very markedly over the past few years as a result of the incorporation of sociological perspectives. These ideas and methods are therefore less prominent as distinctively 'sociological' but by that very token have deeply influenced the social sciences more widely conceived. Perhaps most importantly, over this period our understanding of the nature of sociology has become considerably altered. Functionalism and naturalism have largely disappeared from view as a result of theoretical and methodological developments. At one point in this process it may have looked as though sociology was on the verge of breaking up, at least as a discipline having some reasonable degree of overall theoretical integration. A jostling variety of theoretical standpoints emerged, the proponents of which seemed to be talking past one another rather than addressing common issues and problems. However, this proved to be something of a transitional phase. There will no doubt always be considerable theoretical diversity in sociology, as in the rest of the social sciences; but new syntheses have emerged, different from the dominant outlooks of twenty years ago. I hope that my efforts to develop structuration theory have made a contribution to these synthesizing endeavours, whatever the shortcomings of my own particular concepts and formulations.

One reaction to the straitened circumstances of sociology over the past few years has been to concentrate upon limited areas of empirical work, especially where these are relevant to policy issues. Many sociologists have often opted for technically sophisticated, hard-edged investigations that give the subject an air of scientificity. I do not think this outlook bodes well for the future of sociology if the subject is to sustain a central place in contemporary intellectual life. 'Hard' research is important, but the intellectual claims of sociology do not rest distinctively upon it. All social research, in my view, no matter how mathematical or quantitative, presumes ethnography. What might be seen as 'soft' styles of research endeavour are actually integral to all types of research activity. Moreover, much of the importance of sociology rests upon theoretical reflection. By this I do not just mean the conventional assertion that research 'needs' theory. Theoretical reflection in sociology has a distinctive status in virtue of the constitutive nature of social knowledge, and takes place at the frontiers between what 'is' and what 'might be' in social life. Professional sociologists by no means have a monopoly over such reflection, but they should be in a position to influence it in fundamental ways.

As a result of this reflexive relation, sociology stands in close connection to social movements: not just to 'progressive' ones but to others also. Social movements have their own reflective engagement with the organizations they confront and the institutions they set out to alter. By definition, social movements do not take the social world for granted, but set themselves against the existing order of things. The study of social movements is a subject in its own right in sociology. Yet social movements have a double relation to sociological analysis because they often also identify previously undiagnosed characteristics of, or imminent possibilities within, a given social order. Several of the most influential 'progressive' social movements today focus exactly upon issues that sociologists have been relatively weak in analysing. A prime instance, in relation to what I have said previously, is the peace movement. Peace movements have forced us to see that the question of controlling the means of violence cannot simply be dealt with in terms of traditional discussions of capitalism and socialism. The women's movement has led sociologists – among others in many other disciplines also – to start to rethink some of their most basic conceptions. Green movements have brought to the fore issues that have been poorly understood in sociology hitherto. Something similar is true of many more 'reactionary' movements also. Religious revivalism, and fundamentalist movements, for example, in their reaction against modernity have something to teach about the limits of modernity and the nature of religiosity. 'Pro-life' movements force onto the sociological, as well as the political, agenda questions concerning the social control of the body.

The challenges facing sociology at the end of the twentieth century reflect the issues the new social movements have brought to the fore, and more besides. The list is a formidable one. On the extensional level, accelerating processes of globalization demand direct analysis and threaten to sweep away sociologists' traditional preoccupation with the study of 'societies'. Perhaps the world is in some sense a single society but, if so, what are its major institutional characteristics and what are the main dynamics transforming it? A global perspective must increasingly become central to sociological work, with all the complexities and difficulties that this entails. On the intensional level, transmutations are occurring in gender relations, personal life and the conditions of day-to-day social activity. How should we seek to interpret these changes in a world in which distance and proximity combine in ever more tangled a fashion? On the level of political systems, changing influences on national sovereignty in western countries are altering the conditions of democratic involvement, while in Eastern Europe and elsewhere far-reaching political and economic reorganization is taking place. Do we see in these developments signs of a world beyond capitalism and socialism? We cannot as yet be sure.

In the midst of all this, pronounced inequalities of wealth and power persist between individuals, collectivities and national communities. The tensions that these produce are not likely to be easily contained. How far the array of high-consequence risks that face all of us today can effectively be coped with is very difficult to gauge. Sociology has a key part to play in exploring the contours of this global milieu, the world of high modernity. It is up to us to ensure that the sociological imagination is not found wanting at such a complex and disturbing period of human social development.

Principal works by Anthony Giddens

For each year first books, then articles, are listed in alphabetical order. Review articles are included but not, with one lengthy exception, untitled book reviews.

1960

'Aspects of the social structure of a university hall of residence', *Sociological Review* 8: 97–108.

1964

a. 'Notes on the concepts of play and leisure', *Sociological Review* 12: 73–89.
b. 'Suicide, attempted suicide, and the suicidal threat', *Man: A Record of Anthropological Science* 64 art. 136: 115–6.

1965

a. 'Georg Simmel', *New Society* 4 (112): 24–5. Reprinted in T. Raison (ed.) (1969) *Founding Fathers of Sociology*, London: Penguin, pp. 136–43.
b. 'The present position of social psychology', *British Journal of Sociology* 16: 365–72.
c. With S.W.F. Holloway: 'Profiting from a comprehensive school: a critical comment', *British Journal of Sociology* 16: 351–3.
d. 'Suicide', *British Journal of Sociology* 16: 164–5.
e. 'The suicide problem in French sociology', *British Journal of Sociology* 16: 3–18. Reprinted in 1971b, Ch. 5; and in 1977a as an appendix to Ch. 10 (see 1977l).
f. 'Theoretical problems in the sociology of suicide', *Advancement of Science* 21: 522–6.

1966

'A typology of suicide', *Archives Européennes de Sociologie* 7: 276–95. Reprinted in 1971b, Ch. 10. Substantially revised version reprinted as 'A theory of suicide' in 1977a, Ch. 9.

1968

'"Power" in the recent writings of Talcott Parsons', *Sociology* 2: 257–72. Reprinted in 1977a, Ch. 10.

1970

a. 'Durkheim as a review critic', *Sociological Review* 18: 171–96.
b. 'Introduction', to T. Masaryk: *Suicide and the Meaning of Civilization*, Chicago: University of Chicago Press.
c. 'Marx, Weber and the development of capitalism', *Sociology* 4: 289–310. Reprinted in 1977a, Ch. 5.
d. 'Recent works on the history of social thought', *Archives Européennes de Sociologie* 11: 130–42.
e. 'Recent works on the position and prospects of contemporary sociology', *Archives Européennes de Sociologie* 11: 143–54.

1971

a. *Capitalism and Modern Social Theory: An analysis of the writings of Marx, Durkheim and Max Weber*, Cambridge: Cambridge University Press (261 pp.).
b. Editor: *The Sociology of Suicide*, London: Cass (424 pp.). In addition to 1965e and 1966 includes 'Introduction' (pp. ix–xviii); introductions to parts I to V, 'Durkheim and his contemporaries' (pp. 3–4), 'Theories of suicide' (pp. 55–7), 'Suicide in non-western societies' (pp. 155–7), 'Suicide in relation to social factors' (pp. 243–5) and 'The social context of the suicidal act' (pp. 317–19); and an appendix, 'The statistics of suicide' (pp. 419–24).
c. 'Durkheim's political sociology', *Sociological Review* 19: 477–519. Reprinted in 1977a, Ch. 7.
d. 'The "individual" in the writings of Emile Durkheim', *Archives Européennes de Sociologie* 12: 210–28. Reprinted in 1977a, Ch. 8.
e. 'Marx and Weber: a reply to Mr Walton', *Sociology* 5: 395–7.

1972

a. Editor and translator: *Emile Durkheim: Selected Writings*, Cambridge: Cambridge University Press (272 pp.). Includes 'Introduction: Durkheim's writings in sociology and social philosophy' (pp. 1–50).
b. *Politics and Sociology in the Thought of Max Weber*, London:

Macmillan; New York: Pall Mall (64 pp.).
c.   'Elites', art. 7 in series on Social Stratification, *New Society* 22 (258): 389–92.
d.   'Elites in the British class structure', *Sociological Review* 20:345–72. Reprinted in 1974b, Ch. 1.
e.   'Four Myths in the history of social thought', *Economy and Society* 1: 357–85. Reprinted in 1977a, Ch. 6.

1973

The Class Structure of the Advanced Societies, London: Hutchinson; New York: Harper & Row (336 pp.). Revised edn, 1981 (see 1981e).

1974

a.   Editor: *Positivism and Sociology*, London: Heinemann; New York: Basic Books (244 pp.). Includes 'Introduction' (pp. 1–22).
b.   Joint editor with P.H. Stanworth: *Elites and Power in British Society*, Cambridge: Cambridge University Press (261 pp.). Includes reprint of 1972d as Ch. 1.
c.   With P.H. Stanworth: 'An economic elite: a demographic profile of company chairmen', in 1974b, Ch. 5.

1975

a.   With P.H. Stanworth: 'The modern corporate economy: interlocking directorships in Britain, 1906–1970', *Sociological Review* 23: 5–28. Reprinted as *University of Cambridge Department of Applied Economics Sociology Reprints*, no. 3.
b.   'The high priest of positivism: Auguste Comte', *The Times Literary Supplement*, 14 November 1975. Reprinted in 1982c, Ch. 5.

1976

a.   *New Rules of Sociological Method: A Positive Critique of Interpretative Sociologies*, London: Hutchinson; New York: Harper & Row (192 pp.).
b.   'Classical social theory and the origins of modern sociology', *American Journal of Sociology* 81: 703–29. Reprinted in 1982c, Ch. 4.
c.   'Functionalism: *Après la Lutte*', *Social Research* 43: 325–66. Reprinted in 1977a, Ch. 2.
d.   'Hermeneutics, ethnomethodology and problems of interpretative analysis', in L. Coser and O. Larson (eds) *The Uses of Controversy in Sociology*, New York: Basic Books. Reprinted in 1977a, Ch. 4.
e.   'The rich', *New Society* 38 (732): 63–6.

1977

a. *Studies in Social and Political Theory*, London: Hutchinson; New York: Basic Books (416 pp.). Includes 'Introduction: some issues in the social sciences today' (pp. 9–28), reprints of 1965e, 1966, 1968, 1970c, 1971c, 1971d, 1972e, 1976c, d and the following new essays: 1977c, g, h, i, k, l.
b. 'Durkheim on social facts', appendix to 1971d in 1977a, Ch. 8.
c. 'Habermas's critique of hermeneutics', in 1977a, Ch. 3; and in J.W. Freiberg (ed.): *Critical Sociology: European Perspectives*, New York: Irvington (1979) pp. 39–70.
d. 'Habermas's social and political theory', *American Journal of Sociology* 83: 198–212. Reprinted in 1982c, Ch. 7.
e. 'Introduction', to M. Weber: *The Protestant Ethic and the Spirit of Capitalism*, London: Allen & Unwin, pp. 1–12b.
f. 'Marx and Weber: problems of class structure', appendix to 1970c in 1977a, Ch. 5.
g. 'Max Weber on facts and values', appendix to 1977j in 1977a, Ch. 1.
h. 'Max Weber on interpretative sociology', appendix to 1976d in 1977a, Ch. 4.
i. 'Notes on the theory of structuration', appendix to 1976c in 1977a, Ch. 2.
j. 'Positivism and its critics', in 1977a, Ch. 2; and in T.B. Bottomore and R. Nisbet (eds): *A History of Sociological Analysis*, London: Heinemann, Ch. 7.
k. 'Remarks on the theory of power', appendix to 1968 in 1977a, Ch. 10.
l. 'A theory of suicide', in 1977a, Ch. 9. Substantially revised version of 1966.

1978

a. *Durkheim*, London: Fontana; New York: Penguin (125 pp.).
b. 'Class and classless society', *Partisan Review* 45: 133–45.
c. 'Foreword', to M. Halbwachs: *The Causes of Suicide*, London: Routledge & Kegan Paul, pp. xvi–xx.
d. With P.H. Stanworth: 'Elites and privileges', in P. Abrams (ed.) *Work, Urbanism and Inequality: U.K. Society Today*, London: Weidenfeld & Nicolson, Ch. 4.

1979

a. *Central Problems in Social Theory*, London: Macmillan; Berkeley: University of California Press (294 pp.). Includes 'Introduction' (pp. 1–8) and 1979h.
b. 'An anatomy of the British ruling class', *New Society* 50 (887): 8–10.
c. 'Literature and society: Raymond Williams', *The Times Higher Education Supplement*, 14 December 1979. Reprinted in 1982c, Ch. 10.

Bibliography I

d. 'The prospects for social theory today', *Berkeley Journal of Sociology* 23: 201–23. Also published as Ch. 7 of 1979a.
e. 'Schutz and Parsons: problems of meaning and subjectivity', *Contemporary Sociology* 8: 682–5. Reprinted in 1982c, Ch. 6.

1980

'Classes, capitalism and the state. A discussion of F. Parkin: *Marxism and Class Theory: A Bourgeois Critique* [London, Tavistock, 1976]', *Theory and Society* 9: 877–90. Reprinted in 1982c, Ch. 13.

1981

a. A Contemporary Critique of Historical Materialism, vol. 1: *Power, Property and the State,* London: Macmillan; Berkeley, University of California Press (294 pp.).
b. 'Agency, institution, and time-space analysis', in K. Knorr-Cetina and A.V. Cicourel (eds), *Advances in Social Theory and Methodology: Toward an Integration of Micro- and Macro-Sociologies,* London: Routledge & Kegan Paul, Ch. 5.
c. 'Durkheim, Socialism and Marxism' in A. Izzo and others (eds), *Durkheim,* Rome, Institute of Sociology. Reprinted in 1982c, Ch. 9.
d. 'Modernism and post-modernism', *New German Critique* 22: 15–18.
e. 'Postscript', to 2nd edn of 1973a, pp. 295–320 (notes pp. 343–6).
f. 'Sociology and philosophy', in P. Secord (ed.), *Action Theory and Structural Analysis,* Oxford: Blackwell.
g. 'Time and space in social theory: critical remarks upon functionalism', in S.G. McNall and G.N. Howe (eds) *Current Perspectives in Social Theory,* vol. 2: 3–13, Greenwich, Conn.: JAI Press.
h. 'Trends in the philosophy of the social sciences', in D. Lawton (ed.), *Current Perspectives in Education,* London: Methuen.

1982

a. Joint editor with G. Mackenzie: *Classes and the Division of Labour: Essays in Honour of Ilya Neustadt,* Cambridge: Cambridge University Press (337 pp.). Includes editors' 'Introduction' (pp. 1–11) and 1982m.
b. Joint editor with D. Held, *Classes, Power and Conflict: Classical and Contemporary Debates,* London: Macmillan; Berkeley: University of California Press (646 pp.). Includes editors' 'Introduction' (pp. 3–11) and introductions to each of eight parts, and a reprint of pp. 105–17 and 296–311 of 1973a.
c. *Profiles and Critiques in Social Theory,* London: Macmillan; Berkeley: University of California Press (239 pp.). Includes reprints of 1975b, 1976b, 1977d, 1979c and e, 1980, 1981c; and the following previously unpublished essays: 1982i and j. In addition duplicates

1982i, k, most of l, and m (with some amendments). Also includes as Ch. 2 'The theory of structuration: a critique' by F. Dallmayr with a response (pp. 26–7) from Giddens and a rejoinder to the response.

d.   *Sociology: A Brief but Critical Introduction*, London: Macmillan; New York: Harcourt Brace, Jovanowitch (179 pp.).

e.   'Class division, class conflict and citizenship rights', in 1982c, Ch. 12.

f.   'Commentary on the debate [on Marxism, functionalism, game theory]', *Theory and Society* 11: 527–39.

g.   'From Marx to Nietzsche? Neo-conservatism, Foucault, and problems in contemporary political theory', in 1982c, Ch. 15.

h.   'Historical materialism today: an interview with Anthony Giddens', *Theory, Culture and Society* 1: 63–77.

i.   'Hermeneutics and social theory', in 1982c, Ch. 1. Reprinted with editors' amendments in G. Shapiro and A. Sica (eds), *Hermeneutics: Questions and Prospects*, Amherst: University of Massachusetts Press, 1984.

j.   'The improbable guru: re-reading Marcuse', in 1982c, Ch. 11.

k.   'Labour and interaction', in J. Thompson and D. Held (eds) *Habermas: Critical Debates*, London: Macmillan, Ch. 8. Also in 1982c, Ch. 8.

l.   'On the relation of sociology to philosophy', in P.F. Secord (ed.) *Explaining Human Behaviour*, Beverley Hills: Sage, Ch. 9. Largely duplicated in 1982c, Ch. 3, 'Action, structure, power'.

m.   'Power, the dialectic of control and class structuration', in 1982a, pp. 29–45. Also in 1982c, Ch. 14, with slight amendments.

n.   'A reply to my critics', *Theory, Culture and Society* 1: 107–13.

o.   'Reason without revolution: Habermas's *Theorie des Kommunikativen Handelns*', *Praxis International* 2: 318–38. Reprinted in R.J. Bernstein (ed.) *Habermas and Modernity*, Cambridge, Polity Press, 1985, 1987a, Ch. 10.

p.   Contribution to a review symposium of U. Himmelstand, G. Ahrne, L. Lundberg and L. Lundberg: *Beyond Welfare Capitalism* (London: Heinemann, 1981), *Acta Sociologica* 25: 308–13.

q.   'Space, time and politics in social theory: an interview with Anthony Giddens', *Society and Space* 2: 123–32.

1983

a.   'Comments on the theory of structuration', *Journal for the Theory of Social Behaviour* 13: 75–80.

b.   'Four theses on ideology', *Canadian Journal of Political and Social Theory* 7: 18–21.

1984

a.   *The Constitution of Society: Outline of the Theory of Structuration*, Cambridge: Polity Press; Berkeley: University of California Press (402 pp.).

b. 'Nation-states and violence', in W.W. Powell and R. Robbins (eds) *Conflict and Consensus: A Festschrift in Honour of Lewis Coser*, New York: Free Press. Reprinted in 1987a, Ch. 7.

1985

a. *The Nation-State and Violence*, vol. 2 of *A Contemporary Critique of Historical Materialism*, Cambridge: Polity Press; Berkeley: University of California Press (399 pp.).
b. 'Alvin Gouldner and the intellectuals', *The Times Literary Supplement*, 6 September 1985. Revised version published in 1987a, Ch. 11.
c. 'Jürgen Habermas', in Q. Skinner (ed.) *The Return of Grand Theory in the Human Sciences*, Cambridge: Cambridge University Press, Ch. 7.
d. 'Liberalism and sociology', *Contemporary Sociology* 14: 320–2.
e. 'Marx's correct views on everything (with apologies to L. Kolokowski)' *Theory and Society* 14: 167–74.
f. 'Time, space and regionalisation', in D. Gregory and J. Urry (eds) *Social Research and Spatial Relations*, London: Macmillan, Ch. 12.

1986

a. Editor: *Durkheim on Politics and the State*, Cambridge: Polity Press; Stanford: Stanford University Press (250 pp.). Includes editor's 'Introduction', pp. 1–31.
b. 'Action, subjectivity, and the constitution of meaning', *Social Research* 53: 529–45.

1987

a. *Social Theory and Modern Sociology*, Cambridge: Polity Press; Stanford: Stanford University Press (310 pp.). Includes reprints of 1982o, 1984b and 1985b (revised) and the following previously unpublished essays: 1987c – k.
b. Joint editor with J.H. Turner: *Social Theory Today*, Cambridge: Polity Press. Includes editors' 'Introduction' (pp. 1–10) and 1987i.
c. 'Erving Goffman as a systematic social theorist', in 1987a, Ch. 5.
d. 'Nine theses on the future of sociology', in 1987a, Ch. 2.
e. 'Out of the orrery: E.P. Thompson on consciousness and history', in 1987a, Ch. 9.
f. 'The perils of punditry: Gorz and the end of the working class', in 1987a, Ch. 12.
g. 'The social sciences and philosophy – trends in recent social theory', in 1987a, Ch. 3.
h. 'Social theory and problems of macroeconomics', in 1987a, Ch. 8.
i. 'Structuralism, post-structuralism and the production of culture', in 1987a, Ch. 4. Also in 1987b, pp. 195–223.

228

j. 'Time and social organization', in 1987a, Ch. 6.
k. 'What do sociologists do?', University of Cambridge Inaugural Lecture, in 1987a, Ch. 1.

1988

'Globalisation and modern development', in E. Bartocci (ed.) *Social Change and Social Conflict in Neo-Industrial Society*, Rome: Institute of Sociology.

1989

a. *Sociology*, UK edn, Cambridge: Polity Press (815 pp.).
b. 'Comments on Paul Kennedy's *The Rise and Fall of the Great Powers* [London: Unwin Hyman, 1988], contribution to review symposium, *British Journal of Sociology* 40: 328–31.
c. 'Reply to my critics', in D. Held and J.B. Thompson (eds) *Social Theory of Modern Societies: Anthony Giddens and His Critics*, Cambridge: Cambridge University Press, ch. 12.

1990

a. *Sociology*, US edn (some different content from UK edn), New York: Norton.
b. *The Consequences of Modernity*, Cambridge: Polity Press; Stanford: Stanford University Press (186pp.).
c. 'Preface' to T. Scheff: *Microsociology*, Chicago: University of Chicago Press.
d. 'R.K. Merton on Structural Analysis', in J. Clark, C. Modgil and S. Modgil (eds), *Robert Merton: Consensus and Controversy*, London, Falmer Press, Ch. 8.
e. 'Structuration theory and sociological analysis', in J. Clark, C. Modgil and S. Modgil (eds) *Anthony Giddens: Consensus and Controversy*, Brighton: Falmer Press, Ch. 22.
f. 'Structuration theory: past, present and future', in C.G.A. Bryant and D. Jary (eds), *Giddens' Theory of Structuration: A Critical Appreciation*, London: Routledge, Ch. 8.

Other works

This list includes all works cited in the text, except works by Giddens, which are listed in Bibliography I. The list also contains a number of references to commentaries and reviews of Giddens' work that are not cited directly in the text. No attempt has been made, however, to provide a comprehensive listing of all such works.

In the text each reference is identified by the author's surname and year of first publication (or in some cases the year in which the work was first written). In the bibliography the identified year (together with the language, if not English) is given after the author's name. The details of the publications that follow are of the editions used in preparing this book; where this was the first edition the year of publication is not repeated.

Abel, P. (1988) 'The "structuration" of action', in N. Fielding (ed.) *Actions and Structures*, London: Sage.

Abrams, P. (1980) 'History, sociology and historical sociology', *Past and Present* 87: 3–16.

—— (1981) 'The collapse of British sociology?' in P. Abrams, R. Deem, J. Finch and P. Rock (eds) *Practice and Progress: British Sociology 1950–1980*, London: Allen & Unwin.

—— (1982) *Historical Sociology*, London: Open Books.

Adorno, T., Frankel-Brunswick, E., Levinson, D., and Sandford, K. (1950) *The Authoritarian Personality*, New York: Harper & Row.

Agger, B. (1989) *Socio(onto)logy*, Urbana: University of Illinois Press.

Alexander, J. (1987a) *Sociological Theory Since 1945*, London: Heinemann.

—— (1987b) 'The centrality of the classics', in A. Giddens and J. Turner (eds) *Social Theory Today*, Cambridge: Polity Press.

Althusser, L. and Balibar, E. (1970) *Reading Capital*, London: New Left Books.

Anderson, P. (1974a) *Passages from Antiquity to Feudalism*, London: New Left Books.

—— (1974b) *Lineages of the Absolutist State*, London: New Left Books.

—— (1986) 'Those in authority', review of Mann (1986), in *Times Literary Supplement*, 12 December: 1405–6.

Appelbaum, R. (1988) 'Giddens joins UC-SB Sociology Department', *Footnotes*, November.
Archer, M. (1982) 'Morphogenesis versus structuration: on combining structure and action', *British Journal of Sociology* 33: 455–83.
—— (1985) 'Structuration versus morphogenesis', in S. Eisenstadt and H. Helle (eds) *Macro-sociological Theory: Perspectives on Sociological Theory*, vol. 1, London: Sage.
Aron, R. (1981) *Peace and War*, Malibur: Kreiger.
Ashley, D. (1982) 'Historical materialism and social evolutionism', *Theory, Culture and Society* 1: 89–92.
Atkinson, D. (1972) *Orthodox Consensus and Radical Alternative*, New York: Basic Books.
Attewell, P. (1974) 'Ethnomethodology since Garfinkel', *Theory and Society* 1: 179–210.
Bagguley, P. (1984) 'Giddens and historical materialism', *Radical Philosophy* 38: 18–24.
Bagguley, P., Mark-Lawson, J., Shapiro, D., Urry, J., Walby, S. and Warde, A. (1989) *Restructuring. Place, Class and Gender*, London: Sage.
Barbalet, J. (1987) 'Structural resources, and agency', *Current Perspectives in Social Theory* 8: 1–24.
Barnes, B. (1974) *Scientific Knowledge and Sociological Theory*, London: Routledge & Kegan Paul.
—— (1980) Review of *Central Problems*, in *Sociological Review* 28: 674–6.
Bauman, Z. (1976) *Towards a Critical Sociology*, London: Routledge & Kegan Paul.
Baynes, K., Bohman, J. and McCarthy, T. (eds) (1987) *After Philosophy: End or Transformation?* London: MIT Press.
Bendix, R. (1977) *Nation Building or Citizenship*, Berkeley: University of California Press.
—— (1978) *Kings or People*, Berkeley: University of California Press.
Berger, P. and Luckmann, T. (1966) *The Social Construction of Reality*, Harmondsworth: Penguin.
Bernstein, R. (1983) *Beyond Objectivism and Relativism*, Oxford: Blackwell.
—— (1986a) 'Structuration as critical theory', *Praxis International* 6: 235–49.
—— (ed.) (1986b) *Habermas and Modernity*, Cambridge: Polity Press.
Bertilsson, M. (1984) 'The theory of structuration: prospects and problems', *Acta Sociologica* 27: 339–53.
Bhaskar, R. (1975) *A Realist Theory of Science*, Leeds: Leeds Books.
—— (1979) *The Possibility of Naturalism: a Philosophical Critique of Contemporary Human Science*, Brighton: Harvester.
—— (1983) 'Beef, structure and place: notes from a critical naturalist perspective', *Journal for the Theory of Social Behaviour* 13: 81–95.
—— (1986) *Scientific Realism and Human Emancipation*, London: Verso.

Blau, P. and Duncan, O. (1967) *American Occupational Structure*, New York: Free Press.

Bleicher, J. (1980) *Contemporary Hermeneutics: Hermeneutics as Method, Philosophy and Critique*, London: Routledge & Kegan Paul.

Bleicher, J. and Featherstone, M. (1982) 'Historical materialism today: an interview with Anthony Giddens', *Theory, Culture and Society* 1: 63–77.

Blum, A. (1974) *Theorizing*, London: Heinemann.

Bourdieu, P. (1977) *Outline of a Theory of Practice*, Cambridge: Cambridge University Press.

—— (1984) *Distinction: A Social Critique of the Judgement of Taste*, London: Routledge.

Bramsted, E. and Melhuish, K. (eds) (1978) *Western Liberalism: A History in Documents from Locke to Croce*, London: Longman.

Braverman, H. (1974) *Labour and Monopoly Capital*, New York: Monthly Review Press.

Brown, R. (1987) 'Norbert Elias in Leicester: some recollections', *Theory, Culture and Society* 4: 533–9.

Bryant, C. (1976) *Sociology in Action: A Critique of Selected Conceptions of the Social Role of the Sociologist*, London: Allen & Unwin.

—— (1987a) 'Developing theories', review of *Social Theory and Modern Society* in *Times Higher Education Supplement*, 24 April.

—— (1987b) 'The constitution of society: Elias, Bhaskar and Giddens compared', Paper presented to the faculty of Social Sciences, University of Utrecht, mimeo.

—— (1989) 'Towards post-empiricist sociological theorizing', *British Journal of Sociology* 40: 319–27.

Bryant, C. and Becker, H. (eds) (1990) *What Has Sociology Achieved?*, London: Macmillan.

Bulmer, M. (1982) *The Uses of Social Research: Social Investigation in Public Policy-Making*, London: Allen & Unwin.

—— (1990) 'Successful applications of sociology', in C. Bryant and H. Becker (eds) *What Has Sociology Achieved?*, London: Macmillan.

Burman, P. (1988) *Killing Time, Losing Ground*, Toronto: Wall & Thompson.

Callinicos, A. (1985) 'Anthony Giddens – a contemporary critique', *Theory and Society* 14: 133–66.

—— (1987) *Making History: Agency, Structure and Change in Social Theory*, Cambridge: Polity Press.

Camic, C. (1989) '*Structure* After 50 Years', *American Journal of Sociology* 95: 38–107.

Carlstein, T. (1981) 'The sociology of structuration in time and space: a time-geographic assessment of Giddens' theory', *Swedish Geographical Yearbook*: 41–57.

Childe, G. (1956) (3rd edn) *Man Makes Himself*, London: Watts.

Clark, J., Modgil, C. and Modgil, F. (eds) (1990) *Anthony Giddens, Consensus and Controversy*, Brighton: Falmer Press.

Clarke, S. (1981) *The Foundations of Structuralism*, Brighton: Harvester.

Cohen, I. (1986) 'The status of structuration theory: a reply to McLennan', *Theory, Culture and Society* 3: 123–33.
—— (1987) 'Structuration theory and social praxis', in A. Giddens and J. Turner (eds) *Social Theory Today*.
Cohen, P. (1968) *Modern Social Theory*, London: Heinemann.
Collingwood, R. (1946) *The Idea of History*, Oxford: Oxford University Press (1973).
Collins R. (1985) *Three Sociological Traditions*, New York: Oxford University Press.
—— (1986) *Weberian Sociological Theory*, Cambridge: Cambridge University Press.
Colson, F. (1926) *The Week*, Westport, Conn: Greenwood Press.
Connell, R. (1987) *Gender and Power*, Cambridge: Polity Press.
Cooper, D. (1972) *The Death of the Family*, Harmondsworth: Penguin.
Craib, I. (1984) *Modern Social Theory From Parsons to Habermas*, Brighton: Wheatsheaf.
—— (1986) 'Back to Utopia: Anthony Giddens and modern social theory', *Radical Philosophy* 43: 17–21.
Dainton, Sir F. (1971) 'The future of the Research Council System', in *A Framework for Government Research and Development*, CMND 4184. London: HMSO.
Dallmayr, F. (1982) 'Agency and structure', *Philosophy of Social Science* 12: 427–38.
Dandeker, C. (1989) *Surveillance, Power and Modernity*, Cambridge: Polity Press.
Daniels, S. and Cosgrove, D. (1988) 'Introduction: iconography and landscape' in D. Cosgrove and S. Daniels (eds) *The Iconography of Landscape*, Cambridge: Cambridge University Press.
Dawe, A. (1970) 'The two sociologies', *British Journal of Sociology* 21: 107–18.
Demerath, N. and Peterson, R. (eds) (1967) *System, Change, and Conflict*, New York: Free Press.
Derrida, J. (1981) *Dissemination*, London: Athlone.
Dickie-Clark, H. (1984) 'Anthony Giddens' theory of structuration', *Canadian Journal of Political and Social Theory* 8: 92–110.
—— (1986) 'The making of a social theory: Anthony Giddens' theory of structuration', *Sociological Focus* 19: 159–76.
Dobson, K. (1979) 'Persons and people: conceptualizing individuality and collectivity through Evelyn Waugh's *The Ordeal of Gilbert Pinfold*', *Leeds Occasional Papers in Sociology*, no. 9.
Donnison, D. (1972) 'Research for policy', in M. Bulmer (ed.) *Social Policy Research*, London: Macmillan.
Durkheim, E. (French 1895) *The Rules of Sociological Method*, Glencoe: Free Press (1938).
Eberhard, W. (1965) *Conquerors and Rulers*, Leiden: Brill.
Edgar, D. (1987) 'The new nostalgia', *Marxism Today*, March: 30–5.
Elchardus, M. (1988) 'The rediscovery of Chronos: the new role of time in sociological theory', *International Sociology* 3: 35–59.

Elias, N. (1969) *Psychiatry in a Changing Society*, London: Tavistock.
—— (German 1939) *The Civilizing Process*, Oxford: Blackwell (1978).
—— (German 1970) *What is Sociology?* London: Hutchinson (1978).
—— (1987) 'The retreat of sociologists into the present', *Theory, Culture and Society* 4: 223–47.
Eisenstadt, S. (1987) 'Macrosociology and sociological theory: some new directions', *Contemporary Sociology* 16: 602–9.
Erikson, E. (1968) *Identity: Youth and Crisis*, London: Faber (1983).
Feyerabend, P. (1975) *Against Method*, London: New Left Books.
—— (1981) *Realism, Rationalism and Scientific Method*, Cambridge: Cambridge University Press (see especially the 'Introduction', pp. vii–xii).
Foucault, M. (French 1961) *Madness and Civilisation*, London: Tavistock (1967).
—— (French 1975) *Discipline and Punish*, London: Allen Lane Press (1977).
—— (1980) in C. Gordon (ed.) *Power/Knowledge: Selected Interviews and other Writings 1972–77*, Brighton: Harvester.
Frampton, K. (1988) 'Place-form and cultural identity', in J. Thackara (ed.) *Design After Postmodernism*, London: Thames & Hudson.
Freeden, M. (1978) *The New Liberalism: an Ideology of Social Reform*, Oxford: Clarendon Press.
Friedland, R. (1987) 'Giddens' golden gloves', *Contemporary Sociology* 16: 40–2.
Friedman, M. (1953) *Essays in Positive Economics*, Chicago: University of Chicago Press.
Fulbrook, M. and Skocpol, T. (1964) 'Destined pathways: the historical sociology of Perry Anderson', in T. Skocpol (ed.) *Vision and Method in Historical Sociology*, Cambridge: Cambridge University Press.
Gadamer, H. (1960) *Truth and Method*, London: Sheed & Ward.
Gane, M. (1983) 'Anthony Giddens and the crisis in social theory', *Economy and Society* 11: 368–98.
Garfinkel, H. (1967) *Studies in Ethnomethodology*, Englewood Cliffs, New Jersey: Prentice Hall.
Gellner, E. (1964) *Thought and Change*, London: Weidenfeld & Nicolson.
—— (1983) *Nations and Nationalism*, Oxford: Blackwell.
Gerth, H. and Mills, C.W. (eds) (1948) *From Max Weber: Essays in Sociology*, London: Routledge & Kegan Paul (1970).
Goffman, E. (1959) *The Presentation of Self in Everyday Life*, New York: Doubleday.
—— (1974) *Frame Analysis*, New York: Harper.
Gottlieb, R. (1986) 'Three contemporary critiques of historical materialism', *Philosophy and Social Criticism* 11: 87–101.
Goudsblom, J. (1977) *Sociology in the Balance*, Oxford: Blackwell.
Gouldner, A. (1970) *The Coming Crisis of Western Sociology*, New York: Basic Books.
Gregory, D. (1984) 'Space, time and politics in social theory: an interview

with Anthony Giddens', *Society and Space* 2: 123–32.

—— (1985) 'Suspended animation: the stasis of diffusion theory', in D. Gregory and J. Urry (eds) *Social Relations and Spatial Structures*, London: Macmillan.

—— (1989) 'Presences and absences: time-space relations and structuration theory', in D. Held and J. Thompson (eds) *Social Theory of Modern Societies: Anthony Giddens and His Critics*, Cambridge: Cambridge University Press.

Gregory, D. and Urry, J. (eds) (1985) *Social Relations and Spatial Structures*, London: Macmillan.

Gregson, N. (1986) 'On duality and dualism: the case of structuration and time-geography', *Progress in Human Geography* 10: 184–205.

Gross, D. (1982) 'Time-space relations in Giddens' social theory', *Theory, Culture and Society* 1: 83–4.

Gruneau, R. (1983) *Class, Sports and Social Development*, Amherst: University of Massachusetts Press.

Gurvitch, G. (ed.) (1958) *Traité de Sociologie*, Paris: Presses Universitaires de France, vol. 1.

Habermas, J (German 1968) *Knowledge and Human Interests*, London: Heinemann (1972).

—— (1970) 'On systematically distorted communication', *Inquiry* 13: 205–18.

—— (German 1973) *Legitimation Crisis*, London: Heineman (1976).

—— (German 1976) 'What is universal pragmatics?', in his *Communication and the Evolution of Society*, London: Heinemann.

Hägerstrand, T. (1953) *Innovation as a Spatial Process*, Chicago: University of Chicago Press (1976).

—— (1975) 'Space, time and human conditions', in A. Karlquist (ed.) *Dynamic Allocation of Urban Space*, Farnborough: Saxon House.

Hall, J. (1984) Review of *Nation-State and Violence*, *Sociological Review* 35: 430–4.

Halsey, A. (1989) 'A turning of the tide? The prospects for sociology in Britain', *British Journal of Sociology* 40: 353–73.

Harley, J. (1988) 'Maps, knowledge and power', in D. Cosgrove and S. Daniels (eds) *The Iconography of Landscape*, Cambridge: Cambridge University Press.

Harré, R. (1979) *Social Being*, Oxford: Blackwell.

Harvey, D. (1985) 'The geopolitics of capitalism', in D. Gregory and J. Urry (eds) *Social Relations and Spatial Structures*, London: Macmillan.

Hazelrigg, L. (1989a) *Wilderness of Mirrors*, Gainesville: University Presses of Florida.

—— (1989b) *Claims of Knowledge*, Gainesville: University Presses of Florida.

Hechter, M. (1987) Review of *Nation-State and Violence*, *American Journal of Sociology* 93: 516–8.

Hegel, G. (German 1807) *The Phenomenology of the Mind*, 2 vols, London: Sonnenschein (1910).

Heidegger, M. (1978) *Being and Time*, Oxford: Blackwell.

Held, D. and Thompson, J. (eds) (1989) *Social Theory of Modern Socie-ties: Anthony Giddens and His Critics*, Cambridge: Cambridge University Press.

Heritage, J. (1987) 'Ethnomethodology', in A. Giddens and J. Turner (eds) *Social Theory Today*, Cambridge: Polity Press.

Hesse, M. (1980) 'In defence of objectivity', in her *Revolutions and Reconstructions in the Philosophy of Science*, Brighton: Harvester.

Hewison, R. (1987) *The Heritage Industry*, London: Methuen.

Hill, R. and Crittenden, K. (eds) (1968) *The Proceedings of the Purdue Symposium on Ethnomethodology*, Lafayette: Indiana.

Hindess, B. (1977) Review of *New Rules*, *British Journal of Sociology* 30: 510–12.

Hindess, B. and Hirst, P. (1975) *Pre-capitalist Modes of Production*, London: Routledge & Kegan Paul.

Hirst, P. (1982) 'The social theory of Anthony Giddens: a new syncretism', *Theory, Culture and Society* 1: 78–82.

Hoffman, L. (1982) 'From instinct to identity: implications of changing psychoanalytic concepts of social life from Freud to Erikson', *Journal of the History of the Behavioural Sciences* 18: 130–46.

Horkheimer, M. and Adorno, T. (1947) *The Dialectic of Enlightenment*, New York: Herder & Herder (1972).

Howard, R. (1986) *Brave New Workplace*, New York: Penguin.

Jacobs, J. (1970) *The Economy of Cities*, London: Cape.

Jameson, F. (1984) 'Postmodernism and consumer society', in H. Foster (ed.) *Postmodern Culture*, London: Pluto Press.

Janelle, D. (1968) 'Central place development in a time-space framework', *Professional Geographer* 20: 5–10.

—— (1969) 'Spatial reorganization: a model and concept', *Annals of the Association of American Geographers* 58: 348–64.

Janowitz, M. (1971) *Sociological Models and Social Policy*, New York: General Learning Press.

Jary, D. (1981) 'The "new realism" in sociological theory', in P. Abrams and P. Laithwaite (eds) *Development and Diversity: British Sociology*, 1950–80, vol. 2, London: BSA.

—— (1984) Review of *Profiles and Critiques*, in *Political Studies* 34: 167–8.

—— (1989) 'Beyond objectivity and relativism: Paul Feyerabend's two "argumentative chains"', *Poznan Studies in the Philosophy of Social Science and Humanities* 20: 1–13.

Jary, D. and Horne, J. (1988) 'The figurational sociology of sport and leisure of Elias and Dunning and its alternatives', *Loisir et Société* 10: 177–94.

Joas, H (1987) 'Giddens' theory of structuration: introductory remarks on a sociological transformation of the philosophy of praxis', *International Sociology* 2: 13–26.

Johnson, T., Dandeker, C. and Ashworth, C. (1984) *The Structure of Social Theory*, London: Macmillan.

Kern, S. (1983) *The Culture of Time and Space, 1880–1918*, London:

Weidenfeld & Nicolson.

Kilminster, R. (1979) *Praxis and Method: a Sociological Dialogue with Lukàcs, Gramsci and the Early Frankfurt School*, London: Routledge & Kegan Paul.

—— 'Zur Utopiediskussion aus soziologischer Sicht', in W. Vosskamp (ed.) *Utopieforschung*, vol. 2, Stuttgart: Metzler Verlag.

—— (1989) 'Sociology and the professional culture of philosophers', in H. Haferkamp (ed.) *Social Structure and Culture*, Berlin and New York: Walter de Gruyter.

Knorr-Cetina, K. and Cicourel, A. (1981) *Advances in Social Theory and Methodology: Toward an Integration of Micro- and Macro-Sociologies*, London: Routledge & Kegan Paul.

Kroker, A. and Cook, D. (1986) *The Postmodern Scene*, New York: St Martin's Press.

Kuhn, T. (1962) *The Structure of Scientific Revolutions*, 2nd edn, Chicago: Chicago University Press (1970).

Laeyendecker, L. (1990) 'What Dutch sociology has achieved', in C. Bryant and H. Becker (eds) *What Has Sociology Achieved?*, London: Macmillan.

Landes, D. (1983) *Revolution in Time: Clocks and the Making of the Modern World*, Cambridge, Mass: Harvard University Press.

Lane, T. (1982) 'The unions: caught on an ebb tide', *Marxism Today*, September: 6–13.

LaPierre, R. (1960) *The Freudian Ethic: an Analysis of the Subversion of Western Character*, London: Allen & Unwin.

Lash, S. and Urry, J. (1984) 'The new Marxism of collective action: a critical analysis', *Sociology* 18: 33–51.

—— (1987) *The End of Organized Capitalism*, Cambridge: Polity Press.

Layder, D. (1981) *Structure, Interaction and Social Theory*, London: Routledge & Kegan Paul.

—— (1982) Review of *Contemporary Critique* in *Sociological Review* 30: 518–60.

—— (1985) 'Power structure and agency', *Journal for the Theory of Social Behaviour* 15: 131–49.

—— (1987) 'Key issues in structuration theory', *Current Perspectives in Social Theory* 8: 25–46.

Lenski, G. (1966) *Power and Privilege: a Theory of Social Stratification*, New York: McGraw Hill.

Levine, A. and Wright, E. (1980) 'Rationality and the class struggle', *New Left Review* (123): 47–68.

Lévi-Strauss, C. (French 1962) *The Savage Mind*, London: Weidenfeld & Nicolson (1976).

—— (French 1964) *The Raw and the Cooked*, New York: Harper & Row (1975).

Lindblom, C. and Cohen, D. (1979) *Usable Knowledge: Social Science and Social Problem Solving*, New Haven: Yale University Press.

Lipsey, R.G. (1963–89) *An Introduction to Positive Economics*, London: Weidenfeld & Nicolson, 1st to 7th edns.

Livesay, J. (1985) 'Normative grounding and praxis: Habermas, Giddens, and a contradiction within critical theory', *Sociological Theory* 3: 66–76.

Lockwood, D. (1956) 'Some remarks on the social system', *British Journal of Sociology* 7: 134–43.

Louch, A. (1967) *Explanation and Human Action*, Oxford: Blackwell.

McHugh, P., Raffel, S., Foss, D. and Blum, A. (1974) *On the Beginning of Social Enquiry*, London: Routledge & Kegan Paul.

Macintosh, N. and Scapens, R. (1987) 'Giddens' structuration theory: its implications for empirical research in management accounting', *Working Papers in Accountancy*, no. 10, Queens University, Kingston: Canada.

MacKenzie, J. and Richards, J. (1986) *The Railway Station. A Social History*, Oxford: Oxford University Press.

McLennan, G. (1984) 'Critical or positive theory? A comment on the status of Anthony Giddens' social theory', *Theory, Culture and Society* 2: 123–9.

—— (1985) 'Agency and totality', a review of *Constitution of Society*, in *Radical Philosophy* 40: 33.

—— (1988) 'Structuration theory and post-empiricist philosophy: a rejoinder', *Theory, Culture and Society* 5: 101–9.

Manicas, P. (1980) 'The concept of social structure', *Journal for the Theory of Social Behaviour* 10: 65–82.

Mann, M. (1986) *The Sources of Social Power (Vol. 1) – A History of Power From the Beginning to A.D. 1760*, Cambridge: Cambridge University Press.

Mannheim, K. (German 1928) 'Competition as a Cultural Phenomenon', *Essays on the Sociology of Knowledge*, London: Routledge & Kegan Paul (1952).

—— (German 1929) *Ideology and Utopia*, London: Routledge & Kegan Paul (1960).

Marglin, S. (1976) 'What do the bosses do?' in A. Gorz (ed.) *The Division of Labour*, Brighton: Hassocks.

Marshall, T.H. (1973) *Class, Citizenship and Social Development*, Westport: Greenwood Press.

—— (1982) 'Foreword' to A. Giddens and G. Mackenzie (eds) *Social Class and the Division of Labour: Essays in Honour of Ilya Neustadt*, Cambridge: Cambridge University Press.

Martins, H. (1974) 'Time and theory in sociology' in J. Rex (ed.) *Approaches to Sociology: an Introduction to Major Trends in British Sociology*, London: Routledge & Kegan Paul.

Marx, K. (German 1857–8) *Grundrisse*, Harmondsworth: Penguin (1973).

—— (German 1867, ph 1885, ph 1894) *Capital*, Moscow: Foreign Languages Publishing House (vol. 1, 1954; vol. 2, 1957; vol. 3, 1962).

Massey, D. (1984) *Spatial Divisions of Labour*, London: Macmillan.

Merton, R. (1965) *On the Shoulders of Giants*, New York: Harcourt Brace Jovanovich.

—— (1968a) *Social Theory and Social Structure*, London: Collier Macmillan.

—— (1968b) 'On the history and systematics of sociological theory', in R. Merton (1968) *Social Theory and Social Structure*, London: Collier Macmillan.

—— (1981) 'Foreward: Remarks on theoretical pluralism', in R. Merton and P. Blau (eds), *Continuities in Structural Inquiry*, Beverley Hills: Sage.

Moore, B. (1969) *The Social Origins of Dictatorship and Democracy*, London: Allen Lane Press.

Mouzelis, N. (1989) 'Restructuring structuration theory', *Sociological Review* 37: 613–35.

Mullan, B. (1987) 'Anthony Giddens', in his *Sociologists on Sociology*, London: Croom Helm.

Mumford, E. (1960) 'Universal city', in C. Kraeling and R. Adams (eds) *City Invisible*, Chicago: University of Chicago Press.

Nairn, T. (1977) *The Break-up of Britain*, London: New Left Books.

Neustadt, I. (1965) *Teaching Sociology: an Inaugural Lecture*, Leicester: Leicester University Press.

Outhwaite, W. (1983) *Concept Formation in Social Science*, London: Routledge & Kegan Paul.

—— (1985) 'Hans-Georg Gadamer', in Q. Skinner (ed.) *The Return of Grand Theory in the Human Sciences*, Cambridge: Cambridge University Press.

Owen, D. (1951) *Social Romanticism in France, 1830–48*, Oxford: Oxford University Press.

Parsons, T. (1937) *The Structure of Social Action*, Glencoe: Free Press (1949).

—— (1938) 'The role of theory in social research' in P. Hamilton (ed.) (1985) *Readings from Talcott Parsons*, London: Tavistock.

Piaget, J. (1971) *Structuralism*, London: Routledge & Kegan Paul.

Popper, J. (1961) *The Poverty of Historicism*, London: Routledge & Kegan Paul.

Pred, A. (1977) 'The choreography of existence: comments on Hägerstrand's time-geography and its usefulness', *Economic Geography* 53: 207–21.

—— (1983) 'Structuration and place: on the becoming sense of place and structure of feeling', *Journal for the Theory of Social Behaviour* 13: 45–68.

—— (1985) 'The social becomes the spatial, the spatial becomes the social: enclosures, social change and the becoming of place in the Swedish province of Skane', in D. Gregory and J. Urry (eds) *Social Relations and Spatial Structures*, London: Macmillan.

Rawls, J. (1971) *A Theory of Justice*, Cambridge, Mass.: Harvard University Press.

Reich, W. (German 1933a) *Character Analysis* (3rd edn, D. Carfagno (tr.)), New York: Simon & Shuster (1961).

—— (German 1933b) *Mass Psychology of Fascism* (tr. D. Carfagno),

New York: Simon & Shuster (1969).

—— (1972) *Sex-Pol: Essays, 1929–1934* (L. Baxandall (ed.), A. Bostock (tr.)), New York: Vintage.

Robertson, R. and Lechner, F. (1985) 'Modernization, globalization and the problem of culture and world-systems theory', *Theory, Culture and Society* 2: 103–17.

Roche, M. (1987) 'Social theory and the life-world', *British Journal of Sociology* 38: 283–7.

Roethlisberger, F. and Dickson, W. (1939) *Management and the Worker*, Cambridge, Mass.: Harvard University Press.

Rorty, R. (1982) 'Philosophy in America today', in his *Consequences of Pragmatism*, Brighton: Harvester.

Rose, H. (1988) 'Social power, employment relations and organisational control', PhD Thesis, University College Cardiff.

Rothschild, Lord (1971) 'The organisation and management of government R and D' in *A Framework for Government Research and Development*, CMND 4184. London: HMSO.

Runciman, W. (1980) 'Comparative sociology or narrative history? A note on the methodology of Perry Anderson', *Archives européennes de sociologie* 22: 162–80.

Sanderson, S. (1987) 'Eclecticism and its alternatives', in J. Wilson (ed.) *Current Perspectives in Social Theory: A Research Annual*, vol. 8, London: Jai Press.

Sandywell, B. (1975) *Problems of Reflexivity and Dialectics in Sociological Inquiry: Language Theorizing Difference*, London: Routledge & Kegan Paul.

Schivelbusch, W. (1986) *Railway Journey: Industrialization and Perception of Time and Space*, London: Berg.

Schutz, A. (1962) *The Problem of Social Reality: Collected Papers vol. 1*, The Hague: Martinus Nijhoff.

Scott, R. and Shore, A. (1979) *Why Sociology Does Not Apply: A Study of the Use of Sociology in Public Policy*, New York: Elsevier.

Seidman, S. (1983) *Liberalism and the Origins of European Social Theory*, Oxford: Blackwell.

Shapiro, G. and Sica, A. (eds) (1984) *Hermeneutics: Questions and Prospects*, Amherst: University of Massachusetts Press.

Shils, E. (1970) 'Tradition, ecology and institution in the history of sociology', *Daedalus* 99: 760–825.

Shotter, J. (1983) ' "Duality of structure" and "intellectuality" in an ecological psychology', *Journal for the Theory of Social Behaviour* 13: 19–43.

Sica, A. (1983) Review of *A Contemporary Critique of Historical Materialism*, in *Social Forces* 61: 1260–2.

—— (1986) 'Locating the 17th book of Giddens', review of *The Constitution of Society*, in *Contemporary Sociology* 15: 344–6.

—— (1987) Review of P. Sztompka, *Robert Merton*, in *Isis* 78: 283–5.

Skocpol, T. (ed.) (1984) *Vision and Method in Historical Sociology*, Cambridge: Cambridge University Press.

240

—— (1987) Review of *Nation-State and Violence*, in *Social Forces* 66: 294–6.

Smart, B. (1982) 'Foucault, sociology and the problem of human agency', *Theory and Society* 11: 121–41.

Smith, D. (1978) 'Domination and contamination: an approach to modernisation', *Comparative Studies in Society and History* 20: 177–213.

—— (1982a) 'Put not your trust in princes – a commentary on Anthony Giddens and the absolutist state', *Theory, Culture and Society* 1: 93–9.

—— (1982b) 'Social history and sociology – just good friends', *Sociological Review* 30: 286–308.

Smith, J. and Turner, B. (1986) 'Constructing social theory and constituting society', *Theory, Culture and Society* 3: 125–33.

Spybey, T. (1984) 'Traditional and professional frames of meaning for managers', *Sociology* 18: 550–62.

—— (1987) 'Some problems on Giddens' structuration theory', paper presented at the University of Uppsala, mimeo.

Stant, M. (1977) Review of *New Rules*, in *British Journal of Sociology* 11: 369–73.

Stauth, G. and Turner, B. (1988) 'Nostalgia, postmodernism and the critique of mass culture', *Theory, Culture and Society* 2/3: 509–26.

Stewart, J. (1985) 'Beyond explanation and understanding: the refiguration of social theory', *Studies in Symbolic Interaction* 6: 31–58.

Stinchcombe, A. (1978) *Theoretical Method in Social Theory*, New York: Academic Press.

—— (1986) 'Milieu and structure updated', *Theory and Society* 15: 901–14.

Sztompka, P. (1986) *Robert Merton*, New York: St Martins.

Taylor, C. (1983) 'Political theory and practice', in C. Lloyd (ed.) *Social Theory and Political Practice*, Oxford: Clarendon Press.

Therborn, G. (1971) 'Habermas: a new eclectic', *New Left Review* 67: 69–85.

Thompson, E.P. (1967) 'Time, work-discipline and industrial capitalism', *Past and Present* 38: 56–97.

Thompson, J. (1984a) *Studies in the Theory of Ideology*, Cambridge: Polity Press.

—— (1984b) 'The theory of structuration: an assessment of the contribution of Anthony Giddens', in J. Thompson (1984a) *Studies in the Theory of Ideology*, Cambridge: Polity Press.

—— (1984c) 'Rethinking history: for and against Marx', *Philosophy of the Social Sciences* 14: 543–51.

Thompson, J. and Held, D. (eds) (1982) *Habermas: Critical Debates*, London: Macmillan.

Thompson, K. (1979) Review of *Studies in Social and Political Theory*, in *British Journal of Sociology* 30: 375–6.

Thrift, N. (1983) 'On the determination of action in space and time', *Society and Space* 1: 23–57.

—— (1984) Review of *Contemporary Critique* in *Progress in Human Geography* 8: 131–42.

—— (1985a) 'Bear and mouse or bear and tree? Anthony Giddens' reconstruction of social theory', *Sociology* 19: 609–23.

—— (1985b) 'Flies and germs: a geography of knowledge', in D. Gregory and J. Urry (eds) *Social Relations and Spatial Structures*, London: Macmillan.

Tijssen, I. (1988) *Kwaliteit Noodt Tot Meer Gebruik*, Nijmegen, Catholic University of Nijmegen doctoral thesis.

Tilly, C. (ed.) (1975) *The Formation of Nation-states in Western Europe*, Princeton: Princeton University Press.

—— (1981) *As Sociology Meets History*, New York: Academic Press.

Tonkin, B. (1989) 'States of emergency', *New Statesman*, 19 May: 14–15.

Touraine, A. (1965) *Sociologie de l'action*, Paris: Seuil.

—— (1973) *Production de la société*, Paris: Seuil.

Turner, B. (1988) *Status*, Milton Keynes: Open University Press.

Turner, J. (1986a) *The Structure of Sociological Theory*, Chicago: Dorsey Press.

—— (1986b) 'The theory of structuration – review essay', review of *Constitution of Society*, in *American Journal of Sociology* 91: 969–77.

—— (1988) *A Theory of Interaction*, Stanford: Stanford University Press.

Turner, S. (1983) 'Durkheim as methodologist', Part 1 'Realism, Teleology and Action', *The Philosophy of Social Science* 13: 425–50.

Urry, J. (1977) Review of *New Rules*, in *Sociological Review* 25: 911–15.

—— (1982) 'Duality of structure: some critical issues', *Theory, Culture and Society* 1: 100–6.

—— (1985) 'Social relations, space and time', in D. Gregory and J. Urry (eds) *Social Relations and Spatial Structures*, London: Macmillan.

—— (1986) Review of *Constitution of Society*, in *Sociologial Review* 34: 434–7.

—— (1987) 'Society, space and locality', *Environment and Planning D Society and Space* 6: 435–44.

Veyne, P. (1984) *Writing History*, Manchester: Manchester University Press.

Walby, S. (1986) *Patriarchy at Work*, Cambridge: Polity Press.

Wallerstein, I. (1974) *The Modern World System*, New York: Academic Press.

—— (1979) *The Capitalist World Economy*, Cambridge: Cambridge University Press.

Weber, M. (German 1904) '"Objectivity" in social science and social policy', in his *The Methodology of the Social Sciences*, Glencoe: Free Press (1949).

—— (German 1922) *Economy and Society*, vol. 1, New York: Bedminster Press (1968).

Weiss, C. (1979) 'The many meanings of research utilization', in M. Bulmer (ed.) *Social Science and Social Policy*, London: Allen & Unwin (1986).

—— (1983) 'Ideology, interests and information: the basis of policy positions', in D. Callahan and B. Jennings (eds) *Ethics, the Social*

Sciences, and Policy Analysis, New York: Plenum Press.

Weiss, C. and Bucuvalas, M. (1980) *Social Science Research and Decision-Making*, New York: Columbia University Press.

Williams, R. (1973) 'Base and superstructure in Marxist cultural theory', *New Left Review* (82): 3–16.

Willis, P. (1977) *Learning to Labour – How Working Class Kids Get Working Class Jobs*, Farnborough: Saxon House.

Willmott, H. (1986) 'Unconscious sources of motivation in the theory of the subject: an exploration and critique of Giddens' dualistic models of action and personality', *Journal for the Theory of Social Behaviour* 16: 105–21.

Wilson, B. (ed.) (1970) *Rationality*, Oxford: Blackwell.

Winch, P. (1958) *The Idea of a Social Science*, London: Routledge & Kegan Paul.

—— (1964) 'Understanding a primitive society', *American Philosophical Quarterly* 1: 307–24.

Wittkower, R. (1965) 'Imitation, eclecticism and genius' in E. Wasserman (ed.) *Aspects of the Eighteenth Century*, London and Baltimore: Johns Hopkins University Press.

Wright, E. Olin (1983) 'Giddens' critique of Marxism', *New Left Review* 138: 11–33.

—— (1984) 'Review essays: Is Marxism really functionalist, class reductionist and teleological?', *American Journal of Sociology* 89: 452–9.

Zukin, S. (1988) *Loft Living*, London: Constable.

Index

244

Index